Rubric Nation

Critical Inquiries on the Impact of Rubrics in Education

Rubric Nation

Critical Inquiries on the Impact of Rubrics in Education

edited by

Michelle Tenam-Zemach
Nova Southeastern University

Joseph E. Flynn, Jr.
Northern Illinois University

INFORMATION AGE PUBLISHING, INC.
Charlotte, NC • www.infoagepub.com

Library of Congress Cataloging-in-Publication Data

A CIP record for this book is available from the Library of Congress
http://www.loc.gov

ISBN: 978-1-62396-961-5 (Paperback)
      978-1-62396-962-2 (Hardcover)
      978-1-62396-963-9 (ebook)

CONTENTS

FOREWORD

Joel Westheimer

In a popular scene from the 1989 movie, *Dead Poets Society*, the eccentric Mr. Keating (played by Robin Williams) asks one of his students to read aloud from the preface of a high school poetry textbook:

> To fully understand poetry, we must first be fluent with its meter, rhyme, and figures of speech, then ask two questions: 1) How artfully has the objective of the poem been rendered, and 2) How important is that objective? Question 1 rates the poem's perfection; question 2 rates its importance. And once these questions have been answered, determining the poem's greatness becomes a relatively simple matter. If the poem's score for perfection is plotted on the horizontal of a graph and its importance is plotted on the vertical, then calculating the total area of the poem yields the measure of its greatness.

The fictional author of the text, Dr. J. Evans Pritchard, PhD, continues with an example:

> A sonnet by Byron might score high on the vertical but only average on the horizontal. A Shakespearean sonnet, on the other hand, would score high both horizontally and vertically, yielding a massive total area, thereby revealing the poem to be truly great.

Rubric Nation, pages vii–x
Copyright © 2015 by Information Age Publishing

Pritchard concludes by asking students to practice this rating method (using the provided rubric) because "as your ability to evaluate poems in this matter grows, so will your enjoyment and understanding of poetry."

Although both the textbook and its author are fictional, the satire is worrisomely apt. In fact, the fictional passage was based closely on a real text found in a popular 1950s poetry textbook currently in its 12th edition and still used by high school students across the country: Laurence Perrine's *Sound and Sense: An Introduction to Poetry*.

As the chapters in *Rubric Nation* make clear, the demand for standardized measures of quality and success in education has not abated but increased. The relatively uncritical and universal acceptance among school reformers of the importance of rubrics for teaching and learning is at once predictable and misguided. It is predictable because the idea that we should clearly articulate educational goals and then devise methods for determining whether those goals are met is irresistibly tidy. After all, how can teachers pursue high quality lessons if they do not know what they are trying to teach and whether students are learning? Uncritical acceptance of even such a commonsense-seeming idea, however, is misguided for the following reason: education is first and foremost about human relationship and interaction, and as anyone who tried to create a rubric for family fealty or for love or for trust would discover, any effort to quantify complex human interactions quickly devolves into a fool's errand.

This does not mean that there is no place for evaluative rubrics in education (or for standards, testing, and common curriculum frameworks). Many of the chapters that follow make the need for thoughtful measures and learning frameworks clear. Moreover, I have rarely met a teacher who did not have standards; most have their own forms of rubrics or evaluative frameworks as well. But "No Child Left Behind" and "Race to the Top" legislation and related reforms that call for evermore standardized rubrics and frameworks have severely restricted teachers' abilities to act in a professional capacity and exercise professional judgment on behalf of their students.

Finnish educator Pasi Sahlberg calls the kind of school reform that elevates the pursuit of rubrics and standardization above all other educational considerations GERM (for Global Education Reform Movement). He describes GERM as follows:

> It is like an epidemic that spreads and infects education systems through a virus. It travels with pundits, media and politicians. Education systems borrow policies from others and get infected. As a consequence, schools get ill, teachers don't feel well, and kids learn less.[1]

Not only do kids learn less, what they learn also tends to follow prescriptive formulas that match the standardized tests. In the process, more complex and difficult-to-measure learning outcomes get left behind. These include creativity and emotional and social development as well as the kinds of thinking skills associated with robust civic engagement. As a result, teachers' ability to teach critical thinking and students' ability to think and act critically are diminished.

Almost every school mission statement these days boasts broad goals related to critical thinking, global citizenship, environmental stewardship, and moral character. Yet beneath the rhetoric, increasingly narrow curriculum goals, accountability measures, standardized testing, and an obsession with rubrics have reduced too many classroom lessons to the cold, stark pursuit of information and skills without context and without social meaning—what the late education philosopher Maxine Greene called mean and repellent facts. It is not that facts are bad or that they should be ignored. But democratic societies require more than citizens who are fact-full. They require citizens who can think and act in ethically thoughtful ways. Schools need the kinds of classroom practices that teach students to recognize ambiguity and conflict in "factual" content and to see human conditions and aspirations as complex and contested.

As our cultural obsession with standardization, rubrics, and accountability measures in only two subject areas (math and literacy) increasingly dominates school reform, the most common complaint I now hear from both teachers and administrators is this: *I have been stripped of my professional judgment, creativity, and freedom to make decisions in the best interests of my students.* When education reforms turn away from an emphasis on supporting positive conditions of practice and move toward technocratic strategies for "compliance," the profession suffers, and so do students. Many teachers would echo the sentiments of Gloria, a teacher in a recent study I conducted of the tenth-grade civics curriculum in Ontario. She told us this:

> In my 22 years of teaching, never have I experienced a climate that has turned all educational problems into problems of measurement until now. Poor citizenship skills? Raise their math and literacy scores. Poor participation? Doesn't matter. Poverty? Inequality? The solution is always always to give the students more tests. These days pedagogically, I feel like I can't breathe.

But education goals, particularly in democratic societies, have always been about more than narrow measures of success, and teachers have often been called upon and appreciated for instilling in their students a sense of purpose, meaning, community, compassion, integrity, imagination, and commitment. Every teacher accomplishes these more artful and ambiguous tasks in different ways. Much as Darwin's theory of natural selection depends on genetic variation, any theory of teaching in a democratic society depends on a multiplicity of ideas, perspectives, and approaches to exploring and seeking solutions to complex issues of widespread concern.

Parents, administrators, and politicians alike all must acknowledge that educators in a democratic society have a responsibility to create learning environments that teach students a broad variety of lessons—including but not limited to the kinds of learning goals easily captured by rubrics.

Talented teachers need the freedom and professional autonomy to work the magic of their art in myriad ways that defy standardization and regimentation of practice. Talented teachers need manageable class sizes in which they can provide the right conditions for that magic to take root. And talented teachers need policymakers who have the courage to marshal the resources necessary to create the best possible conditions of practice and then let teachers do their jobs free of interference and corrosive mistrust. To the extent rubrics can aid in these efforts, they may be useful; but if they hinder these goals, they must be criticized.

That's why this book is so timely. Neither thoughtlessly dismissing the idea of rubrics nor embracing them uncritically, the contributing authors have, together, created a space for dialogue around the tensions inherent in the teaching profession between autonomy and committee rule, between spontaneity and uniformity. Far from allowing the poetry of teaching and learning to be reduced to facile measurements, the authors demand a more careful consideration of rubrics as an educational tool, useful at times, inherently flawed, always open to question.

You may recall in *Dead Poets Society* that after allowing his students to listen attentively to the detailed instructions on measuring the quality of poetry (even drawing a graph on the blackboard to show just how to execute the formula for evaluation), Keating proceeds to demand that students rip out that entire chapter from the text. "Begone J. Evans Pritchard, PhD!" he exclaims to the sound of students tearing out the offending pages. He was asking them, of course, to revel in the radical possibility of unquantifiable teaching and learning. I suggest reading this book with just such an attitude.

NOTE

1. Sahlberg, P. (2012, June 29). How GERM is infecting schools around the world. *The Washington Post.* [The Answer Sheet web log by Valerie Strauss]. Retrieved from http://www.washingtonpost.com/blogs/answer-sheet/post/how-germ-is-infecting-schools-around-the-world/2012/06/29/gJQAVELZAW_blog.html

WHY A BOOK ON RUBRICS?

Problematizing the Unquestioned

**Joseph E. Flynn, Jr., Michelle Tenam-Zemach,
and Leslie David Burns**

This book strives to raise questions that will challenge educators and other stakeholders in public schooling to consider the nature and effects of rubrics. In developing chapters that reflect myriad issues related to these topics, we respond to them through multiple dialectic processes. How do rubrics work? Why are they so prominent in the United States' education system today? What political roles do rubrics play, and whose interests do they serve? And, since a rubric is nothing more than a fixed set of limited and ultimately subjective criteria, what challenges and opportunities might lie in evaluating educators' value and quality based on the atomized procedures of their basic jobs, rather than the holistic entirety of their complex professional practices?

In our quest for answers and alternatives, we began to look in all the familiar places. We conducted systematic literature searches through all the major databases related to education: ERIC, JSTOR, Wilson, ProQuest, Google Scholar, etc. We also checked libraries and Amazon.com. The lion's

Rubric Nation, pages xi–xxx
Copyright © 2015 by Information Age Publishing

share of literature about rubrics addresses how to create them, or how to connect them to standards. Little research exists about whether and especially *how* they work or not (Andrade, 2005; Moskal & Leydens, 2000; Airasian, & Russell, 2008). This seemed puzzling to us, and through our consternation, we engaged in heated discussions in hopes of understanding how the field of education was contending with a mystery that had attained such unquestioned prominence in our professional accountability systems. We repeated and deepened our literature searches and met the same conclusion we did initially: There is a dearth of scholarly literature that critically examines the histories and impacts of rubrics on teaching, learning, and teacher education.

We did, however, discover some research that speaks to the benefits of utilizing rubrics in teaching and learning more generally. Research in higher education has suggested an overall positive relationship between rubric use and student achievement, improved instruction, and program evaluation (Reddy & Andrade, 2010). In their study, Andrade and Du (2005) suggest that rubrics support undergraduate students' own learning and achievement, pointing out that rubrics help students generate a "vision of success" (p. 1). Keefer-Reynolds (2010) explores how rubrics influence pre-service teachers' learning. Her findings align with those of earlier studies: students' view rubrics in tremendously positive ways and often rely on them as maps to success. Schneider (2006) found rubrics to be worthwhile tools to facilitate students in generating "high quality work" (p. 44). Yet, despite the evidence that well-designed rubrics may offer some benefits to students in some contexts, scant research critically examines or situates rubrics in terms of their effects, especially as they are applied in the assessment of teachers and teacher educators themselves.

In our discussions we hypothesized that rubrics became commonplace as more and more teacher preparation programs were corralled under the auspices of National Council for Accreditation of Teacher Education (NCATE) and the discourses of accountability in standards-based education reform efforts. Nevertheless, a simple question loomed: How did rubrics become such ubiquitous tools for pre-service and in-service teacher evaluation when so little empirical evidence speaks to the efficacy of their use? The question required us to examine U.S. education reform as a whole.

REFORM IN U.S. EDUCATION

Standards-based education has become an omnipresent ongoing set of political reform movements, in part because of the rhetoric advocates of standards-based reform tend to use. That rhetoric asserts that if we offer rigorous high standards, hold students, teachers, and administrators accountable, and severely penalize those who fail, we will reach a utopian state wherein everyone succeeds (Jackson, 2003; Vinson & Ross, 2003). This rhetoric is superficially powerful. It is clear and concise, and appears innocuous because it is presented as a means to universal public goods. After all, who would argue against higher standards, and who would argue that we should not work constantly to improve? Such broad, seemingly self-evident statements position people to accept a vision of a greater, more equitable America they should aspire to attain (McDonnell & Weatherford, 2013). In addition to lending an air of credibility to standards-based reform, the rhetoric represents such reforms as simple matters of becoming more consistent and forever improving. Asserting that consistency and consistent improvement is the solution to all of our problems in public education makes it easier to argue for the simplistic development of easily replicated systems. Simpler systems, in turn, make design, implementation, and assessment appear to be simple projects too. In turn, this dual layer of simplistic assertions creates impulses to design tools that will reflect and confirm the ideologies that originate them in the apparent interest of establishing quality control that either maintains a particular status quo or instantiates a new one. The reduction of evaluation according to standards via the design and implementation of rubrics promotes that exact, superficial appearance of seemingly objective, straight-forward, efficient evaluation (Taubman, 2009). Rubrics appear to offer a straight-forward, one-size-fits-all approach to determining who and what is helping a system succeed or not. On its face, this is a simple proposition that has become the norm in education, almost without question. Its present status as a tool of common sense assessment and evaluation also comes at a high cost.

The simplistic ideologies and resulting actions of standards-based reform advocates, including their uncritical (and unfounded) claim that higher standards will lead to student success and global economic competitiveness is the basis of a persistent stranglehold on educational decision-making processes, administrative policymaking, teacher professionalization, and student success (Commoncore.org; McDonnell & Weatherford, 2013; Ravitch, 2013). It is these simplistic treatments of standards-based reform and its relationship to rubrics, as well as the anxiety those treatments generate among professionals who recognize that the system is vastly complex, that set us on the quest to produce additional inquiry and more nuanced understandings of how and why the system operates as it does. Consequently, we seek to understand how it might be made healthier to the benefit of all. We begin with a brief exploration of standards, their proliferation in education reform, and their role in education accountability discourses.

STANDARDS, STANDARDS, AND MORE STANDARDS

In his research on what teachers learn during the National Board Certification processes, Lustick (2010) uncovered connections between Lee Shulman's notion of pedagogical content knowledge (1986), the development of national standards for teachers through the National Board for the Professionalization of Teachers (NBPT), the meteoric rise of the National Council for Accreditation of Teacher Education (NCATE) as the arbiter of accountability for that profession, and the development of presumed need for such standards (and the rubrics required to assess their attainment) as a primary tool of education accountability that emerged in the wake of *A Nation at Risk* (1983). Shulman's notion of pedagogical content knowledge was key in the development of standards for teachers because, according to Shulman (1986), pedagogical content knowledge is "that special amalgam of content and pedagogy that is uniquely the province of teachers, their own special form of professional understanding" (p. 8). Shulman promoted this idea in reflection of the findings and proscriptions expressed by the Holmes Group Report and the Carnegie Task Force (Sedlak, 1987; Shulman, 1986; Wiggins, 1986). Both documents were extensions of the larger national policy conversations about creating higher standards for teacher preparation that could then serve as means for bolstering our nation's performance in education overall, following suit from the Standards Based Reform Movement (SBRM). We refer to these extensions and their subsequent domination of reform as the rise of what we call the Rubric Nation.

One explanation about the rise of the Rubric Nation may be found by examining the larger movement in the United States. The notion that there is a single, unchanging and specific body of standards that can or will lead to student achievement is a widely held belief and oft repeated refrain by proponents of teacher accountability systems (Delandshere & Petrosky, 2004). These systems are based on various ideologies, and there is no shortage of alternatives given their widespread proliferation across interest groups at the professional, national, state, and local levels for the past several decades. Nearly every subject-area professional organization in the U.S. issues some form of standards for professionals on a regular basis, and there are numerous national and state organizations that also create and mandate standards to drive the development of teachers in their preparation programs as well as their accountability systems.

For example, the International Society for Technology in Education (ISTE) has developed a rubric for their National Educational Technology Standards (NETS). According to ISTE's website, "NETS for teachers are the standards for evaluating the skills and knowledge educators need to teach, work, and learn in an increasingly connected global and digital society" (http://www.iste.org/standards/nets-for-teachers). The two page rubric that accompanies these standards is focused on teachers' behaviors in relation to the use of technologies in classrooms and schools. For instance, one "essential condition" (the nomenclature for the criteria) states, "The community and school partners provide expertise, support and resources" (http://electronicportfolios.com/reflect/EssenCondRubric.pdf). Another essential condition posits, "There is proactive leadership and support for the implementation of technology in teaching and learning from the entire educational system" (http://electronicportfolios. com/reflect/ EssenCondRubric.pdf).

Other standards for teachers and teacher educators have been issued by the Council of Chief State School Officers' (CCSSO) Interstate Teacher Assessment and Support Consortium (InTASC). The CCSSO claims to be a

> nonpartisan, nationwide, nonprofit organization of public officials who head departments of elementary and secondary education in the states, the District of Columbia, the Department of Defense Education Activity, and five U.S. extra-state jurisdictions. CCSSO provides leadership, advocacy, and technical assistance on major educational issues. (http://www.ccsso.org/ documents/2011/intasc_model_core_teaching_standards _2011.pdf)

The CCSSO contends its InTASC standards offer a model for essential teaching skills that underscores what all educators should know and be able to do so that their students will be academically successful and "ready to enter college or the workforce in today's world" (http://www.ccsso.org/ Documents/2013/2013_INTASC_Learning_Progressions_for_Teachers .pdf). They also claim that these "Model Core Teaching Standards" reflect what "effective teaching and learning looks like in a transformed public education system" (http://www. ccsso.org/Documents/2013/2013_ INTASC_Learning_Progressions_for_Teachers.pdf). However, where the evidence to support these claims lies is somewhat dubious at best, and much of it actually contradicts the CCSSO's claims (Stotsky, 2013).

Another influential body of teaching standards is the National Council of Accreditation Teachers of Education (NCATE) standards, also now known as the Council for the Accreditation of Educator Preparation (CAEP) since their merger with the Teacher Education Accreditation Council (TEAC). There are six unit standards that are guided by a college of education's Conceptual Framework. Each of the standards guide a college's development of assessments that "Indicate that candidates meet professional, state, and institutional standards" (http://www.ncate.org/Standards/Unit Standards/UnitStandardsinEffect2008/tabid/476/Default.aspx). In order to evaluate the extent to which a candidate has met the target, a rubric is developed to gauge the level of proficiency that has been met across each standard. There are three levels for NCATE rubrics: Unacceptable, Acceptable, and Target. Colleges and teacher education programs are allowed to create their own assessments and rubrics, but data must be collected and submitted as part of the college's annual report.

Yet another additional body of pervasive teaching standards, ones that supposedly increase teacher quality toward full mastery, similar to the claims made by NCATE, is the National Board for Professional Teaching Standards (NBPTS). There are five core propositions promoted by the National Board. Based on these propositions, NBPTS developed standards for "accomplished teaching" across 16 different content areas addressing various developmental levels of students (http://www.nbpts.org/national-board-standards). These and other benchmarks have largely been set by those who advocate a *Nation at Risk*-style standards-based approach to teacher training and national education reform, development and evaluation of standardized teacher preparation in all contexts, and the utilization of rubrics as a key instrument in teacher and teacher education accountability. They represent what Bowers (2010) terms a double bind thinking approach to teacher education and teacher accountability in general, wherein proposed solutions of a problem are generated from the problem itself.

For the propagators of SBRM for teacher education and student performance, rubrics became *the* tool for answering a seemingly simple question: How do we know standards are being effectively achieved? This focus on assessment using rubrics as the primary mode was an important step in understanding their rise as an institutional response to preparing teachers and assessing teacher education quality. Rubrics became a central means for tracking the faithful implementation of standards and expectations as manifested in the behaviors and performances of anyone seeking in a professional education role.

In *A Nation at Risk* (1983), the authors declared that "the educational foundations of our society are presently being eroded by a rising tide of mediocrity that threatens our very future as a Nation and a people" (p. 9). In fact, Meier (2000) contends that those who gathered around the report to advocate for its proposals argued for the privatization of public schools, blaming either the nature of public schools as institutions, the supposedly low quality of teachers and teacher education programs, and/or the nature and problem of local control by the very rising tide of mediocrity the authors of the report sought to reform. Meier (2000) states,

> The cure would have to combine more competition from the private or semi-private sector and more rigorous control by external experts who understood the demands of our economy and had the clout to impose change. This latter viewpoint has dominated the standards-based movement. (p. 11)

Since the publication of *A Nation at Risk* and the standards-based reform movement that continues to play out ever since, those choosing to enter the education profession have been placed under dramatic scrutiny by multiple stakeholders using standards and rubrics.

Standards and Rubrics

Concerning teacher education reform, Edelfelt and Raths (1999) point out that "Almost from the beginning of formal teacher education, teacher educators have been concerned about standards for their programs and candidates" (p. 1). This concern reflects an assumption that teachers should be able to implement universally appropriate "best practices" that will improve *all* students' learning outcomes—an assumption that is contrary to most of what we know about how teaching and learning function in highly variable and asynchronous ways depending on the contexts in which they occur. It also reflects the erroneous assumption that some pedagogical practices are universally best in that they are always "better than others" (Edelfelt & Raths, 1999, p. 1) This assumption fails to consider the need for additional inquiries about when, where, and for whom a given method of teaching is in fact better or not compared to others (in itself a fool's game that requires us to assume that all children learn in the same ways for the same reasons at the same times at the same rates with the same breadth and depth—a practical absurdity).

Nevertheless, when and exactly where rubrics became a default mechanism for evaluating pre-service and in-service teachers according to standards is unclear. What is apparent is that standards, and the rubrics that followed them, have become enormously widespread and institutionalized tools for evaluation of all elements in our education system because various stakeholders have argued that teachers must be held accountable (NCATE, 2007). Furthermore, it is claimed that these tools need to be based on criteria that are treated as neutral and universally applicable across all contexts. They are generally represented as linear, hierarchical, simple, efficient, concise, and objective, even though criteria for educational quality are always, by definition, value-laden and subjective (Delandshere & Petrosky, 2004). Once standards are set and rubrics are derived from them to assess their attainment, further subjective judgments about teacher quality are connected to these instruments via their subjective application by individual assessors themselves who bring their own additional criteria and interpretations of the rubrics and standards to the assessment process. Rubrics, treated as simple templates derived from broad, seemingly inarguable standards of quality, provide a convenient means to standardize expectations for quality teaching and learning in an efficient format that is administratively expedient (whether such expedience is pedagogically justifiable or not).

There is nothing particularly novel or surprising about any of this. And we would not argue that standards and quality are unnecessary, nor that teaching and learning should not be assessed. They should. And, if appropriate and mindful, rubrics could serve as useful tools in such processes. One question that arises through their use, however, is how their relations to standards may affect the entire enterprise of education in the United States in unexpected, unintended, and/or undesirable ways. There is considerable evidence that current standards for K–12 and teacher education are being produced by education outsiders explicitly to de-professionalize public education and thereby enable powerful corporate interests to intervene and profit from the system (Apple, 2006; Giroux, 2012; Ravitch, 2013; Saltman, 2005). How? Through the production of more standards, the rubric systems required to assess them, and the various resources needed to train personnel for their implementation (Burns, 2012).

We must ask whose interests are served (and whose are not) by utilizing standards and rubrics in SBRM as they are now. We must question how they shape the educational landscape and understand how their uses can potentially disempower those directly involved in the processes of public education (e.g, professors, teachers, students, etc.). As Bourdieu and Passerson (1990) point out, "Every power to exert symbolic violence, i.e., every power which manages to impose meanings and to impose them as legitimate by concealing power relations which are the basis of its force, adds its own specifically symbolic force to those power relations" (p. 4). If rubrics offer roadmaps to achieving particular outcomes related to particular standards, for example, who is determining the outcomes that will matter most (or at all), for whom, how, and to what effects? In the next section, we begin with a more specific discussion of what rubrics are and how they are typically created.

Rubrics and the Transformation of U.S. Educational Assessment

Before we discuss the ontology of rubrics and how they are generated, we offer this qualification: While we do not advocate the wholesale use of rubrics, we do recognize that, under the current standards-based education reform paradigm, by definition, rubrics are categorizing instruments that when used in conjunction with other assessment instruments can be useful to assess and guide teaching and learning processes. In concrete terms, rubrics typically assign a score or rating, a rank, or a descriptor that represents the gradations of quality in a particular category based on values for that category that are generally determined prior to performance (Andrade, 2000). Oftentimes, complex functions are broken down into simpler pieces in order to align with the a priori assumptions of rubrics, then, even when there are complicating, contextual, and conditional factors that muddle scoring, rating, and even the categories themselves. Learning and performance are messy, complex processes, but the assignment of a single score is a move of efficiency that oftentimes disregards, masks, or attempts to reduce that messiness, not because it is pedagogically justifiable but because it is administratively expedient to reduce complexity and thereby make assessment less time-consuming, less expensive, and easier to understand or quantify for use in large standardized systems.

Assessment of learning, including learning based on standards, should always be treated as a complex social process because learning is, definitively, a complex social process. Except in the broadest ways and in certain very limited contexts, objective assessment of teaching and learning cannot be sufficiently accomplished by breaking such complex processes down into neutral or even discrete categories that are incapable of adaptation to the full range of ways a learner might demonstrate understanding or a teacher might demonstrate sophisticated pedagogies. Implementers of any rubric-based assessment of teaching and/or learning will always create constraints on complexity through their uses of the rubric in that perceptions of quality for criteria in the rubric's already subjective categories will also reflect the opinions and limited perceptions of those individuals applying it.

In this sense, rubrics create and sustain frameworks that conserve status quos, at least the status quos within the contexts where they are used to assess. Rubrics pre-order perception, limit scope and variation by imposing categories a priori, and encapsulate peoples' understandings of the work they are charged with doing by ensuring users adhere to and comply with the standards to which the rubric pertains. They bracket experience according to their standards-based categories in overtly limited ways that are non-negotiable. Rubrics have, for many, become familiar, comfortable, and simple in their constance as easy-to-use guides. However, ultimately they are likely to have at least potential for creating miseducative experiences that limit those who are assessed by them and forced to reside and identify themselves based on the results. In other words, rubrics provide structures that anchor standards in practice, help conserve those standards and ensure fidelity to them. But they can also minimize the potentials of the actual learning that they are intended to assess, including by constraining how and to what degree an individual conforms. Rubrics, used unmindfully, can become de facto instruments that shape both the standards they assess and the subjectivities of all those who use them.

Indeed, today national teacher education accrediting groups like NCATE formally require all programs seeking formal recognition to include detailed rubrics specific to each assessment used in every course as a matter of policy. Rubrics are no longer merely tools used by professionals to support their assessment of students' learning. They have become highly standardized, rigid, and limiting instruments that, unintentionally or not, govern a great deal of what is taught (and what can be taught) in a given classroom as well as how students are to use and respond to course content in certain ways instead of others. What began as a tool supposedly designed to help teachers and students learn has been revealed to have constant potential for doing harm by constraining flexibility, limiting categories, and thus creating inauthentic contexts and content that are harmful.

Since rubrics have become such an entrenched instrument of teaching, we have had to create many over the years. We have found we often violate our own rubric demands and are required by necessity to determine students' grades based on our discretion when those rubrics have merely produced pre-determined responses where we sought critical thinking and creative use of ideas. The fact of the matter is that rubrics frequently do not account for the full range of student skills and expectations (Wilson, 2006). However, given the current standardized approach to education, it is both necessary and important for educators to consider the ways in which rubrics can be used effectively. As with any tool, in a standardized system, a rubric can be useful when designed and used well. Likewise, rubrics can be poorly designed and/or used ineffectively, despite the fact that we have been told that rubrics help ensure that we remain *effective*.

Noting that the word *effective* in this context means having a predictable result rather than referring to authentic learning (Burns, 2014), we asked the question, "When did rubrics become an unavoidable, institutionalized aspect of everything we do in teacher education?" While acknowledging that the concept of *effective teaching* has become a central frame and goal for much of our nation's current reform efforts, we note that it is in fact a proxy term for *successful teaching* that has long since taken on a life and power of its own in political and policy groups (Burns, 2014). For the purposes of bureaucratic reform, which generally require at least some level of standardization rather than widespread variation, the discourse of effectiveness makes administrative sense. However, while it may be bureaucratically expedient to seek an *effective* system for teaching, decades of constructivist, cognitivist, developmentalist, linguistic, and sociocultural research from across the spectrum of social sciences demonstrate that predictable uniformity of teacher quality and outcomes is impossible due to the nature of constructivist learning, which is always context dependent, deeply complex and variable, and entirely dependent on professionals' abilities to adjust, adapt, and vary their practices in the interest of success, which we define as attainment of a stated goal. According to Berliner (2005), measuring the quality of teaching at all with respect to its full complexity is a practical impossibility.

Rubrics, Accountability, and Teacher Education

While we cannot precisely pinpoint exactly why or when rubrics took hold of teacher education programs and education in general, we do know that currently rubrics for assessment purposes exist in all areas of education, most notably teacher preparation and teacher evaluation. As early as 2007, NCATE Standard 2 specified "The unit [for teacher education] establishes scoring guides, *which may be rubrics*, for determining levels of candidate accomplishment and completing their programs (2007, p. 18, emphasis added). Our concern with this statement about scoring guides and rubrics has become a driving force behind much of what is considered evaluation and assessment of work products as well as student/teacher behaviors. Rubrics are often perceived as a means to an end. That is, if learners are provided a rubric, they will have the means to determine the extent to which they have met minimum criteria for success. Rubrics have become an apparatus to standardize the work being evaluated and inform the producers of that work how well they have accomplished the predetermined goals set for them.

On the surface, setting predetermined goals at all seems more or less harmless. They are intended to offer clear, uniform means for assigning ratings across a number of qualitative categories that relate to the criteria by which one's work will be judged. The argument goes that if we know what it is that we want to achieve, then we should be clear and explicit when articulating those expectations to those who are meant to achieve it (Stevens & Levi, 2013; Andrade, 2000). If we manage to clearly set forth the deliverables, then everyone will be able to follow the path to excellence. How can one argue with that? While the literature demonstrates that well-designed rubrics can indeed increase student achievement in some cases by offering clear expectations and goals (Andrade & Du, 2005), there is scant literature that speaks to the effects of rubrics as evaluative approaches applied to education overall, or to teacher education programs or teachers and their quality in particular.

It would be a far simpler world if the use of rubrics was as simple as it seems on the surface. If it was, then we would not have to look beneath and examine their dark underbellies to understand why so many educators use them with high anxiety and a sense of unease that has become part and parcel with their mandatory use in high stakes processes that may not be valid or reliable. As one reviewer of this book stated in response to the institutionalization of rubrics, "They are so ubiquitous and they are also so evil!" (Personal communication, February 14, 2014). This visceral response suggests the use of rubrics requires challenging questions and critiques about how they shape teaching, learning, thought, and behavior. As Giroux (2012) contends, "the use of test scores to measure teacher quality has both limited teacher autonomy and undermined the possibility of critical teaching and visionary goals for student learning" (p. 2). Thus, given the critical inquiries needed to understand the effect of rubrics on teaching, learning, and the field of education, this book attempts to engage in critical dialogue from a number of different perspectives.

Rubrics render complex outcomes down to numeric values or achievement rankings similar to standardized tests, and thus they consistently reflect impulses originating in corporate theories of Taylorism (Littler, 1978) and Fordism (Doray, 1990). Via Taylorist corporate models of education, rubrics entail the atomization of complex tasks into standardized and invariable procedures that can then (supposedly) be measured and refined for efficiency to the point of perfection. Via Fordist corporate approaches, they can then also be used to generate literal production line-style procedures that (supposedly) assure that the same actions will result in the same outcomes everywhere, every time, regardless of context. In light of the historical fact that both Taylorism and Fordism were systematically applied far beyond their originally intended contexts of factory production to include the standardization of social systems (Clark, 1990), rubrics must be considered as at least potential instruments for use in the de-professionalization of teaching and teacher education, both of which require workers who must be afforded significant levels of autonomy and flexibility in order to be successful.

Rubrics and Standardization

In light of the discussion so far, the research and theories associated with the topic, and the questions our inquiry has generated, rubrics may arguably be seen as part of a larger agenda intended to control teachers using an instrumentalist rationale that positions teachers as mere technical laborers whose main responsibility is to follow and guide pre-determined procedures toward pre-determined outcomes to ensure success in high-stakes accountability systems. The use of rubrics as a primary instrument for assessing teachers-as-technicians potentially disempowers educators by limiting their capacity to produce new knowledge or perspectives, use data to adapt to change in response to diversity, and facilitate student learning (among other problems). Consequently, rubrics may limit teachers' ability to optimize students' chances to learn beyond the most basic levels—if only because rubrics are typically designed in ways that underscore *minimum* requirements rather than *maximum* potential. Thus, the mandatory use of rubrics, enforced without question, may disempower all participants in many educational contexts, especially at the classroom or program levels where professionals most need the authority to work in variable ways depending on local circumstances.

In national and state contexts at least, teachers and teacher educators are not perceived as highly credentialed and well-educated experts and professionals in the teaching-learning continuum. As many advocates of standards-based reform would have it, if they were, then standards and rubrics for evaluation and accountability would not be necessary. Using faulty data that asserts incorrectly that U.S. schools, students, and teachers are failing in comparison to those in other nations (Berliner, Glass, & Associates, 2014), teachers in the U.S. have been excoriated as largely incapable of unsupervised performance and subjected to severe controls via the standards and rubrics that hold them accountable. Lalonde, Gorlewski, and Gorlewski (this volume) point out in their chapter, "(Dis)positioning learners: Rubrics and Identity in Teacher Education," that "As part of accreditation processes across higher education, rubrics are becoming a mandated aspect of assessment and, therefore, have a tremendous influence on instruction and learning" (p. 135). Giroux, (2012) concurs stating, "They [teachers] are now forced to simply implement predetermined instructional procedures and standardized content at best and at worst put their imaginative powers on hold while using precious time to teach students how to master the skill of test taking" (p. 2). Knowledge and power maintain an intimate connection in this situation and often limit who is allowed to exert agency. Because education is a value-laden cultural enterprise, many groups vie to gain control of it to their own goals. Those who do manage to gain control of any of education's various aspects often realize that they will maintain power only so long as they are able to dictate what knowledge is worth knowing and how that knowledge will be demonstrated and recognized (or not). Bourdieu recognized this and coined the term *cultural capital* to represent the value of products in education (Grenfell & James, 1998).

But education is not an isolated enterprise; it functions in intimate and multiple complex relations with other societal, political and cultural forces. In their chapter entitled "The Rubricization of "Teacherhood and Studenthood: Intertextuality, Identity, and the Standardization of Self," Patterson and Perhamus (this volume) discuss how rubrics are tools functioning within a 'culture of technique' (as cited in Palmer, 2001, p. 4). Their point speaks to the inherent potential of rubrics to generate governmentality in which professionals abdicate their own agency in favor of compliance and regardless of what they know is right (Weber, 1983; Foucault, 1978). Instead, rubrics become tools of bureaucracy that determine educators' decision making and during teaching and learning processes. Simply put, the imposition of rubrics as tools for governing thought and behavior creates a cultural context for students, teachers, principals, and others that promotes a certain set of dispositions, skills, and expectations.

CONCLUSION: RUBRIC NATION

In 1977, Bowles and Gintis (2011) introduced the correspondence principle that underscores the connection between educative practices and the larger economic structures of the United States. As they point out, schools, depending on the economic communities in which they are located, will utilize approaches and expectations that reproduce current economic conditions. Low income schools likely position students to occupy lower income jobs at least partly via rubricization, while upper/middle class schools will position students to occupy the strata of traditionally upper and middle class jobs, respectively. While individuals may periodically transcend the categories of rubricization in their local contexts, thereby maintaining the ultimate status quo ideal of *the American Dream* in which hard work is always rewarded with success, these individuals are exceptions that prove Bowles and Gintis' rule. The power of the correspondence principle rests in its ability to connect school practices with economic conditions, and one major instrument for exercising conservative power in that correspondence right now is rubrics.

As the roles and powers of corporations have grown over the past few decades, and the entrenchment of corporate reform has become the status quo today, rubrics may operate to acculturate rather than educate students. In this way, rubrics may unintentionally or otherwise acculturate users to adopt, believe in, and normalize relatively weak and unproductive ways of thinking in ways that prevent healthy growth. Alternately, we might educate students in ways that highlight the fact that education is definitively a project and process of change rather than conservation. This is so even where professional educators and other stakeholders may choose to use traditional foundations and/or employ rubrics in some cases. The key is mindful use and purposeful, intentional, strategic uses of the instruments we have at our disposal as professionals. Rubrics are *one* type of tool, and this book in part interrogates the risks of making a single tool so central to a complex endeavor as important as the improvement of any nation's education system.

Used poorly, rubrics may position users to fulfill predefined or unanticipated/undesirable outcomes, satisfy predetermined roles that normalize tradition and preclude progress, and especially lead users to abandon their identities and autonomies to the categories they are required to submit themselves to via rubrics. In teacher education and in-service professional work, rubrics that are poorly designed or implemented to evaluate teachers have seriously dangerous potentials to socialize a teaching force that is trained to comply with predetermined behaviors simply to maintain their positions (and in some cases avoid removal from the profession due to lack of compliance). Bowles and Gintis (2011) argue that the social relationships of education exist in "the vertical authority lines" (p. 131), noting that "the relationships between administrators and teachers, teachers and students, students and students, and students and their work- replicate the hierarchical division of labor" (p. 131). However, under corporate reform models, state and federal leaders and bureaucracies, along with their most wealthy and therefore politically powerful financial underwriters, have become dominant in this vertical line of authority. For instance, in order for states to qualify for Race to the Top (RTT) monies, local educators who might once have exercised greater professional autonomy must now employ teacher evaluation systems that include value-added measures, merit pay based on student performance on standardized tests, and, perhaps most importantly, policies that eliminate teacher "tenure" so that even the most expert and experienced professional educator can be fired without any due process or cause whatsoever beyond an employer's (or stakeholder's) say so (Ravitch, 2013). Used poorly, or with intent to these ends, rubrics could easily be used to not only manifest but normalize the vertical lines and negative exercises of authority that Bowles and Gintis' research describe.

Given the use of rubrics now in nearly every aspect of the U.S. education system, oftentimes those being evaluated (students, teachers, professors, institutions, etc.), we worry that professionals, policymakers, and stakeholders in our nation's public schools now focus less on educating individuals to understand and use content knowledge, principled practices based on that knowledge, and the larger significance and utility of standards as means for ongoing professional improvement. We worry that, instead, this Rubric Nation will now focus more on complying with over-simplified and even simplistic expectations and criteria that may be required to construct a rubric for practical use but actually render such rubrics dangerously conservative tools of limitation. In a schooling regime that uses rubrics almost entirely to assess, evaluate, label, and govern, there is a tendency to not actually read standards of practice to *understand* them, but rather an impulse to read them in order to simply comply and get by. We worry that this could be a fundamentally unprofessional use and a dangerous way to frame discourses of education in our society. As teachers, teacher educators, and professional education scholars, we find these phenomena disturbing and antithetical to realizing healthy and socially just notions of an educated citizenry (Tenam-Zemach & Flynn, 2011; Burns & Miller, under review).

QUESTIONING THE RUBRIC NATION

In this book, we explore a number of critical questions related to historical, contemporary, and possible future applications of rubrics and rubricization in U.S. public education contexts, especially those related to teaching and teacher education. In Chapter 1, Tenam-Zemach asks how the Maslow's (1948) concept of *rubricization* and its accompanying processes of implementation can arrest opportunities for educators to realize, attain, and embody diverse professional identities, and what the consequences are. In chapter 2, Patterson and Perhamus explore how rubrics directly impact the experience of being teachers and students.

In Chapter 3, Masko demonstrates the "philosophical schism" generated by the use of rubrics utilized in her writing pedagogy courses, while Parkison, in chapter 4, examines how educators can reframe rubrics to maintain flexible curricula and methods to the benefit of students' while escaping pitfalls that could result in rigidity and compliance mentalities in schools. Lynch, in Chapter 5, interrogates the ways in which computer-designed and technology-driven rubrics manipulate perceptions of professional educators' quality. While Boostrom, in chapter 6, examines how policies affect rubric designs in ways that affect curricula along with both teachers' and students' abilities to think critically. In Chapter 7, Gist asks how rubrics might serve as tools for exercising power in public school contexts, and how resulting power-relations affect discourses of teacher quality. In Chapter 8, Haraway and Flinders examine the challenges of using rubrics in relation to particular norms and structures of schooling. Subsequently in chapter 9, Lalonde, Gorlewski, and Gorlewski analyze the mandatory design and implementation of rubrics for use in quantifying teacher quality in U.S. public education. Dreyer and Thomas use Chapter 10 to explore whether rubrics are appropriate tools for high-stakes teacher assessment in today's schools. Marshall, a veteran school principal, asks in chapter 11, how rubrics might help or hinder attempts to provide professional educators with common language for discussing and assessing the quality of their work. Burns examines in chapter 12 how rubrics for evaluating teacher quality can actually negate research-based knowledge about teaching, learning, and education as complex and definitively variable social processes that defy categorization (and therefore rubricization). In Chapter 13, using ideas and frameworks from Whiteness Studies, Flynn considers how rubrics reflect and privilege Whiteness and inadvertently contribute to the perpetuation of institutional and systemic racism.

While *Rubric Nation* is explicitly written as a critical exercise and fundamental critique of the present system's reliance on rubrics as instruments of assessment and evaluation of teaching, learning, and educational quality, that does not mean we are blind to potential and actual healthy implementations of such tools. The point of this text is not to argue obstinately that rubrics are inherently evil or even poor tools of no use. Under the current standards based system, rubrics can be made well, implemented appropriately, and used in healthy ways. However, we feel there are significant reasons for concern, and that those concerns are not and should not be limited to those who practice as teachers and teacher educators.

We hope this book will help those audiences consider how to operate professionally to the benefit of all, of course, but we also hope this book will help other public education constituents understand rubrics more deeply as they help make policies, decisions, and resources that will be used to evaluate both our nation's teachers and our nation's children. While the following chapters often reach negative conclusions about rubrics in contemporary education, it is important to understand that they do not necessarily preclude the notion that rubrics might operate as a useful *part* of education in our nation. As Gore and Morrison (2001) quote Foucault to explain their work, our critiques are intended to be more than attempts to highlight what is wrong or harmful, actually or potentially. Rather, we seek to examine "what kinds of assumptions, what kinds of familiar, unchallenged, unconsidered modes of thought the practices we accept rest" (cited in Gore & Morrison, 2001, p. 568).

While the use of rubrics may constitute a logical result of rational policy decision-making (Bardach, 2005), in that rubrics are designed to support the efficient evaluation of policy implementation, Stone's (2002) scholarship has definitively demonstrated that such supposedly *rational* policies often have *irrational* and unpredictable consequences when implemented. Some of these consequences, by design or not, have benefits while others do harm. Rubrics are also often functions of fabricated consensus (Apple, 1990; Burns, 2014) manufactured by diverse stakeholders in complex political processes. In such cases, rubrics may in fact manifest as insufficient representations of the larger systems they are meant to account for simply because the criteria that constitute them are literally compromises about both *what knowledge* and *whose knowledge* counts at a given moment in a given discourse (Chouliaraki & Fairclough, 1999).

As Cherryholmes (1988) expresses, no policy or tool in education can ever be treated as an ahistorical, atemporal, decontextual, and/or universal public good without risking the perpetuation of significant social disparities and even injustices. *Rubric Nation* proceeds with these premises in mind so that educators and their partners may act in ways that do not seek to stratify, categorize, and normalize human beings in certain ways to the exclusion of others. Rather, this book is intended to help educators act in ways that recognize that public schooling is a Democratic project in which diversity is valued not for its use in categorization, but for its use in growth, expansion, innovation, critical thinking, and the preparation of vibrant new generations that can use their ever-evolving knowledge and experience to make the world a better place for everyone rather than only some.

REFERENCES

Airasian, P. W., & Russell, M. K. (2008). *Classroom assessment: Concepts and applications* (6th ed.). New York, NY: McGraw-Hill

Andrade, H.G. (2000). Using rubrics to promote thinking and learning. *Educational Leadership, 57*(5), 13–18.

Andrade, H. (2005). Teaching with rubrics: The good, the bad, and the ugly. *College Teaching, 53*(1), 27–30.

Andrade, H. G., & Du, Y. (2005). Student perspectives on rubric-referenced assessment. Practical Assessment, *Research and Evaluation, 10*(3). Retrieved August 25, 2014 from http://pareonline.net/pdf/v10n3.pdf.

Apple, M. W. (1990). *Ideology and curriculum.* New York, NY: Routledge.

Apple, M. W. (2006). *Educating the "right" way: Markets, standards, God, and inequality* (2nd ed.). New York, NY: Routledge.

Bardach, E. (2005). *A practical guide to policy analysis: The eightfold path to more effective problem solving* (2nd ed.).Washington, DC: CQ.

Berliner, D. C. (2005). The near impossibility of testing for teacher quality. *Journal of Teacher Education, 56*(3), 205–213.

Berliner, D. C., Glass, G. V., & Associates. (2014). *50 myths and lies that threaten America's public schools: The real crisis in education.* New York, NY: Teachers College Press.

Bourdieu, P., & Passeron, J. (1990). *Reproduction in education, society and culture.* Thousand Oakes, CA:Sage

Bowers, C.A. (2010). *Educating for eco-justice and community.* Athens, GA: University of Georgia Press.

Bowles, H. & Gintis, S. (2011). *Schooling in capitalist America: Educational reform and the contradictions of economic life (Reprint Ed.).* Chicago, IL: Haymarket Books.

Burns, L. D., & Miller, S. J. (under review). Social justice policymaking in teacher education from conception to application: Realizing Standard VI. *American Educational Research Journal.*

Burns, L. D. (2012). Standards, policy paradoxes, and the new literacy studies: A call to professional political action. *Journal of Adolescent and Adult Literacy, 56*(2), 93–97.

Burns, L. D. (2014). *Moving targets: A critical discourse analysis of standards and teacher preparation in English language arts.* Saarbrücken, Germany: Scholar's Press.

Cherryholmes, C. (1988). *Power and criticism: Poststructural investigations in education.* New York, NY: Teachers College Press.

Chouliaraki, L. & Fairclough, N. (1999). *Discourse in late modernity: Rethinking critical discourse analysis.* Edinburgh: Edinburgh University Press.

Clark, S. (1990, April). What in the F——'s name is Fordism? Paper presented at the British Sociological Association Conference, University of Surrey, Surrey, England.

Delandshere, G., & Petrosky, A. (2004). Political rationales and ideological stances of the standards-based reform of teacher education in the US. *Teaching and Teacher Education, 20,* 1–15.

Doray, B. (1990). *From Taylorism to Fordism: A rational madness.* London: Free Assn Books.

Edelfelt, R. A., & Raths, J. D. (1999). A brief history of standards in teacher education. (Report No. SP038072). Reston, VA: Association of Teacher Educators. (ED461627).

Foucault, M. (1978). The subject and power. *Critical Inquiry, 8*(4), 777–795.

Giroux, H. A. (2012). *Education and the crisis of public values: Challenging the assault on teachers, students, & public education.* New York, NY: Peter Lang.

Gore, J., & Morrison, K. (2001). The perpetuation of a (semi-)profession: Challenges in the governance of teacher education. *Teaching and Teacher Education, 17*(5): 567–582.

Grenfell, M. & James, D. (1998). *Bourdieu and education: Acts of practical theory.* London: Falmer Press.

Interstate Teacher Assessment and Support Consortium. (2011). *InTASC model core teaching standards: A resource for state dialogue.* Retrieved August 25, 2014, from http://www.ccsso.org/Documents/2011/InTASC_Model_Core_Teaching_Standards_2011.pdf

International Society for Technology in Education. (n.d.). *Essential conditions rubric: ISTE national educational technology standards.* Retrieved on August 25, 2014, from http://electronicportfolios.com/reflect/EssenCondRubric.pdf

Jackson, S. (2003). Commentary on the rhetoric of reform: a twenty-year retrospective. In K. J. Saltman & D. A. Gabbard (Eds.), *Education as enforcement: The militarization and corporatization of schools* (pp. 223–238). New York, NY: Routledge Falmer.

Reynolds-Keefer, L. (2010). Rubric-referenced assessment in teacher preparation: An opportunity to learn by using. *Practical Assessment, Research, and Evaluation, 15*(8). Retrieved August 25, 2014 from http://pareonline.net/pdf/v15n8.pdf

Lalonde, C., Gorlewski, J., & Gorlewski, D. (2014). (Dis)positioning learners: Rubrics and identity in teacher education. In M. Tenam-Zemach & J. Flynn (Eds.) *A rubric nation: Critical reflections on the uses and impact of rubrics in education.* Charlotte, NC: Information Age Publishing.

Littler, C. R. (1978). Understanding Taylorism. *The British Journal of Sociology, 29*(2), 185–202.

Lustick, D. (2010). *Certifiable: Teaching, learning, and national board certification.* Lanham, MD: R&L Publishing.

Maslow, A. (1948). Cognition of the particular and of the generic. *Psychological Review, 55*(1), 22–40.

McDonnell, L. M., & Weatherford, M. S. (2013). Organized interests and the common core. *Educational Researcher, 42*(9), 488–497.

Meier, D. (2000). *Will standards save public education?* Boston, MA: Beacon Press.

Moskal, B. M., & Leydens, J. A. (2000). Scoring rubric development: Validity and reliability. *Practical Assessment, Research & Evaluation, 7*(10). Retrieved August 25, 2014 from http://pareonline.net/getvn.asp?v=7&n=10.

National Board for Professional Teaching Standards. (2014). National Board Standards. Retrieved August 25, 2014, from http://www.nbpts.org/national-board-standards.

National Commission of Excellence in Education. (1983). *A nation at risk: The imperative for educational reform.* Washington, DC: U.S. Government Printing Office.

National Council for the Accreditation of Teacher Education. (2007). The NCATE unit standards. Retrieved August 25, 2014 from http://www.ncate.org/documents/standards/ UnitStandardsMay07.pdf

National Council for the Accreditation of Teacher Education. (2010). Unit standards in effect 2008. Retrieved on August 25, 2014, from http://www.ncate.org/Standards/UnitStandards/UnitStandardsinEffect2008/tabid/476/Default.aspx

Palmer, P. (2001). *The courage to teach: Exploring the inner landscape of a teacher's life* (first ed.). San Francisco, CA: Jossey Bass.

Patterson, N. & Perhamus, L. (2014). Teacherhood and Studenthood: Intertextuality, Identity, and the Standardization of Self. In M. Tenam-Zemach & J. Flynn (Eds.) *A rubric nation: Critical reflections on the uses and impact of rubrics in education.* Charlotte, NC: Information Age Publishing.

Ravitch, D. (2013). *Reign of error: The hoax of the privatization movement and the danger to America's public schools.* New York, NY: Knopff.

Reddy, Y. M., & Andrade, H. (2010). A review of rubric use in higher education. *Assessment & Evaluation, 35*(4), 445–448.

Saltman, K. J. (2005). *The Edison schools.* New York, NY: Routledge.

Schneider, F. J. (2006). Rubrics for teacher education in community college. *The Community College Enterprise, 12*(1), 39–55.

Sedlak, M. (1987). Tomorrow's teachers: The essential arguments of the Holmes Group report. *Teachers College Record, 88*(3), 314–325.

Shulman, L. S. (1986). Those who understand: Knowledge growth in teaching. *Educational Researcher, 15*(2), 4–14.

Stevens, D. D., & Levi, A. J. (2013). *Introduction to rubrics: An assessment tool to save grading time, convey feedback, and promote student learning.* Sterling, VA: Stylus.

Stone, D. (2002). *Policy paradox: The art of political decision making* (Rev. Ed.). New York, NY: W.W. Norton.

Stotsky, S. (2012). Common core standards miss the mark. Retrieved August 25, 2014 from www.susanohanian.org/show_nclb_outrages.php?id=3989.

Taubman, P. (2009). *Teaching by the numbers: Deconstructing the discourse of standards and accountability in education.* New York, NY: Routledge Taylor and Francis Group.

Tenam-Zemach, M., & Flynn, J. (2011). America's rise [race] to the top: Our fall from grace. *Curriculum and Teaching Dialogue, 13*(2), 113–124.

Vinson, K.D. & Ross, W. (2003).Controlling images: The power of high stakes testing. In K. J. Saltman & D. A. Gabbard (Eds.), *Education as enforcement: The militarization and corporatization of schools* (pp. 241–257). New York, NY: Routledge Falmer.

Weber, M. (1983). *Max Weber on capitalism, bureaucracy, and religion: A selection of texts.* New York, NY: Allen and Unwin.

Wiggins, S.P. (1986). Revolution in the teaching profession: A comparative review of two reform reports. *Educational Leadership, 44*(2), 56–59.

Wilson, M. (2006). *Rethinking rubrics.* Portsmouth, NH: Heinmann Publishing.

CHAPTER 1

THE RUBRICIZATION OF EXPERIENCE

Michelle Tenam-Zemach

*Each one of us has within him a whole world of things, each man of us his own
special world. And how can we ever come to an understanding if I put in the words
I utter the sense and value of things as I see them, while you who listen to me must
inevitably translate them according to the conception of things each one of you has
within himself. We think we understand each other, but we never really do.*

—Kernan (1965, p. 2)

I have always held a profound distrust of categorization or classification
of experience. I am, for better and for worse, a constructivist. I have been
trained to believe and think that all experiences are mediated through
subjective processes. When I was an undergraduate, I majored in English
literature. As anyone who has experienced this impressionable discipline,
studying literature is an immeasurably complex and influencing process.
It requires one to read myriad authors and go through many transformations of self. Despite the number of changes I have experienced, I have
steadfastly held onto the belief that no one ever seems to understand
completely the nature of meaning from my perspective. If I intend one

Rubric Nation, pages 1–19
Copyright © 2015 by Information Age Publishing
All rights of reproduction in any form reserved.

meaning, before I have the opportunity to complete the expression of that idea, my thoughts, ideas, and perspectives have already been pigeonholed. That is, frequently the person I am communicating with has developed a preconceived understanding of what I mean to say. The epigram for this chapter eloquently expresses this ontological and epistemological dilemma, and as this chapter will demonstrate, so does the work of Abraham Maslow.

In 1948, Abraham Maslow introduced a term, *rubricizing*, to explain humans' predisposition for classification and categorization. While his theory of rubricization is decades old, it offers a current and relevant theoretical framework to analyze and critique education reformers' current obsession with utilizing rubrics across the educational spectrum. The purpose of this chapter is to explore the realm of Maslow's (1948) theory of "cognition of the particular and the generic" (p. 22) and to argue that rubrics, because of their uniformity and predetermined meanings, represent a threat to both the teachers' and learners' understandings of self in the act of the learning process. Whether one is a teacher or a student, all involved in the classroom environment are learners, or at least potentially can be if they reframe how they perceive the context of the learning experience. As Maslow articulates, all experience, all behavior, all individuals can be reacted to by the psychologist (or, in the case of this evaluator) in two ways:

> He may study an experience or a behavior in its own right, as unique and idiosyncratic, i.e., as different from any other experience, or person or behavior in the whole world. Or he may respond to the experience not as unique, but as typical, i.e., as an example or representative of one or another class, category or rubric of experience. (p. 22)

When a person is perceived or attended to in a manner that immediately classifies or categorizes any (or all) aspect of a particular reality, according to Maslow (1948), that person is being *rubricized*. As he states, "Even where it (reason) confesses that it does not know the object presented to it, it believes that its ignorance consists only in not knowing which one of its time-honored categories suits the new object" (Maslow, 1948, p. 22). Humans are predisposed to place their perceptions in small boxes, or as Maslow (1948) refers to it as a "drawer full of folders" (p. 26). Seen from another perspective, humans are limited by their own impulses to categorize themselves and each other (Dewey, 1938/2008). The format of this chapter will mirror Maslow's article, entitled "Cognition of the Particular and of the Generic," a manuscript published in 1948 that presciently underscores, theorizes upon, and provides clarity and insight into today's teachers and students' rubricized experiences.

Attending to Our Learning

As Maslow (1948) points out, each person is a unique individual who can react and be reacted to in different ways. He argues that how a person attends to an experience, compared to how that person perceives it, is with "relatively greater stress on selective, preparatory, organizing and mobilizing actions" (p. 23). It is not just the nature of reality itself that determines a person's reaction, but who that person is as an individual that determines how she attends to a particular event or reality. The point of greater concern, for Maslow and for those who utilize rubrics, is the necessity of questioning whether it is possible for one to "discern in the attending responses the dichotomy between fresh, idiosyncratic attending to the unique event and stereotyped, *rubricized* recognition in the outside world of a set of categories which already exist in the mind of the attending person" (p. 23; emphasis added). Basically, Maslow posits that our nature is to attend to the world in a way so that it already conforms to how we perceive it. It is a human's way of maintaining the "status quo, rather than a true recognition of change, novelty and flux" (p. 23). We tend to force what is new to align as much as possible with what is familiar and comfortable based on our experiences and identities. While this argument may make sense or seem evident, there clearly are both positive and negative implications, particularly for how it affects and influences those who are being stereotyped or judged. One obvious implication is that rubricization could easily be imposed on people who failed to acknowledge it for what it actually is (a subjective projection that does not reflect the totality of their reality). In turn, they subject themselves to such rubricization so much so that they "learn from experience" to conform to that "other," subjective, and limited definition of who they are or ought to be in a given context. The act of rubricizing, therefore is a dangerous outcome in many education contexts. In fact, Maslow argues that rubricizing is one reason education in the United States fails to meet its goals:

> As might be expected, such a position has certain implications for helping us to understand why education in this country falls so far short of its goals. We shall stress only one point here, namely, that education makes little effort to teach the individual to examine reality directly and freshly. Rather it gives him a complete set of pre-fabricated spectacles with which to look at the world in every aspect, e.g., what to believe, what to like, what to approve of, what to feel guilty about. Rarely is each person's individuality made much of, rarely is he encouraged to be bold enough to see reality in his own style, or to be iconoclastic or "different." (p. 36)

Additionally, we do not, as Maslow (1948) points out, need to put our full attention to the act of "mere rubricizing" (p. 23) of an experience.

Instead, we only need to follow our preconceived notions about the experience when evaluating or judging it. He provides some examples of "testimony" (p. 23) for his conclusion: streamlined reading, abridged novels, and formulaic responses. I would add to these examples rubrics themselves. Rubrics provide schematics for the act of *rubricizing* and make the processes of evaluating automatic and rote rather than a thoughtful, engaging, and meaningful experience; "in a word, we do not have to 'notice' or pay attention to the familiar elements of experience" (pp. 23–24). Consequently, we run the risk of abdicating our obligations, no longer being required to attend to people as autonomous, significant individuals; it is far easier to dissociate from them, to depersonalize processes of rubrication in the name of objectivity, and place the individuals we rubricize into *a priori* categories which we have arbitrarily determined that they must fit.

Maslow (1948) argues that there is a contradiction inherent in this process. "It is simultaneously true that we tend (a) *not* to notice that which does not fit into the already constructed set of rubrics, i.e., the strange, and (b) it is the unusual, the unfamiliar, the dangerous or threatening which are *most* attention-compelling" (p. 24, emphasis in original). This particular theoretical argument potentially explains, in part, why some teachers are so often provided a high rating on their evaluations (Sawchuck, 2013). Their instructional behaviors, especially if they are traditional, are familiar to most observers, and as such will conform to an evaluator's expectations; the teachers' acts do not threaten evaluators or challenge their expectations. This is also one of the reasons why many in the field of education (not to mention policymakers) have argued for complete overhaul of teacher evaluation systems (Duncan, 2011; Weisberg, Sexton, Mulhern, & Keeling, 2009). They argue that too many teachers receive high evaluations compared to the number of underperforming students on high-stakes, standardized exams. Maslow's theory does shed some light on why those who insist on stringent teacher evaluation systems argue that using a rubric to evaluate teachers' performances should be adopted (and in most states, has already been). By utilizing rubrics to evaluate teachers, those in power will be free to categorize teachers based upon predefined, numerical scales that are always, by definition, limited, subjective, and subject to the preexisting expectations and biases of users. Teachers who are rated highly can keep their jobs (until they no longer are capable of doing so anyway), but those who are not, and those who cannot be remediated to submit to rubrication, can and will be eliminated from the system. As one editorial in the *New York Times* states when discussing the new teacher evaluation system adopted by the state of New York, and citing John King, the Commissioner of Education, "Good teachers will become better ones and ineffective teachers can be removed from the classroom" (Channing, 2013). The use of rubrics to evaluate teachers is an example of an administrative and policy mechanism of how such tools can be used as instruments of control and deprofessionalization. Rubrics could facilitate and justify sanctions against teachers because so much of it is already about compliance to *a priori* expectations and false/faulty categorization of teachers' acts.

But what of the dangers Maslow (1948) previously alludes to in his discussion? He points out that when we feel threatened, we are prone to pay "fullest attention" (p. 24). He also states that "least attention is given to the familiar-safe" (p. 24), and what appears to us to be a moderate amount of unfamiliarity is "transformed into familiar-safe, i.e., rubricized" (p. 24) as a near automatic psychological tendency that maintains any given status quo we might embrace. We opt to make certain experiences familiar and not pay them the attention needed to experience them in their in the most educative ways possible unless we feel susceptible in some way or acquire an impulse to learn.

According to Dewey (1938/2008), a miseducative experience is one that results in the individual becoming less likely to desire, seek out, and engage with new experiences that can then result in additional learning. Often, the concept of miseducation is interpreted as experience that is perceived by individuals as unpleasant or negative. However, positive experiences that please individuals and/or make them comfortable may also be miseducative. Rubrics, by definition, offer categories designed to simplify, categorize, and thereby comfort users (both teachers and students) by generating predictability. That standardized predictability can often feel comforting and become familiar and thus more pleasant if it is not addressed cautiously. When teachers create a rubric to evaluate students' performance, for example, it is in the abstract that they hope students will fulfill specific outcomes. In reality, successful performance often can be far different than success as stipulated beforehand during the design of a rubric (Turley & Gallagher, 2008; Wilson, 2006). In this way, rubrics can result in placing limits on learning, what counts as success, and how students and teachers can innovate and make positive progress.

But what type of reality does society, in the pursuit of educating and being educated, want to achieve? Do we want to attend to our daily pursuits in the manner of conforming to what is safe and known via rubricization, or would we instead prefer to develop understandings and awareness of unknowns? While there are inarguably multiple purposes to education (Labaree, 1997; Tenam-Zemach & Flynn, 2011) educators contend that education should facilitate a learner's quest for that which is generative, despite whether what is new is perceived by learners as threatening and/or challenging (Gardner & Boix-Mansilla, 1994). In their discussion of the philosopher Agamben's paradigms, Meskin and Shapiro (2014) argue for the importance of extending Agamben's work to the field of education. According to the authors, Agamben's philosophy is similar to Maslow's theory of rubricization, but Agamben advances the paradigm by disrupting presumptions that classification and categorization of experience are ever simple or sufficient. Meskin and Shapiro explain,

> Agambenian paradigms, drawing on the fecundity of an analogical thinking at least partly freed from preconception and prejudgment, display a combination of great utility for educators today: the combination of ongoing intellectual generativity with an aspiration to discover and delve into moments of disharmony between a singular object and the pre-established scheme or class into which it is supposed to fit. (p. 422)

When we consider the utilization of any rubric for evaluative purposes, we understand that the expectations for behaviors are codified by the cells of the rubric. Whether we are using that rubric to codify how a writer has organized his ideas or developed her thesis for a particular audience, for instance, we have predetermined a particular, and, by definition, finite set of possible outcomes to which we hold the writer accountable. The same is true with a principal called upon to observe and evaluate a teacher. The particular behaviors that the principal evaluates are viewed through both her pedagogic lenses and expectations based on subjective prior experiences as well as the lenses of the rubric. Agamben would argue that it is in between the cells of a rubric where action and meaningful assessment truly occur. A rubric, however, denies the evaluator the capacity to acknowledge those uncategorized but most meaningful behaviors and actions as relevant. This is profound. The consequent lack of acknowledgement has significant consequences for not only the individuals being evaluated (e.g., teachers whose jobs and/or pay will be determined by their compliance to their evaluation rubrics; a professor not receiving tenure for apparently failing to meet a subjective criterion on a rubric; a student being denied admission to a university for failing to meet a specific [and possibly tacit] subjective expectation) but also for the field of education as a whole. Thus, I argue that rubrics and the rubricization of experience constitute serious threats to teachers and students, as this chapter will explicate. And what of those people who are required to use a rubric to evaluate others? How does it affect their experiences? How does the use of rubrics limit the potential aesthetic experience of the evaluator?

Experience: Science or Art

"It is my thesis that teaching is an art guided by educational values, personal needs, and by a variety of beliefs or generalizations that the teacher holds to be true" (Eisner, 2002, p. 154). Historically, the science of education began with educational psychology. In questioning why schools often pursue mechanistic approaches to solving educational problems, Eisner (1985) credits the "assumptions of those who have shaped the thinking of the curriculum field ... [to] the aspiration to develop a scientifically based technology of education" (p. 8). Two of the individuals he references are John Dewey and Edward L. Thorndike. While a discussion of both these theorists is beyond the scope and purpose of this chapter, both, according to Eisner, "regarded science as the optimal model for inquiry" (p. 9). Our current modus operandi in schools remains in this tradition. But here too Maslow (1948) provides us a theoretical position that justifies caution of such scientific models. He states,

> The Scientist fundamentally seeks to classify the experience, to relate it to all other experience, to put it into its place in a unitary philosophy of the world to look for the respects in which this experience is similar to and different from all other experiences. (p. 25)

Scientists, Maslow posits, are determined to make sense of the world through classification and categorization, but the underlying assumption of this approach is that there is more similarity than difference between experiences. Eisner's quote above states something entirely different. Experience is determined by the individual's values, needs, and beliefs. Rubricizing experiences aligns to an unhealthy, overdetermined scientific model; it precludes acknowledgement of and value for that which is unique or different. If one supposes, however, that teaching and all human experience for that matter, can be approached as Art rather than as Science (or in conjunction with it), then a dramatically different set of paradigms emerges. Potentially, this shift opens the way to healthier and more inclusive and generative alternatives.

The Artist, according to Maslow (1948) and in the most modernist sense, "is interested only in the unique and idiosyncratic character of experience" (p. 25). Maslow's Artist treats experiences based on individual perception and attention. She understands the idiosyncratic nature of expression and experience, and attends to the experience as an individual. Maslow, citing one critic speaking of a particular artist, states, "He [the artist] sees what others only look at" (p. 25). That is, Maslow's Artist interprets each experience in a new and particular way. It is his purpose "to freeze the experience in some way so that perhaps perspicuous people may also see it fresh" (p. 25). Even reading these words provokes an array of possibilities in terms of what teachers and students can bring to the learning experiences via such an Artistic approach to education. One could imagine a context that promoted learning from the perspective of the new, the unnamed, and the unknown as perspectives that are not just useful but also valuable and essential to authentic education. For an educational milieu to insist on

individuality of expression and thought seems anathema to current education reform initiatives because their foundations in rubricization render
them largely unable to cope with the kinds of divergence that are inherent in constructivist learning by definition. The notion that each teacher
may have a different idea about the meaning of a poem, a math problem,
or scientific theory, provokes outrage and angst among many rubricized
reformers. The current rhetoric of uniformity via standards and accountability (i.e., Common Core State Standards, InTASC, etc.), dampens hope
and precludes most efforts to generate a dialogue among policymakers and
educational stakeholders about Maslow's theories of artistry and the particular as they might relate to educational experiences in the current U.S.
system. In fact, today, we are more focused on rubricizing all experiences
than ever before, not just in K–12 contexts but *all* contexts.

Nevertheless, the emphasis on a systematic approach to education, and
curriculum more specifically, is rooted in the history of America's education system. Null (2011), in discussing the deliberative curriculum tradition, reminds us that

> the attempt to turn curriculum making into a science took over pedagogical
> philosophy in the United States more than a century ago. As the idea of cur-
> riculum as a systems problem gained power, art as a guiding factor in curricu-
> lum and teaching was banished as vague, soft, and immeasurable. (p. 162)

Yet, all true learning—learning which excites the mind, engages the spirit, and motivates the soul to want to learn more—is not something that
is always scientifically measurable or quantifiable. Maslow's invocation of
the Artist provides opportunities for eliminating or ameliorating the rubricization of experience in education and offers a reframing of learning
possibilities.

Rubricizing in Perception

In the next section of Maslow's (1948) discussion of rubricizing experience, Maslow explicates how humans tend to rubricize perception. When
attending to an experience, humans tend to either ignore that which does
not fit into their preconstructed boxes or only attend to that which is most
"attention compelling" (p. 24). One's perceptions tend to label an experience rather than examine it. Maslow insists that for those who fail to perceive what is truly there to be experienced should instead be calling it "by
a name other than true perceiving" (p. 26). In other words, perception is
an act of labeling rather than actual understanding or the "absorption or
registration of the intrinsic nature of the real event" (p. 26). Instead of

regarding each individual person as a "unique individual" (p. 26), rubricization positions people to actually misperceive others by forcing them to fit some arbitrary "representation of a category" (p. 26). For instance, when a teacher meets a new student on the first day of class, she is predisposed, according to Maslow, to ascribe that student preconceived stereotypes that concord with the teacher's preexisting schematic templates. To put it another way,

> The person engaged in stereotyped perceiving ought to be compared, if we wish to be honest, to a file clerk rather than a camera. The file clerk has a drawer full of folders and her task is to put every letter on the desk into its appropriate folder under the A's or the B's or whatever. (p. 26)

There is nothing particularly revolutionary about Maslow's (1948) argument. Teachers, students, administrators and most individuals involved in the educational enterprise have been placing each other in file drawers under specific categories within the system since the inception of a systematic approach to education (Null, 2011). What are of particular importance in relation to Maslow's theorizing are the consequences of this behavior. Clearly, stereotyping any given aspect of the learning experience poses many consequences to the student, to that student's education, as well as the system of education in its entirety. For instance, tracking, a practice that separates students according to academic achievement, constructs different curriculum outcomes for students. This practice is universal in U.S. education. Yet, Oakes (n.d.) contends that this approach to grouping students generates inequalities in both the quality of education children receive and their long-term outcomes. She states that "the curriculum and instruction in various tracks are tailored to the perceived needs and abilities of the students assigned to them" (n.d.). This perception, however, is quite often based on stereotypes of student categories of students. Steele and Aronson (1995) offer some insight into this issue. They state that

> the existence of such a stereotype [widely known negative stereotype] means that anything one does or any of one's features that conform to it make the stereotype more plausible as a self characterization in the eyes of others, and perhaps even in one's own eyes. (p. 797)

Ruby Payne's (2005) *A Framework for Understanding Poverty* (Framework) is an insidious example of stereotyping through perception. This particular text has sold (as stated on the cover) more than 800,000 copies; yet its premises promote and rely entirely on a series of unfounded stereotypes about student identity groups, in particular, student groups whose identities manifest in impoverished conditions. Payne's Framework is an immensely popular training tool for school districts nationwide (Bomer,

Dworin, May, & Semingson, 2008) that contributes to the book's high sales rate. Yet, as Bomer et al. (2008) inquire, "What happens when a category of student is constructed, through language, as a uniform group in need of improvement" (p. 2498), as is the case throughout Payne's Framework. Maslow would argue that once we have perceived a particular individual as representative of a stereotyped and fixed category, we simply file that person away and preclude that learner's opportunities to grow and change as the result of new educative experiences. Payne's Framework enables teachers and school administrators to get away with oversimplifying their approaches to addressing students in poverty, and even positions them to conclude that such students are beyond helping because of the "fact" of their rubricized category. Once a student has been identified as a student in poverty, educators merely have to follow the Framework's suggestions to handle that student and comply with federal requirements.

A detailed examination of Payne's (2005) approach to professionally developing teachers to "understand" and "address" students of poverty in their classrooms is beyond the intent and scope of this chapter. However, the acceptance of Payne's work in our present national educational context powerfully illustrates the lengths to which educational stakeholders will go to rubricize individuals so that they comply with mainstream or local expectations in their system. More importantly, it allows those responsible for educating students to avoid perceiving each individual as a unique person with idiosyncratic traits and tendencies and therefore fulfilling professional obligations to attend to those individuals' diverse needs.

Maslow (1948) cites the tendency to perceive in seven ways: (a) the hackneyed; (b) the schematized and abstract; (c) the organized, structured, and univalent; (d) the named or nameable; (e) the meaningful; (f) the conventional; and (g) the expected (p. 26). When we are confronted with the "concrete," disorganized, unnameable, "meaningless," "unconventional or unexpected" (p. 26), we tend to reshape our perception of individuals related to it and force it all into a schematic with which we are already familiar and comfortable. While some may call such behavior an understandable and human impulse, in the context of public education it is incumbent upon professionals to resist such impulses because we know they do harm to the children, communities, and society we seek to serve. Rubrics impede professional resistance to such impulses.

Payne's (2005) framework offers a heinous example of this sort of unmindful stereotyping (actually, there are countless examples in the book; I offer only one). In one case study from her Framework, Payne writes of a student named LaKeitha, who is one day rude to her teacher. The teacher informs the student that she cannot return to class until the teacher has spoken to the mom (yes, the mother, not the father or parent). Accordingly, LaKeitha tells the teacher that LaKeitha's mom will come to school the next morning. But *of course*, in Payne's scenario, the mother does not show up. LaKeitha is waiting for the teacher the next day at school and apologizes relentlessly crying the entire time. She tells the teacher, "Her dad is in jail. She is the oldest of five children. Her mother works two jobs, and LaKeitha works from 5:00 to 9:00 pm at Burger King every day to bring in money" (p. 71). Oh, and if this scenario does not illustrate almost every negative stereotype associated with African American students in poverty, LaKeitha's mother is now in jail as well because of an expired inspection sticker that was identified when she was pulled over by the police (at least Payne spared the reader potentially more racist rationales for pulling the mother over and arresting her in the first place). I offer this rather sordid example in detail to demonstrate the extent to which stereotypes may position us to "perceive events more easily as representatives of categories than in their own right, as unique and idiosyncratic" (Maslow, 1948, pp. 26–27).

Even if LaKeitha's situation is typical as it relates to the experiences (of teachers being trained by Payne and her associates), wouldn't it be in the best interest of both the teachers and the students to see LaKeith with fresh eyes? Isn't it possible to conceive of LaKeitha's situation as one that differs from the readily accepted and even anticipated stereotypes to which Payne limits her scenarios? Maslow's theories explain why professional development experiences offered by the likes of Ruby Payne are predictably desired and accepted by many people, including educators: they reinforce what individuals tend to already believe about "others" rather than requiring us to inquire carefully and without preconceptions about various student populations and individuals in all their idiosyncrasies. There is no responsibility to design novel and unique approaches for strategically helping these "other" students be successful, and there is tremendous pressure to accept and operate on the premise that such "others," whether people of color, impoverished, both, or otherwise, are worth any effort at all because their behaviors and conditions are perceived as intractable rather than consequences of one's own decision to embrace rubricization.

Furthermore, Payne's (2005) stereotypical approach to perception, experience, and representation of her subjects validates some individuals' own ignorance (willful or accidental) and further promotes a worldview in which "others" are not helped so much as fixed or marginalized due to their lack of conformity with the norms dictated by rubricization of their identities. Payne's approach is much easier than actually redressing a racist system or attempting to eradicate the manifold inequities engendered by it (Apple, 2006; Lipman, 2011). Maslow (1948) expands on his discussion of perception and helps us understand how and why perspectives like Payne's do so much harm in education by stating that "true perception" is a much more time-consuming process than the "fraction of a second which is all that is necessary for labelling and cataloging" (p. 27). Payne's (2005) work exemplifies this point as well.

It is much more expeditious to provide teachers a chart that indicates potential "explanations of behaviors along with suggested interventions" (Payne, 2005, p. 79) than it is to "encompass the object, soak it in, and understand it" (Maslow, 1948, p. 27). Moreover, once these students are placed into these rubrics of poverty and the approaches to addressing them are also rubricized, it is almost impossible to envision such students another way. "One who has already been put into a rubric tends very strongly to be kept there" (Maslow, 1948, p. 27). Even if that particular person or group's behavior challenges rubricized categorizations, their behavior is often dismissed as anomalous and therefore not taken seriously. One would wonder why, despite the vast body of scholarly literature that challenges our understanding of the culture of poverty (Bomer et al., 2008; Foley, 1997), so many educators maintain a deficit perspective of many student groups, especially those whose identities include poverty and/or minority status. Maslow responds to this wonderment by arguing that it is the act of rubricizing itself that provides the answer to this "age-old problem of how people continually believe in a falsehood even when the truth stares them in the face year after year" (Maslow, 1948, p. 27). Rubricization in education enables ignorance of harsh truths and necessary actions that would otherwise be required if we truly sought to attain our oft-stated goals of successful education for all children in a diverse and democratic society.

Rubricizing in Learning and Thinking

In his discussion of rubricizing the act of learning and thinking, Maslow (1948) concludes with two major points: first, all attempts to rubricize experience constitute an "attempt to 'freeze the world'" (p. 28), because humans have impulses to rubricize experiences in order to be able to cope with and understand them for the maintenance of our personal status quo. Second, despite our need to staticize the world around us, it remains in constant motion or "flux" (p. 28), whether we like it or not. Furthermore, he argues that while the tendency for humans is to staticize our environment and generate habits that are then reinforced in our behavior to maintain that stasis, such habits are impediments to our capacity for handling the ever-vacillating problems we confront within the world, or even merely our own classrooms. While rubricizing may help us personally adjust to the world around us, make sense of it, and feel more comfortable, it typically "hinders us in our inventiveness and creativeness" (p. 31) and prevents us from adapting to the world (rather than vice versa). Thus, we need to develop dispositions to approach novel problems and issues of difference and variation in education with "fresh, unrubricized thinking... of solutions to new problems" (p. 31).

How do we apply Maslow's (2005) theoretical constructs to teaching, learning, and thinking? This is a particularly interesting question in the era of the implementation of a nationalized curriculum (i.e., Common Core State Standards) and high-stakes testing and assessments (i.e., PARCC and Smarter Balanced Consortium). The Common Core State Standards (CCSS) are a body of language arts and mathematics standards that provide learning goals regarding "what a student should know and be able to do at the end of each grade" (CCSS, 2014a). Some 46 states originally adopted the CCSS, however, since initial adoption, several states have opted out (Schneider, 2014). Nevertheless, and irrespective of the contentious nature of these standards, any common set of standards shared by the majority of classrooms across the United States will most likely lead to increased rubricization of teaching, learning, and thinking rather than what Maslow argues for: a paradigm that enables teaching, learning, and thinking and promotes creativity and inventiveness. Any curriculum that prescribes specific criteria or outcomes and measures them against a predetermined body of standards is, by definition, rubricized. These standards, and their accompanying assessments, potentially eliminate any opportunity for students to address the "changing, fluctuating aspects of the world with problems which are unique, novel, [or] never before met with" (Maslow, 1948, p. 31).

Interestingly, however, the Common Core website, when discussing the English Language Arts/Literacy standards, claims that the "standards also lay out a vision of what it means to be a literate person who is prepared for success in the 21st century" (CCSS, 2014b). Despite the fact that there is little if any evidence to support the claims made by CCSS proponents (Ravitch, 2013), these claims are rampant in the media and some of the literature on the CCSS. For example, in a 2010 Thomas B. Fordham Institute report, researchers graded all the state standards used in the United States, analyzed the CCS standards, and compared them. Carmichael, Martino, Porter-Magee, and Wilson (2010) gave some states' standards higher marks than the CCSS. Yet, despite their own findings that these universal standards may be inferior, the Fordham Institute continues to push for CCSS implementation across all states. Mercedes Schneider, a public school teacher and education activist known for her watchdog approach to CCSS proponents' claims, discusses these issues in an article entitled, "Fordham's Mike Petrilli: Selling Common Core in States With Better Standards" (Schneider, 2014). Schneider's article vilifies the Fordham Institute's report and those involved in it, in particular, Mike Petrilli, the Institute's vice president. Schneider accuses Petrilli, a self-proclaimed trustworthy education analyst, as untrustworthy because "he uses such trust to exploit—his undeniable goal being to manipulate states into keeping CCSS—even if his own think tank graded a state's standards as being better than the CCSS" (Schneider, 2014). Tom Loveless, an educational researcher at the Brookings Institution, reinforces this perspective and questions whether or not the Common Core even matters. In an article in *Education Week*, Loveless (2012) concludes that "on the basis of past experience with standards, the most reasonable prediction is that the common core will have little to no effect on student achievement" (p. 32). Both Schneider's attack on the Foundation's report and Loveless' perspective of the CCSS not only illustrate the contentious mass media rhetoric surrounding the CCSS, but more importantly, also underscores the lack of evidence as to the efficacy of wholesale implementation of a rubricized education system. This returns us to the issues associated with insisting on having students learn a predetermined body of standards and how that approach further rubricizes their experiences.

In his book, *Why School*, Mike Rose (2009) points out that standards "often are applied to students' work in ways that shut down rather than foster learning" (p. 101). Rose further points out that this approach to education, one that focuses on testing and competition, leads to "reductive definitions of teaching and learning" (p. 57). None of what is currently occurring in public education leads us to a Maslowian view of learning. Actually, it is quite the opposite. This standardized approach further rubricizes educational experiences and limits students' capacities to adequately address novel and relevant problems. As Maslow states, "The first effort of that person who tends strongly to rubricize will ordinarily be to avoid or overlook problems of any kind" (1948, p. 33). These people, Maslow argues, become seriously threatened whenever a problem is posed that demands an innovative or creative solution and requires more than a "ready made answer, i.e., which demands self-confidence, courage, and security" (p. 33). With regard to perception, the standardization of the curriculum potentially threatens teachers and students' ability to develop the skill of approaching a problem in a fresh, actual, ambiguous manner. How will future leaders contend with the unnameable if they are only ever conditioned and trained to rubricize their new experiences and maintain the status quo? How will they address the unconventional and unexpected when they only know how to schematize their experiences based on the familiar?

Given major technological and climatic shifts that are occurring in our natural environment across the globe, for instance, how will today's students be prepared for their future, and what capacities will they have to address those problems in innovative and unique ways that will almost certainly be required for success? Where in the CCSS discourse is the language for coping with chaos and meaninglessness that so often is inherent in daily experiences? How do the CCSS specifically (if at all) prepare students to be independent, mindful thinkers and problem solvers involved in "thinking activity" (Maslow, 1948, p. 35). As Maslow states, "Thinking is the technique whereby mankind creates something new, which in turn implies that thinking must be revolutionary in the sense of occasionally conflicting with what has already been concluded" (1948, p. 35). How many opportunities for this type of thinking are offered in any body of standards? In a recent commentary in *Education Week,* Prensky (2014) criticizes the CCSS on this account, stating,

> Rather than putting so much into creating and implementing the common-core standards, we would do far better to design "accomplishment-based education" whereby our kids have the means to become the kinds of people we want them to be. When they leave school, with a strong résumé to their credit, they should be creative and effective thinkers, communicators, and doers. Anyone who thinks we've arrived at that goal is fooling himself. (p. 40)

Even if standards offer students an opportunity to "problem solve," how ambiguous, abstract, unconventional, or unexpected could they be when they are expected to end up at the same place at the same time? How does a common body of standards enable teaching students to become individual thinkers, producers, or citizens who can think independently, creatively, and critically? Maslow (1948) considers similar issues when discussing the implications of rubricizing in higher education. He states,

> Proof for the contention of stereotyping in higher education can be obtained in practically any college catalogue in which all of shifting, ineffable and mysterious reality is neatly divided into three credit slices which, by some miraculous coincidence, are exactly sixteen weeks long, and which fall apart neatly into completely independent departments. If ever there was a perfect example of a set of rubrics imposed *upon* reality rather than *by* reality, this is it. (p. 36, emphasis in original)

Maslow's perspective of education, one written over 60 years ago, should compel all those involved in the education enterprise to reconsider what society's aims, goals, and aspirations are for preparing students for life and success. If we continue to rubricize teaching and learning experiences (irrespective of their level in our education system) and the curriculum, then we are doomed to a shared but false reality that feels familiar but does us harm.

What to Do About It?

Despite a recent move in the United States to a national standardized body of content standards in P–12 education, and an overreliance and emphasis on the use of rubrics, Maslow (1948) offers us insight and possible approaches to consider in lieu of this direction. He states, "One idea strongly suggested by an examination of rubricized thinking is a decreased absorption with rubrics and an increased concern with fresh experiences, with concrete and particular realities" (p. 36). How does this translate to educational practice? Clearly, the use of rubrics for teacher evaluation systems will not change as long as both federal and state policies insist on this form of evaluation. However, by critically engaging in meaningful dialogue with superintendents, school administrators, and school boards, as well as parents and local politicians, educational stakeholders can influence the overreliance on these tools. Maslow offers us a language by which to engage in such dialogues, which can shift people's understanding of the negative implications of an overdependence on such limiting instruments as rubrics. Additionally, by sharing Maslow's theoretical ideas with educators, a deeper, more pervasive understanding of the need to shift both pedagogic and curricular practices becomes justified. In citing Whitehead, Maslow offers us an additional perspective:

> My own criticism of our traditional educational methods is that they are far too much occupied with intellectual analysis, and with the acquirement of formularized information. What I mean is, that we neglect to strengthen habits of concrete appreciation of the individual facts in their full interplay of emergent values, and that we merely emphasize abstract formulations which ignore this aspect of the interplay of diverse values" (p. 36)

Students, thus, need opportunities to see beyond formulaic thinking and instead spend time problematizing. Pedagogic models such as Problem-Based Learning (Eggen & Kauchak, 2012; Kain, 2003) and Differentiated Instruction (Sousa & Tomlinson, 2011; Tomlinson, 2001) are just some of the alternative models that may facilitate a shift in rubricized methods of teaching and learning. As Maslow (1948), citing Whitehead, argues, "The general training should aim at eliciting our concrete apprehensions, and should satisfy the itch of youth to be doing something" (pp. 36–37). Providing students with greater and more frequent opportunities to "do" rather than to just be fed information is an appropriate place to start. Minimizing standardized testing both at the local and state levels would also ameliorate the damage done by the rubricization of educational experiences. We must shift the focus from purely content-driven teaching and testing to individualized, problematized learning and decision making, and Maslow's theory of rubricization offers us a means to justify why and how to accomplish this.

CONCLUSION

Maslow's theory of rubricizing experience is as relevant today as it was in 1948, if not more so. For the first time in the history of the United States, this country has a national curriculum. Despite various stakeholders' relentless resistance to a national curriculum, those who exert the most influence and power have been able to achieve this goal. And while the jury is still out on whether or not these standards will positively or negatively influence educational (and thus societal) outcomes, one thing is for certain: by mandating that all children learn the same content at the same time, and often in the same ways, the ambiguous, the unnamed, and the unknown will have little if any space in the curriculum.

Today, more than any other time in recent history, teachers feel under constant threat of being fired, being labeled as failures, and having no influence over the curriculum that they must implement. Students too feel threatened and overwhelmed by the endless barrage of assessments and high-stakes exams. These threats, as Maslow (1948) argues, only reinforce impulses to rubricize how teachers attend to and perceive the students in their classrooms and the curriculum that they teach. Within this paradigm of education, how will teachers encourage students to accept the ambiguous and grapple with the unknown? How will students approach learning unashamed of what they do not know and cannot name? Such questions abound, but little of the current rhetoric of reform provides any unique or inventive solutions.

As Maslow (1948) reminds us, "There is a certain contrast between classifying experiences and appreciating them, between using them and enjoying them" (p. 37). Just as I do not want others to rubricize my experiences for me, I do not want to be guilty of rubricizing them for myself or others. Personally, I prefer to appreciate and enjoy my experiences. I want to approach my experiences in unsullied, idiosyncratic ways. How different would the educational landscape appear if each teacher and each student approached the other and their learning experiences in this manner? What impact could this paradigmatic shift have on the lives of all those involved in education? Unfortunately, with the rubricization that comes with the Common Core State Standards and the national assessment storm that is now blinding us, we probably will not find out any time soon.

REFERENCES

Apple, M. (2006). *Educating the "right way": Markets, standards, God and inequality.* New York, NY: Routledge/Falmer.

Bomer, R., Dworin, J. E., May, L., & Semingson, P. (2008). Miseducating teachers about the poor: A critical analysis of Ruby Payne's claims about poverty. *Teachers College Record, 110*(12), 2497–2531. Retrieved from http://www.tcrecord.org/content.asp?contentid=14591

Carmichael, S. B., Martino, G., Porter-Magee, K., & Wilson, W. S. (2010). State of the statestandards—and the common core—in 2010. Retrieved from http://www.math.jhu.edu/~wsw/FORD/SOSSandCC2010_FullReportFINAL.pdf

Channing, J. (2013, June 1). New York to evaluate teachers with new system. [Editorial]. *The New York Times.* Retrieved June 2, 2013, from http://www.nytimes.com/2013/06/02/nyregion/new-evaluation-system-for-new-york-teachers.html?hpw

Common Core State Standards (CCSS). (2014a). *About the standards.* Retrieved from http://www.corestandards.org/about-the-standards/

Common Core State Standards (CCSS). (2014b). *English language arts standards.* Retrieved from http://www.corestandards.org/ ELA-Literacy/

Dewey, J. (2008). *Experience and education.* New York, NY: Touchstone. (Original work published 1938)

Duncan, A. (2011). Working toward "wow": A vision for a new teaching profession [Press release]. Retrieved from http://www.ed.gov/news/speeches/working-toward -wow-vision-new-teaching-profession

Eggen, P., & Kauchak, D. (2012). *Strategies and models for teachers: Teaching content and thinking skills* (6th ed.). New York, NY: Pearson.

Eisner, E. (1985). *The educational imagination: On the design and evaluation of school programs* (2nd ed.). New York, NY: Macmillan.

Eisner, E. (2002). *The educational imagination: On the design and evaluation of school programs* (3rd ed.). New York, NY: Macmillan.

Foley, D. E. (1997). Deficit thinking models based on culture: The anthropological protest. In R. Valencia (Ed.), *The evolution of deficit thinking: Educational thought and practice.* London, UK: Falmer.

Gardner, H., & Boix-Mansilla, V. (1994). Teaching for understanding: Within and across disciplines. *Educational Leadership, 51*(5), 14–18.

Kain, D. L. (2003). *Problem-based learning for teachers grades 6–12.* Boston, MA: Ablongman.

Kernan, A. B. (Ed.). (1965). *Classics of the modern theater: Realism and after.* New York, NY: Harcourt Brace.

Labaree, D. F. (1997). Public goods, private goods: The American struggle over educational goals. *American Educational Research Journal, 34*(1), 39–81.

Lipman, P. (2011). *The new political economy of urban education: Neoliberalism, race and the right to the city.* New York, NY: Routledge/Falmer.

Loveless, T. (2012, April 18). Does the common core matter? *Education Week, 32*(31), 28. Retrieved from http://www.edweek.org/ew/articles/2012/04/18/28loveless_ep.h31.html

Maslow, A. (1948). Cognition of the particular and of the generic. *Psychological Review, 55*(1), 22–40.

Meskin, J., & Shapiro, H. (2014). 'To give an example is a complex act': Agamben's pedagogy of the paradigm. *Educational Philosophy and Theory, 46*(4), 421–440.

Null, W. (2011). *Curriculum: From theory to practice.* New York, NY: Rowman & Littlefield.

Oakes, J. (n.d.). Keeping track, part 1: The policy and practice of curriculum inequality. *Equity Materials.* Retrieved July 25, 2104, from http://academic.sun.ac.za/mathed/174/Oakes.pdf

Payne, R. (2005). *A framework for understanding poverty* (4th ed.). Highlands, TX: aha Process.

Prensky, M. (2014). The goal of education is becoming. *Education Week, 33*(30), 40.

Ravitch, D. (2013). *Reign of error: The hoax of the privatization movement and the danger to America's public schools.* New York, NY: Knopf.

Rose, M. (2009) *Why schools?: Reclaiming education for all of us.* New York, NY: New Press.

Sawchuck, S. (2013). Teachers' ratings still high despite new measures. *Edweek, 32*(20), 18–19. Retrieved from http://www.edweek.org/ew/articles/2013/02/06/20evaluate_ep.h32.html

Schneider, M. (2014, April 9). Fordham's Mike Petrilli: Selling common core in states with better standards. *Huffington Post.* Retrieved May 15, 2014, from http://www.huffingtonpost.com/mercedes-schneider/fordhams-mike-petrilli-se_b_5102434.html

Sousa D. A., & Tomlinson, C. A. (2011). *Differentiation and the brain: How neuroscience supports the learner-friendly classroom.* Bloomington, IN: Solution Tree.

Steele, C. M., & Aronson, J. (1995). Stereotype threat and the intellectual test performance of African Americans. *Journal of Personality and Social Psychology, 69*(5), 797–811.

Tenam-Zemach, M. & Flynn, J. (2011). America's race [rise] to the top: Our fall from grace. *Curriculum Teaching Dialogue, 13*(2), 113–124.

Tomlinson, C. A. (2001). *How to differentiate instruction in mixed-ability classrooms* (2nd ed.). Upper Saddle River, NJ: Pearson

Turley, E. D., & Gallagher, C. W. (2008). On the *uses* of rubrics: Reframing the great rubric debate. *English Journal, 97*(4), 87–92.

Weisberg, D., Sexton, S., Mulhern J., & Keeling, D. (2009, June 8). The Widget Effect: Our national failure to acknowledge and act on differences in teacher effectiveness. *TNTP.* Retrieved from http://widgeteffect.org/downloads/TheWidgetEffect.pdf

Wilson, M. (2006). *Rethinking rubrics.* Portsmouth, NH: Heinmann.

CHAPTER 2

THE RUBRICIZATION OF TEACHERHOOD AND STUDENTHOOD

Intertextuality, Identity, and the Standardization of Self

Nancy G. Patterson
Lisa M. Perhamus

It was one of those cramped conference rooms that had too many chairs and a table that looked like an over-sized surfboard. Two women dressed in neatly tailored suits busied themselves in one corner shuffling handouts and over-head transparencies into neat stacks. Nancy, who taught middle school English at the time, was a member of the district's Language Arts Curriculum Committee. Teachers on the committee had been asked to bring a class set of student papers to the meeting.

It was 1992 and the teachers from the committee represented every building in the district. They were going to learn about rubrics. The two women in suits were consultants from the state department of education,

Rubric Nation, pages 21–33
Copyright © 2015 by Information Age Publishing
All rights of reproduction in any form reserved.

and they promised a golden secret: authentic assessment. Assessment that would save teachers time, focus their instruction, clearly articulate student expectations, and muscle change-resistant wayward teachers toward a common curricular vision.

Who could resist?

The committee members were asked to read their students' assignments, but not mark on them. Once they finished reading, they were asked to sort the papers into three categories: Exemplary, Satisfactory, and Unsatisfactory. From there, they paired up and helped each other determine exactly what it was that made the exemplary papers so good. They categorized those qualities, wrote descriptors, and then moved on to the satisfactory and unsatisfactory papers. Several hours later, the committee members had created categories and descriptors for each "level" of paper and tidy charts that could guide them as they assessed each student paper according to the criteria they created. Gone were grades like A, B, C, etc. Now they had numbers. 4 was the best. 0 was the worst. Rather than giving one monolithic "grade," they had five or six or however many assessment designations they wanted, all corresponding to descriptors. The nice women in suits from the department of education anointed committee members with new powers of descriptive objectivity that would allow them to finally assess students, increase achievement, and release teachers from marking up students' papers. The committee had drunk from the wellspring of truth, justice, student centered-ness, and more free time.

But something was wrong. For one thing, the teachers spent significant time "range finding," sorting papers and writing descriptors for the various categories they discovered. Gone was the promise of efficiency. In fact, the process was so labor-intensive that many teachers decided to assign fewer pieces of writing. But there was something more disturbing happening. There were always some papers, though good, that did not lend themselves to the tidy cells on the rubrics. It was easy for group members to assume they simply had not created good enough rubrics, but that proved to not matter. Within months, the state announced that it was adding a writing component to the state literacy assessment. With that announcement came the rubric that would be used. With relief that they no longer had to labor over developing post-writing rubrics, teachers adopted the state's four-point rubric. In practice, though, the rubric became more than just a guide for their in-class writing assessments; it became a declaration of expectation for students and teachers alike.

In this chapter we explore how the effort to meet these expectations affects not just the methods of teaching and learning, but also the experience of being teachers and students. The contemporary standardized educational climate is, in many ways, a regime of rubric measurements. This regime has serious implications as it produces a "rubricized" sense-of-self that positions rubrics as a hegemonic force. Furthermore, the utilization of rubrics as tools mobilizes the components and content of rubrics—operationalizes the expectations, details and standards of rubrics. Once operationalized, these components actively code and shape both the work being evaluated and the people involved in the evaluation process—the rubric "rubricizes."

Wilson (2006) refers to rubrics as a "fixed list" that operates outside the immediate experience of the act of writing and doing and the act of responding to an individual who is in the process of becoming. Both the experience of student and teacher, the very fabric of identity, are too easily set aside by "the reductive categories of rubrics [that] fail to honor the complexity of what we see in writing and what our students try to accomplish" (p. 41). Today's regulatory educational environments that are based on accountabilities and standardized assessments of both students and teachers call for deep analysis of the ways in which teaching and learning relationships have become rubricized.

TEACHERHOOD AND STUDENTHOOD

Rubrics interrupt the relationship between teacher and student and insert a distancing space in the experiential dimensions of teaching and learning. Creating an additional layer through which teaching and learning happen, rubrics impact the human experience of teacherhood and studenthood. Parker Palmer (2001) reminds us that good teachers have a great capacity for "connectedness." Palmer (2001) adds that they "are able to weave a complex web of connections among themselves, their subjects, and their students so that students can learn to weave a world for themselves" (p. 2). He warns us, though, against adopting a "culture of technique" (p. 17) where tools, in this case rubrics, take on greater and greater authority. Even when the teachers mentioned above created rubrics based on actual student work, they struggled with both the technique and the tool. For the teachers on the district language arts committee, good writing slipped through the cracks of the rubric, even when it was custom made. And, perhaps even worse, they began to doubt their own abilities to determine what good writing was. The expectation to follow the rubric began to usurp their own conceptualizations of the nature of effective writing. In Anyon's (1989) terms, the interaction between student and teacher is short-circuited.

So, what happens to the complex web of connectedness when the culture of technique subsumes how teachers and students relate to one another? We argue that once the tool of the rubric is used for assessment, the outlined expectations become operationalized. As these rubric expectations become part of how teachers and students orient their "selves" to the teaching and learning process, the expectations become an inscriptive part of the ongoing process of how teachers and students understand their identities in the education process. In short, the utilization of rubrics inscribes the identities of human beings. They become rubricized, altered by an external technique created by someone who does not know the identities of the students who will be assessed or the teacher who embodies the instruction. As early as 1948, Maslow warned against accepting "staticized abstractions from reality" (p. 23) and challenged us to resist "rubricizing in attention" (p. 24). Maslow defines rubricizing as the act of distancing oneself from experience, of not noticing. He argues that "rubricizing is a partial, token or nominal response rather than a total one. Rubricization, then, embraces an "automaticity of behavior" (p. 24) that allows us permission to rely on "the familiar and hackneyed rather than the unfamiliar and fresh" (p. 26). Rubricization, then, limits our abilities to see each person as an individual. We use this as the operational definition of rubricization.

Rubrics also become the prescription of the identity categories, of teacherhood and studenthood. As a mediating tool, the rubric not only serves to interpret (assess) student work and teacher work, it becomes an interpretive filter through which students and teachers come to know themselves and each other in the communicative process of teaching, assessing and learning. Teachers communicate to students "rubricized" expectations; student learning is thereby rubricized in the process of producing work that is in alignment with the rubric criteria. Rather than students immersing their selves in their work, engaging in the process of thinking, creating, analyzing and learning, and teachers immersing their selves in a similar fashion in response to the work, both students and teachers must filter this process through the layer of the rubric.

We do not accept current arguments that rubrics themselves are neutral and that any flaws in them can be lessened through changes in wording. We argue that rubrics create a distance and too often a mandated layer through which students and teachers communicate. The development of work and the feedback is no longer a direct dialogue between teacher and student. That dialogue is rubricized. To speak about academic work, teachers and students now use words from the text of the rubric for the assessment process; the rubric has become inserted into the teacher-student relationship. For the teachers on the English Language Arts curriculum committee, student work was sorted into categories: exemplary, satisfactory, and unsatisfactory. Conversation amongst the teachers focused on clarification of terms like "writing conventions" and "adequate command of the language" not about the unique attributes of each writer as demonstrated in that moment of writing.

It is critical to consider how this rubricized dialogue, this additional, distancing layer, affects students' and teachers' sense of self. Palmer (2001) helps to elucidate this:

> External tools of power have occasional utility in teaching, but they are no substitute for authority, the authority that comes from the teacher's inner life. The clue is in the word itself, which has author at its core. Authority is granted to people who are perceived as authoring their own words, their own actions, their own lives, rather than playing a scripted role at great remove from their own hearts. When teachers depend on the coercive powers of law or technique, they have no authority at all. (pp. 32–33)

The experiential process of teaching and learning, which is always active and evolving, is interrupted with rubric cells that capture, in snapshot fashion, a moment in the process. The process is blocked, the experiential is defined, and the self is alienated from both. Rubrics are fixed and static tools through which the fluidity of process must pass. Analyses of rubrics must move beyond conventional conversations about rubrics as tools and begin to examine rubrics as text. A fruitful analysis then becomes focused on the intertextuality (Kristeva, 1980) of rubric text and the text of self.

While a number of scholars (Bahktin, 1986; Fairclough, 1992; Foucault, 1972; Gee, 2010; Kristeva, 1980) have taken up the concept of intertextuality in different ways, in its simplest, commonly understood form, intertextuality refers to the relationship between a text (let's call this Text A); the reader of that text (Reader A); previous texts that have contributed to shaping the meaning of Text A (because all texts are influenced by history and knowledge previously produced); previous life experiences of Reader A (because personal histories influence how people interpret texts and make meaning), and all of the anticipated or subsequent texts and readers after Text A and Reader A. This ongoing relational loop among history, meaning-making, words and readers intersect through texts, with each component influencing another—intertextuality.

Fairclough (1992) observes that theories of intertextuality can help us trace how power circulates through the text and the reader–through object and subject, and that tracing this power circulation can help us to understand that *how* we read connects with the social structures of society. He writes:

> For Bahktin, all utterances, both spoken and written ... are oriented retrospectively to the utterances of previous speakers (and texts). Thus 'each utterance is a link in the chain of speech communication' ... 'our speech ... is filled with others' words, varying degrees of otherness and varying degrees of 'our-own-ness,' varying degrees of awareness and detachment. These words of others carry with them their own expression, their own evaluative tone, which we assimilate, rework, and reaccentuate' (Bakhtin 1986, p. 89). That

is, utterances—'texts' in my terms—are inherently intertextual, constituted by elements of other texts...Kristeva observes that intertexuality implies 'the insertion of history (society) into a text and of this text into history (1986, p. 39)...the text absorbs and is built out of texts from the past...the text responds to, reaccentuates, and reworks past texts, and in so doing helps to make history and contributes to wider process of change...this inherent historicity of texts enables them to take on the major roles they have in contemporary society at the leading edge of social and cultural change...The concept of intertextuality points to the productivity of texts, to how texts can transform prior texts and restructure existing conventions to generate new ones...one can...conceptualize intertextual processes and processes of contesting and restructuring orders of discourse as processes of hegemonic struggle...The relationship between intertexuality and hegemony is important.' (pp. 102–103)

In his introduction to Kristeva's *Desire in Language* (1980), Roudiez clarifies this densely complex concept of intertextuality as involving, "...the components of a textual system...(and) the transposition of one or more systems of signs into another, accompanied by a new articulation of the enunciative and denotative position" (cited in Kristeva, 1980, p. 15). The rubric becomes a textual system that is introduced into the existing systems of the classroom.

When a teacher uses a rubric, the "systems of signs" that are the assignment are cyclically transposed into the rubric cells of criteria. And as students complete their assignments with the guidance of the rubric, their work is articulated anew according to the rubric's grading scale that denotes (for the teacher) its position of "exceeds expectations/meets expectations/does not meet expectations." However, let's pursue this thinking further. Is it just the student's work that is being articulated anew according to the measurements of the rubric or is it, in fact, also our teacher and student selves undergoing this process of re-articulation? Maslow (1948) reminds us that it is far easier to categorize than recognize the "unique and idiosyncratic" (p. 27). He argues that rubricizing adds "up to an almost complete guarantee against creativeness and inventiveness" (p. 32). So, what happens to the teacher and student selves when creativeness and inventiveness are weaned away from experience and the act of thinking "amounts to no more than a shuffling about and rearrangement" (p. 34)?

SENSE OF SELF

Every component in the process of teaching and learning is rooted in one's sense-of-self and how this sense-of-self is oriented to the roles we fill (Butler, 1990; Eckerman, 1997; Foucault, 1988; Fox, 1997.). What is happening with one's sense-of-self, at a human, experiential level, is at the core of this entire discussion. How does the use of rubrics potentially rubricize one's sense-of-self through our roles as teachers and students? Teachers and students are expected to mold themselves into the identity categories of teacherhood and studentood. While this has historically been the case, contemporary mandates over the use of rubrics has shaped this historical moment, in particular as one in which teacherhood and studenthood are rubricized identity categories. Selves can only fit if they have taken on a rubricized shape. Haswell and Haswell's (2010) discussion of potentiality and singularity gets at this idea. They argue that creativity, choice, and rhetorical space must be returned to the classroom. When we teach to a narrowed notion of academic writing, Haswell and Haswell say, we fail to ask how that will affect students' potential for writing after graduation. We can use the same analogy with rubrics. When we rubricize instruction and academic work, we must ask how that will affect students' potential as writers and teachers after graduation. Haswell and Haswell theorize that students are now caught in the "terrible binds" (p. 71) of a singular voice. The multiplicity of their voice is re-shaped to the greatest common denominator, to invoke a mathematical term, to a singular expression that matches one of the rubric criteria. This formalistic bind, they argue, plays out in the lives of teachers who have no power to create lessons or assessments that are based on the needs of the students in their classrooms. Everything is provided for them, and their administrators make sure they remain fixed to the program. Many of these programs even provide scripts that usurp teachers' capabilities to use their own language as they provide instruction. The "-hood" of teacherhood and studenthood rubricizes the self (the self of the teacher; the self of the student) and the multiplicity of voices and identity become muted through the expectation of and fidelity to more singular voices. These singular voices "force experience into rubrics" and becomes "a screen between reality and the human being" (Maslow, 1948, p. 39). Student work and teacher feedback travel through the rubric, through the screen, rather than directly to the person. The primary relationship for both teacher and student in the teaching and learning process, in this sense, is to the rubric as opposed to each other. It is important to trace this traveling through the rubric, and to examine how rubrics have framed our identities as teachers.

UNPACKING STATICITY

The ongoing fluidity of human development, experience and expression, that contribute to the ever-changing sense-of-self, "bump up" against the fixed and concrete rubric cells through which the teaching/learning selves must traverse in the journey of education. A contribution of postmodern and post-structural theory is an analytical lens through which we can see how things that are often deemed static are actually fluid, and how staticity gives the appearance of inherent truths that analysis of the fluid reveal as constructed. Though Butler (1990) makes the following argument about the identity category of gender, her insights are helpful in thinking through how the identity category of teacher is constructed through legitimizing apparatuses like rubrics.

> The question of the 'subject' is crucial for politics . . . because juridical sub-jects are invariably produced through certain exclusionary practices that do not "show" once the juridical structure of politics has been established. In other words, the political construction of the subject proceeds within cer-tain legitimating and exclusionary aims, and these political operations are effectively concealed and naturalized by a political analysis that takes juridical structures as their foundation. Juridical power inevitably "produces" what it claims to merely represent. (p. 2)

In this instance, we are using self and subject interchangeably, and we pro-pose that the regulatory reach of rubrics give their implementation juridi-cal power. We must go further in our collective analyses about the impact of rubrics on teaching and learning and examine how the use of rubrics "'produces' what it claims to merely represent."

Foucault (1980) makes similar arguments about the need to trace how various identity categories are constructed throughout history because it is through that tracing that we can see how the politics of an historical mo-ment literally construct categories of identity and subjectivity to serve politi-cal purposes. We must ask questions about the political purposes rubrics now serve, and this includes how the rubricized categories of teacherhood and studenthood are part of the politic. We must understand what is at stake in the intertexuality of using rubrics. We must examine how the cur-rent standardized, rubricized climate is producing a teacherhood and stu-denthood that it claims to merely represent (and improve). And, we must be critically reflective about the ways in which we, as teachers and students, participate in this production. In what ways do we produce our selves as "rubric ready" teachers and students? It is a biopolitical (Foucault, 1980) question that is grounded in the idea that in our desire to be the best teach-ers and students possible, we have, at least in part, learned how to rubricize our subjectivities in order to simultaneously survive the currently restrictive standardized climate and to score the highest number on the performance rating scale.

Analysis of the production of teacherhood, studenthood and the bio-political dimensions of the intertextuality between rubric and self calls us to intimately unpack how the rubric, as a tool, becomes operational-ized. Let's consider how a word, like rubric, that might appear "static," is simultaneously productive. Postmodern discourse often refers to this kind of analysis as problematizing any given concept (Natolo & Hutcheon, 1993). Teachers in a highly regimented literacy program, for example, might be able to identify a problem (a situation representing a dilemma or obstacle) that is born of the restrictive educative environment. Responding to this problem might require considering how to resolve the dilemma or overcome the obstacle. As a noun, a problem is a thing to be analyzed and acted upon. To "problematize," though, shifts the fixed connotation of the noun to a verb that calls for actively "seeing the problems" (the dilemmas and tensions) in what society often deems as static. A teacher who encourages students to problematize the word, "meritocracy," for example, asks students to consider the ways in which meritocracy is sold as an American Dream, the concept that hard work yields social upward mobility and challenges students to consider the social, economic, political and cultural realities that have historically impacted people's capacity to move up the socioeconomic ladder. The act of problematizing demands questioning status quo definitions; seeing multiplicities in what may appear to be singular; and purposively unpacking the fixed or static with an eye toward what is operationalized to create that which is understood to be concrete. A poststructural theoretical lens calls for analyzing the ways in which nouns might operate as verbs (Williams, 2005).

Recognizing the technologies or mechanisms for how a thing becomes operationalized is an important political undertaking, for it encourages analyses that can unmask *how* something is actually working. Without such questioning, things become settled; assumed to be "the way things are;" taken for granted and thereby less resisted. It is difficult to resist that which one cannot see. Unpacking how something is operationalized, seeking ways to understand the verb of the noun, helps us to see the details for analysis if our goal is to more deeply recognize the powerful, active reach of mechanisms that render things invisible. It is precisely because exploitation happens most frequently in those invisible spaces that rendering the invisible visible is important work.

So, what might we see if we examine the ways in which the rubric, most commonly understood as a noun (a tool for assessing student work) operates as a verb (circulating through the student's and teacher's experience of assessment)? Does the act of using rubrics rubricize the human experience of teaching and learning? And, if we acknowledge the degree to which human experience affects our individual and collective sense-of-self, are there ways in which the current "rubric climate" is "rubricizing teacher and student identity?"

During the assessment process, the rubric is a mediating tool through which students and teachers make sense of, negotiate and define academic performance. Less visible, and given less theoretical attention, is the degree to which students and teachers internalize the valuating aspect of rubrics. It is as if in the drive to meet the requirements of the rubric has become so intense (because the 21st century is arguably a rubricized regime of education in the guise of automated essay scoring, rubricized teacher preparation programs, and the language of curriculum standards) that people have swallowed the cells of the rubric and increased the likelihood that what they then produce gets the most points. The current rubricized climate encourages learning and teaching through these rubric cells. The cells are now part of how teachers think, create, understand and define. There is a blurring of cells. In the cells of our beings are the cells of the rubrics. Today is an historical moment in which rubrics are embodied.

THE LAZY TIRED SELF

In order to understand how rubrics are embodied, we have to look at why we so willingly invite them into our experience. Wilson (2006) acknowledges that rubrics bring with them irresistible promises "to save time, to provide an objective grading tool, and to keep our teaching and feedback focused on the most important aspects of good writing" (p. 27). Maslow (1948) agrees. Rubricizing, he says, is far easier and less time consuming than what he refers to as "whole-hearted attending" (p. 23). Rubricizing, according to Maslow, does not require the kind of attention necessary for true understanding and perception. He argues that because the "mind can cognize well only what is static, much of our attending, perceiving, learning, remembering, and thinking actually deals with staticized abstractions from reality or with theoretical constructions rather than with reality itself" (p. 23). Maslow (1954) makes it clear that though we cannot live without abstractions and concepts, they must be "experientially based rather than empty or helium-filled" (p. 205). In other words, we must be willing to do the difficult work of assessing. This is what requires time and a level of understanding and perception, the very things that rubrics promise to provide. But, Maslow (1948) argues that rubrics embody a lazy tired self, a self that does not have to truly notice and respond. Rubrics represent a dismissal of authentic experience through a "partial, token, or nominal response rather than a total one" (p. 23). This token or partial response enables us to perceive merely the familiar and ordinary. Work that falls outside the familiar cells of a rubric, work that is creative, perhaps, or unusual, is approached as strange, or at best, difficult to classify within the boundaries of a rubric. Maslow (1948) says, "where the event is unfamiliar, concrete, ambiguous, unnamed, meaningless, unconventional, or unexpected, we show a strong tendency to twist or force or shape the event into a form that is more familiar, more abstract, more organized, etc." (p. 26). Maslow (1948) also states that, "We tend to perceive events more easily as representatives of categories than in their own right, as unique and idiosyncratic" (pp. 26-27). In a learning environment we then teach to the familiar, to that which is less strange in order to twist that which is to be assessed into a product that will fit the rubric. This, Maslow warns, leads us away from experience and away from viewing individuals as unique. This abstraction and dismissal of individual experience, of the very elements that embody the self, is disrespectful, not only to students, but teachers.

Wilson (2006) gets to the heart of this when she argues that rubrics enable us to approach academic work through the lenses of deficiency and skepticism. When the purpose of assessment is to efficiently rank or rate academic work, we absent our selves from our own experiences as independent and deep thinkers and we dismiss the experiences of students. This enables use to overlook potential, not only in students, but in our selves as teachers. The setting aside of our selves as thinkers and experiencers in favor of the static language of a rubric constrains our own potentiality (Haswell & Haswell, 2010). This devaluing of experience is an act of hegemony.

CONCLUSION

Much of the conceptualization of academic achievement comes out of a history of discourse traditions formed to serve the well-educated classes while simultaneously limiting the advancement of other, less educated groups (Anyon, 1980; Apple, 2004; Fairclough, 1992; Giroux, 1983). This history represents a hegemonic tendency that continues to dismiss other discursive traditions (hooks, 1994). Rubrics advance this hegemonic, marginalizing frame of academic assessment, creating a politically based distance between the act of assessment and the acts of learning. Contemporary utilization of rubrics, in its reification of conformity, marginalizes those who wish to remain rooted in process over product and erodes teachers' and students' sense of authorship and agency. Peter Johnston (2012) writes

> For us to have agency we have to believe that things are changeable, because if they can't be changed, taking action is futile . . . In the talk of the classroom, we want to hear the threads of a dynamic view of intellect—indeed, of self. We want to inoculate . . . against infection by fixed theories; we want . . . to say 'I'm not good at this yet' and to take steps to change that. Indeed, yet is a key word that we should regularly encourage. . . . (p. 21)

The tidy cells on a rubric mute the "yet" of becoming. Rather than marking a passage to greater learning, they now serve as an end mark. Too often the rubric ends a process rather than starts one. Thus, it inoculates us from the "yet." It creates what Haswell and Haswell (2012) refer to as constrained potentiality, and fixes performance rather than enables an act of becoming.

As the act of using a rubric interrupts the "yet" in the narrative, it seduces us into viewing knowledge acquisition as an artifact rather than a process. Wilson (2006) argues that rubrics lull us into a static state that reduces the "yet" to a lower form of achievement. Rubrics assume that academic work will be perfect and that anything that falls outside some sort of pre-determined ideal interrupts our abilities to explore meaning.

Rubrics are not the golden secret of authentic assessment promised by those women in suits who visited Nancy and her colleagues on the language arts curriculum committee. Our identities as teachers who transact with students who are themselves exploring their identities as thinkers, are interrupted not only by rubrics, but by the staticity rubrics impose on the act of becoming, the act of "yet." Wilson notes that "our job as...teachers is to help every student improve, a role at odds with the rubric's intended role as a sorting machine" (pp. 32–33). This is a role, we conclude, that dismisses and constrains the scholarly self of teaching. Assessment at its best is always negotiated between and embodied in the individual identities that people our school environments. It is fluid, not static. It is the work that all of us commit to when we decide to teach.

REFERENCES

Anyon, J. (1980). Social class and the hidden curriculum of work. *Journal of Education, 162*(1), 67–92.

Apple, M. (2004). *Ideology and curriculum.* London, England: Routledge.

Bakhtin, M. (1981). *The dialogical imagination* (M. Holquist, Ed., C. Emerson & M. Holquist, Trans.). Austin: University of Texas Press.

Butler, J. (1990). *Gender trouble: Feminism and the subversion of identity.* New York, NY: Routledge.

Eckerman, L. (1997). Foucault, embodiment and gendered subjectivies: The case of voluntary self-starvation. In A. Petersen & Bunton, R. (Eds.), *Foucault: Health and medicine* (pp. 151–172). London, England: Routledge.

Fairclough, N. (1992). *Discourse and social change.* Malden, MA: Polity Press.

Foucault, M. (1972). *The archeology of knowledge.* London, England: Tavistock Publications.

Foucault, M. (1980). *The history of sexuality, volume 1: An introduction* (R. Hurley, Trans.). New York, NY: Vintage/Random House.

Fox, N. (1997). Is there life after Foucault? Texts, frames and differences. In A. Petersen & Bunton, R. (Eds.), *Foucault: Health and medicine* (pp. 31–52). London, England: Routledge.

Gee, J. (2005). *An introduction to discourse analysis.* New York, NY: Routledge.

Giroux, H. (1983). *The constitution of society: Outline of the theory of structuration.* Cambridge: Polity Press.

Haswell, J., & Haswell, R. (2010). *Authoring: An essay for the English profession on potentiality and singularity.* Logan: Utah State University Press.

hooks, b. (1994). *Teaching to transgress: Teaching as the practice of freedom.* New York, NY: Routledge.

Johnston, P. H. (2012). *Opening minds: Using language to change lives.* Portland, ME: Stenhouse.

Kristeva, J. (1980). *Desire in language: A semiotic approach to literature and art.* New York, NY: Columbia University Press.

Maslow, A. H. (1948). Cognition of the particular and of the generic. *Psychological Review, 55*(1), 22–40.

Natolo, J., & Hutcheon, L. (Eds.) (1993). *A postmodern reader.* Albany: State University of New York.

Palmer, P. (2001). *The courage to teach: Exploring the inner landscape of a teacher's life* (first ed.). San Francisco, CA: Jossey Bass.

Roudiez, L. (1980). Introduction. In J. Kristeva, *Desire in language: A semiotic approach to literature and art* (L. Roudiez, Trans.) (pp. 1–20). New York, NY: Columbia University Press.

Williams, J. (2005). *Understanding poststructuralism.* Chesham, UK: Acumen Publishing Limited.

Wilson, M. (2006). *Rethinking rubrics in writing assessment.* Portsmouth, NH: Heinemann.

Wilson, M. (2010). Rethinking a writing teacher's expertise: Following students under the kitchen table, *English Journal 99*(3), 50–56.

CHAPTER 3

COLLISION COURSE

Postmodern Progressive Composition Pedagogy and Positivist Traditional Assessment

Amy L. Masko

How often in my life is there a schism between theory and practice? I am a progressive educator. A constructivist. A Deweyan. I believe in my core that human beings are seekers of knowledge, and to teach in a constructivist manner is to foster that very humanness. Yet, when my oldest daughter did not want to take an extended family trip, and instead wanted to spend the summer with her friends, I bribed her with getting her ears pierced when we returned. When my son scampered across the muddy yard in his socks because he didn't want to take the time to put on his shoes, I told him he lost the privilege to jump on the trampoline the next day. Sometimes as a parent, I am a behaviorist. Rewards and punishments. A Skinnerian.

Last night, when my middle school son started to write an essay on Chipmunks and their genetic traits and environmental adaptations—which was due the next day—I grabbed the rubric and said, "Did you write about

Rubric Nation, pages 35–46

its habitat? (check)...Did you include one environmental adaptation? (check)...Did you check for sentence variation? (check)... Do you want me to look at your spelling? (check)...Ok, now go to bed." He did not revise. He did not think deeply about his writing. In fact, his only focus on his writing, other than getting words to paper, was to be careful not to plagiarize from the Animal Planet webpage on Chipmunks. This was not constructivist teaching or constructivist learning (Bruner, 1976). This is a theory-to-practice schism that continues to occur in my life, most prominently in the practice of writing. Rubrics rarely support constructivist composition pedagogy. Whether it is in my home when my son starts his homework too late, realizes it is less complete than he thought, and has a mother trying to hurry him to bed, or whether it is in my English education courses where students ask, "Where is the rubric?" before I begin to explain any and every assignment, rubrics serve the purpose of an assignment checklist. It seems, therefore, that rubrics have the potential to limit student writing rather than support student writing. Rubrics are too easily relegated to a checklist of completeness, not a tool to foster deep or reflective thinking about writing, as instructional rubrics are perhaps intended (Wilson, 2006).

Over the past 10 years that I have been in teacher education, I have paused numerous times to consider the theory-to-practice schism that occurs in my university English education courses. This chapter will discuss the ways in which my pedagogy in my university classroom is in conflict with the pedagogical theories with which my students and I grapple. My approach to teaching English education methods can be described as constructivist. I have students examine different curricular paradigms, such as constructivist, progressive education in contrast to more traditional approaches (Null, 2011), challenging students to consider both best practices and their own educational philosophies in examining contemporary teaching practices in schools. In the end, my students place their developing composition pedagogy on a continuum between traditional models and progressive, constructivist models, with most falling toward the progressive, constructivist end of the spectrum for elementary students. Yet, while my practice is constructivist, I often employ a more traditional model of assessment, such as the use of rubrics, which causes a philosophical schism. In no class is this conflict more evident than in my writing pedagogy courses.

CONTEXT OF TEACHING WRITING COURSE

In my elementary composition pedagogy class, Teaching Writing, I ask my undergraduate students to carefully consider how young students write, and how one might go about helping them to become better at it. We read the key authors in the field of progressive writing pedagogy, such as Lucy

Calkins (1994), Katie Wood Ray (2006), and Ralph Fletcher and JoAnn Portalupi (2007). We analyze what these experts can teach us about teaching young people to communicate. We consider the artistry involved in writing and helping children live a "writerly life" (Calkins, 1994, p. 21), and the deep thinking involved when children analyze the writing of published authors to learn craft (Ray, 2006), and how to create mini-lessons that target specific aspects of writing craft (Fletcher & Portalupi, 2007). We consider these authors in conversation with others who have gone before them, as well as with those who offer differing points of view on the teaching of writing, such as Donald Graves (1994) and Donald Murray (1999). I ask them to consider how experts who focus on high school composition can add to the conversation for elementary composition pedagogy. I try to help them see composition pedagogy on a continuum. We read Peter Smagorinsky and his colleagues (2010), Maja Wilson (2006), Nancie Atwell (1998), and George Hillocks (1995). We complicate our understanding of best practice in writing instruction by examining models such as Power Writing. We consider the five-paragraph essay and other kinds of formulaic writing. We work hard to understand where the field is for elementary writing pedagogy, and even as we examine contemporary curriculum and the new Common Core State Standards, we still, in the end, typically settle on a progressive, constructivist model of instructional practices.

I tell them that in no other subject can we, as teachers, get as close to students' learning, as when we read their writing. "Too rarely is the individual teacher so free from the dictation of authoritative supervisor, textbook on methods, prescribed course of study, etc., that he can let his mind come to close quarters with the pupil's mind and the subject matter" (Dewey, 1916, p. 127). Writing teachers have the very unique and all-too-rare opportunity to come to close quarters with their students' minds. We can see how young writers make sense of their world, how they understand a concept, and how they take risks in their writing, which often extends their thinking. We can see the ways that young children internalize phonics rules, and grapple with standard American syntax. Writing is a connection between teachers and students that sometimes even goes beyond the mind and moves into the realm of the heart. Any writing teacher will tell you about students who share their most precious thoughts through their writing, something that rarely happens in other subjects.

Soon into the course, after students have been working on their own creative writing, forming revision groups to give and receive peer feedback on their writing, I give them their first assignment: a literary critique, accompanied by a rubric. I experience a little cognitive dissonance, recognizing that theory and practice are colliding in my course. I plow forward anyway, acknowledging that students want a rubric, and sometimes complain in their student evaluations if they are not provided one. They complain that my assignments are "unclear" or that they "do not know what I want," when they do not have a rubric. Notably, I provide my students with detailed assignment sheets, outlining the specifics of the assignment. There should be no reason for confusion. However, it is often the case that students perceive rubrics to add a certain clarity to an assignment. I propose later in this paper that this is a false sense of clarity.

If rubrics appear to teacher education students to be an essential component to any writing assignment, how have they historically and contemporarily fit into composition pedagogy?

HISTORY OF COMPOSITION PEDAGOGY: 1892 COMMITTEE OF TEN

Examining the curricular and pedagogical history of composition at the K–12 level, we can see some fairly stark differences between the elementary and secondary levels. My students often report to me that they are taught in elementary and middle school to write creatively, to express themselves, to find their voice. And then in high school, they are taught the five-paragraph essay and learn that there is one right way to compose writing. A friend of mine, who is a high school English teacher, told me once that students who take her creative writing class have a very difficult time getting out of the five-paragraph essay form. They have simply forgotten how to write in any other way. In my Teaching Writing course, my teacher-education students support what my friend told me. They go on to complain that they are taught five-paragraph essay as the correct way to write in high school, and yet in college they are told not to limit their writing to a five-paragraph essay. So, why is there a disconnect in the continuity of writing pedagogy between elementary and secondary school? We need to examine the history of composition pedagogy to understand the basis for this pattern.

In 1892 the Committee of Ten was formed (Hobbs & Berlin, 1995; Pinar, Reynolds, Slattery, & Taubman, 1995), with the purpose of reviewing the secondary school curriculum. The Committee of Ten appointed several sub-committees, one called the Conference of English. The sub-committee included a professor from Harvard's newly formed English department, and a girls' high school headmaster from a Boston school, among others (Hobbs & Berlin, 1995). The purpose of this committee was to critically examine and reshape the entire curriculum for secondary schools. Considering that Harvard had only recently established its first English department, we can see that the job of the secondary school was shifting from preparing students in classical languages to preparing them in English studies (Hobbs & Berline, 1995). Writing pedagogy came under review and was about to be shaped. The Conference of English released the following policy statement:

The main direct objects of the teaching of English in schools seems to be two: (1) to enable the pupil to understand the expressed thoughts of others and to give expression to thoughts of his own; and (2) to cultivate a taste for reading, to give the pupil some acquaintance with good literature, and to furnish him with the means of extending that acquaintance. (Hobbs & Berlin, 1995, p. 252)

The Conference of English went on to define the different goals of elementary level writing and secondary level writing, which is our first glimpse at the disconnect my students discuss as their current experience. Hobbs and Berlin (1995) go on to explain that in elementary level writing, the pupil could "furnish his own material, expressing his own thoughts in a natural way…[relying on] his own observations and personal interest" (p. 252). However, secondary level writing was to focus on "training in expression of thought" (p. 253), and the emphasis was on precision, clarity, and conciseness.

Later, in 1917 the United States Office of Education published a report titled *Reorganization of English in the Secondary Schools*, which called for writing to be a progression from creative and individual at the lowest grades to social and more practical at the upper levels (Hobbs & Berlin, 1995). It was suggested that grades seven through nine could have creative writing integrated into the writing curriculum, but that was to decrease by the upper grades, so that only those with special talents would be writing creatively in high school (Hobbs & Berlin, 1995).

We can see evidence of two models of composition pedagogy emerging with these early 20th century policies: for elementary level writing, we see evidence of the Process Approach, and for the secondary level writing, we see evidence of the Current-Traditional Rhetoric model. In the next section I will examine how these two models of writing look in contemporary classrooms.

CONTEMPORARY WRITING MODELS

Current-Traditional Rhetoric Model

The Current-Traditional Rhetoric Model has its epistemological base in positivistic and rational realms, offering writing as an extension of the scientific method (Hobbs & Berlin, 1995). Modes are emphasized in this model. Specifically educators focus on exposition/argument, where the writer's faculty of reason, or *logos*, as Aristotle described, is paramount. The second prominent mode is description/persuasion, where the writer's faculty of emotion or will, or *ethos*, as Aristotle described, is most important. These modes of discourse are seen as "correct," and hence positivist.

Growing from this model is the five-paragraph essay, among other pre-scriptive models of composition pedagogy. I argue that rubrics are also an outgrowth of this model, where a focus on correctness is emphasized and clearly tied to a grade. The notion of writing as an outgrowth of the scientific process suggests that writing can be completed in such a way as to follow a specific, prescribed, pre-determined process. A rubric follows that same line of reasoning; a writing teacher can determine *a priori* what characterizes a quality paper by delineating a set of characteristics that make the writing correct, and the grading process more scientific, and as such, more objective.

Process Approach

The Process Approach to writing, often enacted as a writing workshop, is described by Calkins (1994) as follows:

> Through what writers report about their composing processes, we have begun to recognize that just as researchers often follow a scientific method, writers often follow a process of craft when they work. Some theorists describe the writing process as prewriting, writing, and rewriting; some speak of circling out and circling back; some of collecting and connecting. I prefer Donald Murray's terms: rehearsal, drafting, revision, and editing . . . In our own way and at our own pace, most of us follow a cycle in our writing. (pp. 22–23)

As we can see, the process is recursive, fluid, and different for different writers. We can clearly see its epistemological base in postmodern (Aylesworth, 2013) thought. The Process Approach to composition pedagogy was born out of mimicking what authors do in their own processes of crafting a story or poem or essay. Calkins (1994) and others argue that children need to see themselves as writers, and as such she argues that teachers do, too. We all must live writerly lives. While students learn mode or form in a writing workshop format, they do so by examining models of that form produced by other, more accomplished writers (Ray, 2006), often referred to as mentors. Instead of receiving a graphic organizer that outlines the five paragraphs of an essay, they read essays and pick out features that are particular to that genre. Then they incorporate those features in their own writing.

Finally, in this Process Approach model, students write about what they know. They write about their own lives, the things that are important to them, and their own experiences (Calkins, 1994). This has not changed much since the Committee of Ten's recommendations for elementary writing curriculum in 1892.

While the Process Approach to writing is more common in elementary classrooms, and the Current-Traditional Rhetoric Model is often seen in secondary classrooms, it is not always so. Linda Rief (1992) advocated for implementing the writing workshop in secondary classrooms, as did Nancie Atwell (1998), describing the model for middle schools. Furthermore, the five-paragraph essay and Power Writing[1] are not uncommon in the elementary classroom. To further complicate matters, there are also hybrid models that have emerged such as the Structured Process Approach (Hillocks, 1995; Smagorinsky, Johannessen, Kahn, & McCann, 2010). While we can make an elementary/secondary school dichotomy that is, at least, fairly typical in the split that the 1892 Committee of Ten distinguished, it is not a static dichotomy. There are exceptions, and they are not rare.

RUBRICS AS POSITIVIST

Where do rubrics fit within this writing pedagogy? Rubrics are designed to highlight correctness in writing, and are thus, positivist (Wilson, 2006). Theoretically, therefore, rubrics are a better assessment match for positivist composition pedagogy, such as the Current-Traditional Model. The Current-Traditional Model is based on notions of the scientific method, where rational thought and objectivity are valued (Hobbs & Berlin, 1995). While some have argued that rubrics can be instructional, and as such can highlight the writing process (Andrade, 2001; 2000; Spandel, 2006), it is more typical that rubrics espouse precision and objectivity, and are readily aligned with specific modes of writing. Hence, the Process Approach, which is the approach most commonly taught in elementary teacher education courses,[2] does not lend itself well to the notion of correctness, which is why rubrics cause such a theoretical and philosophical collision in praxis in my Elementary Teaching Writing course. The process approach falls under the postmodern epistemological paradigm, where correctness and one right answer are challenged.

Positivism is a philosophy that derives from scientific reasoning, and espouses that society operates by specific laws, similarly to science, and that these scientific or logical ways of operating are observable (Abraham, 1994). Only knowledge derived from this logical, scientific reasoning can be seen as valid (Abraham, 1994). Rubrics align to this paradigm, as they provide proof of a teacher's judgment on student work, truth that is grounded in logical reasoning and correctness, and is observable and measurable. Positivist thinking argues that good writing can only be described by the five or four or seven characteristics on the scoring rubric. Rubrics function in composition classrooms with positivist notions present in the practice.

Andrade (2000, 2001) defines rubrics as a written document that delineates the expectations for an assignment by listing the criteria and a gradation of quality from exceptional to poor. She continues to outline arguments as to why a rubric helps teachers to teach, as well as evaluate student writing, stating, "instructional rubrics can have positive effects on students' writing and learning about writing" (2001, p. 1). Vicki Spandel, author of the 6-Trait Writing Assessment model for the Northwest Regional Educational Laboratory (NWREL), supports that claim, encouraging educators to think of rubrics as writing guides, arguing that

> it is easy to be dismissive about rubrics if we view them as mere lists of expectations. They are much more than that. In reality, a writing guide has three parts: (1) the written criteria we commit to paper, (2) the examples that show our criteria in action and serve as models for students, and (3) the reader who acts as an interpreter. (Spandel, 2006, p. 20)

She suggests that creating rubrics demands a great deal of thought and reflection about what good writing looks like. For this reason, she suggests, and Andrade (2000, 2001) concurs, that students should be part of the process of creating the rubrics used to evaluate their writing, arguing that when students are involved in the process, they see the rubric less as a scoring guide and more of a writing guide, which can actually function to instruct student writing. "Instructionally useful rubrics are created by readers who think reflectively about how to make their own and others' writing better" (Spandel, 2006, p. 19).

In addition to their promise to be an instructional tool to help guide student writing to higher quality (Spandel, 2006; Andrade, 2000; 2001), rubrics are also touted for their efficiency in grading student writing (Andrade, 2000). Rubrics promise to not only make grading student papers more efficient, effective, and authentic, but also more fair (Spandel, 2006). Students know ahead of time the criteria for their writing and will not be surprised by their teachers' feedback. Spandel (2006) states that, "if we do not make our [criteria] known, we say to students, 'I can't describe it,' 'I prefer not to reveal what I am looking for,' or 'You figure it out' "(p. 20). Andrade (2000) continues this argument to state that rubrics also hold teachers accountable for their judgment, arguing that they help teachers justify to parents and others the grade that they assign. Spandel (2006) agrees stating, "Rubrics help us overcome arbitrariness, inconsistency, and flat-out bias... Rubrics make us accountable for scores or grades that affect human lives" (p. 21).

According to proponents, rubrics serve the purpose of making criteria transparent to students, thus making teachers accountable for their judgment and assignment of grades, as well as making grading student papers more efficient and standardized. They also argue that rubrics further function as an instructional tool for students, making qualities of good writing visible.

THE PROBLEM WITH RUBRICS
OR THE POSTMODERN PARADIGM

Postmodernism is more fluid than positivist structures allow (Bauman, 2007), and so is the process approach to writing. Donald Murray (1999) best describes the postmodern fluidity of the writing process approach as follows:

> Now you and I have experienced the writing process. There is, however, not one writing process, but many. This book is organized on one writing process—the one I most often find effective for me. But I adapt it according to the writing task, my experience with that task, and the way my head works that morning. Sometimes I write away with a river flood of fluency, other days I build a draft slowly like a bricklayer. No matter. I am a writer. I write. And you should as well. Change your process as your thinking style evolves, as you face a new writing task, or as you become more experienced with a particular writing task. (p. 10)

Murray, among other postmodern writing pedagogues, suggests that the process is different for every person (student) and that the role of the teacher is to facilitate the writing process, or as Calkins' (1999) suggests, "we are teaching the writer, not the writing" (p. 225). With this model, how can a rubric be designed *a priori*? Under this paradigm, teachers do not necessarily have preconceived notions of where the entire class will progress, but instead they have goals for each individual writer that they develop over time, through conferring with the writer, reading his or her drafts, and carefully observing and theorizing about that particular student writer. It is about the writer's process, not about the final product. Rubrics are theoretically problematic in such a postmodern paradigm.

Many educators are critical of rubrics, suggesting that rubrics often offer narrow criteria for evaluating quality writing (Kohn, 2006; Wilson, 2006, 2007; Hillocks, 2002). Wilson (2006, 2007) suggests that the qualities that are specified in a rubric may be qualities seen in one great student paper, but not in another. She suggests that if she evaluated her students' writing on content, organization, voice, word choice, conventions, and sentence fluency (the 6-traits of writing espoused by the 6+1 assessment model), it would limit her ability to evaluate on other qualities she values such as "promise, thinking through writing, or risk-taking" (Wilson, 2006, p. 63). Yet, she argues, adding those elements to a rubric wouldn't help matters, as not every paper needed to meet all that she values in good writing.

THEORY TO PRACTICE COLLISION

My Teaching Writing course is designed for elementary teacher candidates. While I teach them about all of the various approaches to composition pedagogy, together we typically settle on a progressive writing pedagogy as the best model for elementary students. So, why do I, on more occasions than

I wish to recount, provide rubrics for my students? Why do I use them to assess their assignments?

Maja Wilson (2006) brings me a little comfort when she says, "If you're anything like me, you have mixed feelings about rubrics. You've used them. In fact, sometimes you really like them" (p. 2). And she's right. Sometimes I do like them. It is easy to justify a student's grade when I can check off a series of boxes on a rubric. Yet, my gut often reminds me that as I espouse postmodern progressive education to be good learning and good teaching, it is in direct contrast to this style of grading. A rubric might make me feel somewhat more "objective," or "scientific" in my assessment of my students' writing, but I know that is not the case. Rubrics provide me with a false sense of "correctness" in my judgment, and they also provide my students with a false sense of organization or clarity to an assignment.

Most significantly, our current college students grew up with rubrics. They are products of No Child Left Behind (NCLB), which promotes positivist practices in everything from curriculum to instruction to assessment. NCLB requires a high level of teacher accountability (Masko & Bosiwah, 2012), and rubrics provide that (Andrade, 2000). Our students are the result of these policies playing out in classrooms across the country. Of course they like rubrics; it is what they know.

Yet, this is the exact reason we should challenge students' over-reliance on rubrics. If we are to change the paradigm of teachers from what they grew up knowing and instead move them toward more progressive pedagogies, we have to take risks in our classrooms and move students out of their comfort zones, in order to push students in their development and help them gain some comfort with ambiguity. We live and learn in a postmodern world, where there are no single truth claims, and often there is more than one correct answer. Ambiguity is our normal state of being in our postmodern world, yet rubrics attempt to label and box specific elements, thus falsely creating the illusion of objectivity, as well as clarity and organization. As Wilson (2006) points out, writers like Ernest Hemingway and Sandra Cisneros would likely fail on a six-trait rubric. We need to model for our students that using a rubric to assess student writing, suggesting that there are six or four or twelve characteristics that make writing correct, is a false truth. We need to put constructivist practices into play in our own classrooms, so our students see that grading without a positivist paradigm can be done. And that it should be done.

As for me, and the theory to practice schism that keeps showing up in my life? Well, I am a work in progress.

NOTES

1. "Traditional Power Writing is based on a numerical approach to the structure of writing. It replaces the ambiguity and abstraction of writing terminology with a numbered structure that students can understand more easily. This numerical structure provides the basis for all forms of writing: expository, persuasive, narrative and descriptive. Power Writing solves the writer's frequent problem of how to say it and in what order.

   Equally important to Power Writing is the sequential teaching process that builds in steps upon the mastery of each concept. Students are taught how to organize their thoughts before their writing begins. Structured writing follows organized thinking. These concepts are taught with age-appropriate exercises to assure that students possess the skills to expand complexity in their thinking and writing" (The Writing Site, retrieved March 20, 2014).

2. A thorough review of the textbook catalogues for Pearson and Heinemann for K–8 Writing Methods indicate that the Process Approach to teaching writing is the most common methodology for teacher education.

REFERENCES

Abraham, J. (1994). Positivism, structuralism and the differentiation-polarisation theory: A reconsideration of Shilling's novelty and primacy thesis. *British Journal of Sociology of Education, 14*, 231–241.

Andrade, H. G. (2001). The effects of instructional rubrics on learning to write. *Current Issues in Education* [On-line], *4(4)*. http://cie.ed.asu.edu/volume4/number4.

Andrade, H. G. (2000). Using rubrics to promote thinking and learning. *Educational Leadership, 57*(5), 13–18.

Atwell, N. (1998). *In the middle: New understandings about writing, reading, and learning*. Portsmouth, NH: Heinemann.

Aylesworth, G. (2013). Postmodernism. In E. N. Zalta (Ed.) *The Stanford encyclopedia of philosophy*. Retrieved from http://plato.stanford.edu/archives/sum2013/entries/postmodernism/.

Bauman, Z. (2007). *Liquid times: Living in an age of uncertainty*. Cambridge, UK: Polity Press.

Bruner, J. (1976). *The process of education*. Boston, MA: Harvard University Press.

Calkins, L. (1994). *The art of teaching writing*, Portsmouth, NH: Heinemann.

Dewey, J. (1916). *Democracy and education*. New York, NY: Macmillan.

Fletcher, R. & Portalupi, J. (2007). *Craft lessons: Teaching writing k–8*. Portland, ME: Stenhouse Publishers.

Graves, D. (1994). *A fresh look at writing*. Portsmouth, NH: Heinemann.

Hillocks, G. (2002). *The testing trap: How state writing assessments control learning*. New York, NY: Teachers College Press.

Hillocks, G. (1995). *Teaching writing as reflective practice: Integrating theories*. New York, NY: Teachers College Press.

Hobbs, C. L., & Berlin, J. A. (1995). A century of writing instruction in school and college english. In J. J. Murphy (Ed.) *A short history of writing instruction: From ancient Greeks to modern America.* New York, NY: Routledge.

Kohn, A. (2006). The trouble with rubrics. *English Journal, 95*(4), 12–15.

Masko, A. L., & Bosiwah, L. (2012). Teacher accountability & student responsibility: A cross-cultural comparison of American & Ghanaian schooling practices and policies and a reflection on NCLB. *Curriculum and Teaching Dialogue, 14,* 39–52.

Murray, D. (1999). *Write to learn* (6th ed). New York, NY: Harcourt Brace College Publishers.

Null, W. (2011). *Curriculum: From theory to practice.* Rowan and Littlefield Publishers.

Pinar, W. F., Reynolds, W. M., Slattery, P., & Taubman, P. M. (1995). *Understanding curriculum.* New York, NY: Peter Lang Publishers.

Ray, K. W. (2006). *Study driven: A framework for planning units of study in the writing workshop.* Portsmouth, NH: Heinemann.

Rief, L. (1992). *Seeking diversity: Language arts with adolescents.* Portsmouth, NH: Heinemann.

Smagorinsky, P., Johannessen, L. R., Kahn, E. A., & McCann, T. M. (2010). *The dynamics of writing instruction: A structured process approach for middle and high school.* Portsmouth, NH: Heinemann.

Spandel, V. (2006). In defense of rubrics. *English Journal, 96*(1), 19–22.

The Writing Site. Retrieved from http://pasdtechtips.pbworks.com/f/An+Overview+to+the+Power+Writing+Approach.pdf

Wilson, M. (2007). Why I won't be using rubrics to respond to students' writing. *English Journal, 96*(4), 62–66.

Wilson, M. (2006). *Rethinking rubrics in writing assessment.* Portsmouth, NH: Heinemann.

CHAPTER 4

RUBRICS REFRAMED

Reappropriating Rubrics
for Assessment and Learning

Paul Parkison

Within the dialogue regarding assessment of outcomes, it is common to focus on content expertise. An alternative framework relies upon an understanding of the instructor as an expert learner. The instructor-as-expert-learner has capabilities with multiple disciplining technologies (learning strategies that have emerged and evolved within our culture in the form of academic disciplines) and is able to discern the technology that will meet the learners' needs most effectively. Expert learners deconstruct disciplining technologies in order to recognize the multiple and varied paths that can be taken to desired learning outcomes.

The instructor-as-expert-learner must also recognize and negotiate the technologies of power (standards and accountability systems that are hegemonic within the current education system) and overcome the assumption that assessment is about accountability and compliance. The instructor-as-expert-learner uses assessment as a tool for instructional decision-making and learning. Within a learning-driven structure, mastery of content

Rubric Nation, pages 47–65
Copyright © 2015 by Information Age Publishing
All rights of reproduction in any form reserved.

becomes less important than mastery of cognitive processes and ways of knowing that characterize disciplinary technologies of power. The focus on content expertise leads rubrics to becoming disciplining technologies that constrain the learning and assessment process and lead to a compliance frame of mind. By reframing rubrics as learning devices and decision guides, it is possible to reappropriate rubrics as valuable assessment tools. Moving away from an accountability and compliance perspective depends upon recognizing assessment and the use of rubrics as an instructional decision-making process directed toward learning.

How do educators reframe rubrics so that the benefits to learning and broadening of the curricula can be maintained while the rigidness of compliance is avoided? At the individual instructor and learner level, as well as the institutional level, rubrics have much to offer. The challenge remains to develop a method for striking a balance between providing guidance and parameters for the performance of learning outcomes and creating a script for the performance of these outcomes. In this chapter, a proposed framework is offered for striking this balance.

Understanding the role of rubrics has become challenging over the last 20 years. Rubrics have become ubiquitous in education and schools, yet their purpose is vaguely understood. Rubrics, when used well, are a mechanism through which educators communicate the performance expectations that exemplify quality work. Informing learners about the desired and expected outcome of their performance seems such a commonsense piece of teaching that when the use of rubrics to communicate these expectations was proposed, opposition was scarce. Letting the learners know the "rules of the game" prior to participating in the learning and what a good and bad exemplar looks like made, and makes, sense (Black & Wiliam, 2006; Wiggins, 1993). This process is part of instruction and helps facilitate learning.

Concurrently, the use of rubrics has developed through the appeal to objectivity in the evaluation of learner's performance of their learning (Wiggins, 1993). As standardized testing in the form of forced-choice question banks came to dominate education, the claim of objectivity of these tests was used to grant legitimacy to the process. Multiple choice, true/false, and matching questions that compose these tests are vetted for bias, and the "correct" answer is reportedly not dependent upon the individual making the evaluation. Educators who recognized the necessity of mediating the influence of these instruments saw rubrics as a method of validating evaluations of more subjective and performance-based learner performances (Archbald & Newmann, 1988; Mehrens, 1992; Wiggins, 1993). Rubrics were asserted to bring rater reliability to the evaluation of authentic student performances (Airasian, 2005). Because educators could be trained to provide reliable evaluations of authentic student performances, it was hoped that these performances could gain credibility with education policymakers and those who govern accountability systems (Mehrens, 1992; Myford & Mislevey, 1995; Wiggins, 1993). An alternative process-driven framework to this accountability model, with its emphasis on rater reliability and verification, will reemphasize learning and the development of disciplinary competence and expertise.

As rubrics have become ingrained within educational institutions, including schools of education and their accrediting bodies, and as outcomes-based curriculum has come to dominate education, rubrics have lost their place as tools for learning and taken on the role of metrics of compliance (Kleijnen, Dolmans, Willems, & Hout, 2013; Lawy & Tedder, 2012; Peck, Gallucci, & Sloan, 2010). Rubrics initially offered the instructor and the learner a tool for communicating expectations for performance; however, they have come to symbolize compliance within high-stakes accountability systems. Once tools for defending more authentic learning and curriculum, rubrics have become the hoops that instructors and learners must jump through in order to receive a stamp of approval from those who enforce the accountability and accreditation systems and certify content expertise. Alignment tables and matrices linking rubric criteria to accreditation and program standards are mandated by accrediting bodies (CAEP, 2013; InTASC, 2013). To reclaim this valuable tool, educators must reframe and reimagine how rubrics can be used to inform instruction and guide learning.

A crucial part of this reframing depends upon a clear distinction between assessment and evaluation. Though these processes are highly related, they are distinct and fulfill different roles within schooling. Assessment is a vital process within educative experiences. Assessment is the process of gathering, aggregating, analyzing, and using evidence about a learning experience and then making instructional decisions regarding the next step to take to achieve the desired outcome (Airasian, 2005; Wiggins, 1993). Evaluation is the process of making judgments about the quality of a learning performance (Airasian 2005; Wiggins 1993). Confusion about the relationship between these distinct processes has resulted in the misappropriation of rubrics as tools for evaluation and accountability judgments and has led to the acceptance of a compliance perspective among educators.

Premises of the Model

At the base of the proposed framework is the belief that education is a continuous and complex process that is contextual and contingent (Tomlinson et. al., 2009). The influence of culture and the funds of knowledge the learner and instructor bring to the educational context dramatically influence the learning processes of all involved (Gonzalez, Moll, & Amanti, 2005). Negotiation of the desired learning outcome by the instructor and the learner is a critical part of the learning process (Arends & Kilcher, 2010; Cornelius-White & Harbaugh, 2010; Gardner, 2000). Recognition that learning outcomes are contingent and negotiated (political) informs a more dynamic process in the development, implementation, and assessment of curriculum and instruction. This recognition also explicitly politicizes the evaluation process. From a compliance perspective, the learning outcomes are seen as constraining rather than enabling. The negotiation of these outcomes is controlled by those whose power is sufficient to capture the language of the standards. Testing and rubrics then align to this standards-driven hegemony (Apple, 2006; Spring, 2011). Instructor evaluations, program evaluations, and accreditation evaluations are political because they are contingent upon the values and perspective of the evaluator and the ideological narrative represented by the standards. By refocusing on the democratic processes that should inform the identification of desired learning outcomes, compliance is replaced by engagement as the mode of being within the process (Habermas, 1994). Essentially, this refocusing relies upon political dialogue to expose and critique the taken-for-granted premises that standardization and high-stakes accountability are built upon. Reempowering the instructor as a curriculum developer and reliable assessor of student learning, and not simply an out-of-the-box (or out-of-the-accreditation-requirement framework) instructional implementer, requires that we co-opt what are appropriately discursive forums in which the instructor is a valued participant.

Teaching, assessment, and curriculum, when effective, emerge within a deliberative process. The challenge is to structure the deliberative process so as to be inclusive, responsive, accountable, and transparent (Parkison, 2013). Collaborative interaction among stakeholders is critical to the success of this process. Collaborative and engaged learning relies upon democratic principles in which the instructor and learners form an interconnected web of interests. This web has no center, but it is bound by the language game at play—the academic literacy or disciplining technologies being addressed in the learning experience (Foucault, 1988). Human beings utilize collective, or intersubjective, worldviews (language games) to create meaning. Ludwig Wittgenstein called these intersubjectively constructed language games "horizons" (Wittgenstein, 1958). Horizons represent the form of life in which human beings are embedded as they interact to create meaning. These horizons shift with context, overlap as participants engage and disengage, and constrain the potential alternative actions and perspectives available. Within the horizon of our experience, we utilize democratically developed institutions in order to create meaning. By shifting from an objective/subjective political structure to an intersubjective political structure within education, the learning experience becomes democratic and collaborative. Instructor and learners cooperatively create horizons in which to communicate, learn, and be accountable.

Within a collaborative, learning focused assessment methodology, special program accreditor standards can be utilized to define the language game that governs the learning experiences and desired learning outcomes of a specific curriculum, course, or program. Any collaboration occurs for a purpose. We do not simply come together to "collaborate." Accreditor standards serve the purpose of defining the academic language through which the learning experience can develop and be discussed. These standards provide the language for collaboration. The objectives for the collaboration that occurs within the learning experience, for both learners and instructor, are premised by, but not necessarily determined by, these standards. If education is approached from this philosophical position, the institutionalization of assessment and the use of instruments like rubrics fundamentally changes to become learning focused. Learning politics become collaborative not by choice of the instructor, but as a necessity. The classroom becomes a horizon in which student/instructor-as-expert-learner interaction occurs (Parkison, 2014).

Disciplining the Classroom

The assumption that external stimuli, rewards, and punishments within an accountability system are the key to educational improvement indicates a confidence in behaviorist strategies and a lack of confidence in constructivist approaches to education (Beane, 2005; Kohn, 1996). Collaborative assessment and the overall collaborative methodology start from a different premise: students and instructor-as-expert-learner are intrinsically motivated when they are empowered as decision-makers (Bandura, 1986; Beane, 2005; Black & Wiliam, 2006; Cornelius-White & Harbaugh, 2010; W. Glasser, 1986; Jackson, Boostrom, & Hansen, 1993; Riggs & Gholar, 2009; Wiggins, 1993).

Thomas Popkewitz (1987) describes a similar concern with the openness of the public space for curriculum and assessment dialogue when he considers evaluation as a "disciplining technology" that prescribes both what individuals should think about and how they should think about it (Popkewitz, 1987, 1997). The implementation of "disciplining technologies" is commonplace within schooling. They come in the form of accountability systems, standardized and high-stakes testing, and scripted curriculum guides (Giroux, 2012). Rubrics can also discipline the classroom and the learning that occurs within it. Even a simplistic understanding of reliability and validity indicate the underlying assumption of the primary role of discipline within the learning context (Mehrens, 1992; Myford & Mislevey, 1995). Rubrics can act as hegemonic horizons that constrain the community or as guides that enable collaboration within the community, depending upon the premise from which instruction begins. They can be interpreted as specifying the recipe to be followed in order to produce a desired outcome or as outcomes that can be attained through multiple pathways. Moving beyond simple communities of learners (groups who are learning but not necessarily engaging) toward engaged communities of learners in which participants not only learn but question the legitimacy of what is being learned is essential to a democratic classroom (Parkison, 2014). Democratic, engaged classrooms recognize that learners are citizens with rights to have a say in what is learned, need a curriculum with a conscience, focus on significant social and personal issues, and are instruments for understanding self, work, and world (Beane, 2005). This does not mean that discipline is unnecessary, but that it is subject to critique—is a contingent and negotiated technology. Like all disciplining technologies, rubrics can be "taken for granted" or problematized and critiqued.

Judith Langer (2011) addresses disciplining technologies in an informative manner by reframing the discussion around academic literacy. Langer's discussion of disciplinary thought and language helps move away from the compliance and evaluation perspective toward a more democratic and process-driven perspective:

> Disciplinary thought and language that serve as markers, ones that carry meaning and are widely understood and used within a discipline. These markers denote the social conventions that are subject—or context-specific, those that people within that field know, understand, and expect others "in the know" to use. (Langer, 2011, p. 3)

This dialogic approach to the role of disciplining technologies provides a basis from which to reappropriate rubrics as technologies of learning and repositions assessment as systematic, process-driven, decision-making within the learning process. If we can reframe rubrics as technologies of learning rather than technologies of discipline or accountability, the potential exists for rubrics to empower both instructors and students as decision-makers and learners.

If we utilize the metaphor of horizon as introduced above to consider the role of a rubric within the learning process, the challenge presented to the reframing of rubrics may become clear. The metaphor of horizon is distinctly different than an outcome or goal. It is not a target or focal point.

Horizons depend upon position and attention. If a rubric specifies content and structural organization for a student performance or artifact, then the student may narrow their focus to only that content and organize their performance according to the recipe provided in the rubric. The student's position with respect to the competencies and knowledge required to be successful may constrain the student's attention. This student is following the directions and utilizing the materials or content that has been certified as appropriate by the rubric.

For example, if students were asked to bake cookies as the desired outcome or performance, then the rubric for that task could take several forms. Each of the rubrics would impact the learning horizon. One rubric could resemble a recipe from the back of the package of chocolate chips. Specific contents/ingredients would be required for successful completion of the outcome or performance. The process for mixing, measuring, baking, and cooling would also be specified. Previous experiences, levels of competence, or interest (position) would not impact the outcome in a dramatic way if the learner followed the directions. Attention to the details would be all that was required. The final performance is relatively predictable and standardized.

On the other hand, the rubric for the desired outcome or performance could focus on engagement and learning. The rubric could focus upon essential components of cookies: flour, sweetener, and fats. It could also specify documentation of process: bake, no-bake, bars, drops, or molded; mixing and measurement; and serving suggestions. Given a rubric of general requirements, students can incorporate their personal experience and preferences for cookies. Their position (life experience) will inform the final product. Documentation of process would direct attention to the details without specifying the exact steps. The final performance is less predictable and standardized, but the competency and knowledge demonstrated is authentic and can inform the practice or learning needed to improve.

If the rubric focuses upon the disciplinary processes required to be successful in the desired performance and provides generalized or conceptual examples of content, then the student will recognize choice and flexibility in the performance. The student will complete the performance in the manner they determine to be appropriate according to their comfort with the disciplinary processes and will utilize specific content that reflects their individual experience and understanding. These students are bringing their funds of knowledge and disciplinary understanding into the process. Their positions are authentic and they will attend to performances that are meaningful within their experience.

The negotiation of position and attention, content and process, is political and part of what the reframing of rubrics attempts to make intentional and explicit. Helping to negotiate both position and attention, rubrics can guide students toward the understanding to be developed. Reframed, rubrics will help teachers recognize where each student is and what they understand, and then allow them to make instructional decisions that build from that position.

By reframing rubrics as embedded within the learning process, instructors are encouraged to consider the experiences that are helpful in leading students from where their life experiences and received understanding have brought them toward desired or disciplinary understanding. By focusing on the tools used to construct and manage contextual understanding, rubrics can encourage reflection and intentional learning. A "process-driven" rubric emphasizes that each individual requires the accumulation of a sophisticated toolkit of technologies (disciplining as well as liberating) that enable them to negotiate for position and understanding within diverse contexts. Instructors utilizing this type of reframed rubric facilitate students taking steps to engage in the unfamiliar, interact with the unknown, and problematize the comfortable. Instructors, through process-driven rubrics, help students develop their toolkit of technologies so that they enter the world with the focal utilities needed to be successful, authentic individuals.

Rubrics as Decision Aids

How rubrics are generated is critical to their effectiveness (Mandinach & Jackson, 2012). Unlike many rubrics implemented by learning institutions, process-driven rubrics are constructed as decision aids, valuable to the instructor and learner and used as prompts to further learning and more complex understanding and performances. Rubrics within process-driven curriculum and assessment systems are directed toward the students' ways of knowing or habits of mind (Costa, 2008; Gonzalez et al., 2005). The desired learning outcomes have more to do with the learner's ability to negotiate, select, and implement disciplining technologies appropriate to specific performance tasks than with mastery of specific content or conformity to a specific disciplining technology. Rubrics, from this perspective, offer a decision aid for the learner and instructor as evidence of learner understanding is assessed and the learning dialogue turns toward identifying the next experience which could have the most significant impact on the learner's proficiency or comprehension.

This shift of focus from student performance evaluation to learning engagement impacts the function of the rubric. Within the accountability and evaluation frame, standards represent disciplining technologies that dictate curriculum and pedagogy. They demand specific student performances in order to demonstrate externally determined proficiencies. These rubrics resemble recipes to be followed by the learner. While these standards should be the topic of dialogue among students and instructors (as well as other community stakeholders), they provide an example of standardized outcomes that limit the learning experiences that could potentially be offered. Rubrics from the perspective of process-driven curriculum and assessment take on a different function. Consider a decision aid a set of criteria and indicators that point toward potential risks and opportunities and that provide guidance for ways of developing learner capacities. Decision aids help to identify decision points within a process. Moments when significant evidence indicates the need for a specific intervention or attention to specific proficiency are used to guide the learning dialogue.

It is possible to look to standards as a horizon from which to build a process-driven rubric. Instructors and students can engage in a dialogue regarding the value of these proficiencies, but once (or if) decided upon as the desired learning for an educational experience, there are steps that can be used to develop decision aids at critical junctures. The desired learning outcome, or role of the course within a program, dramatically influences the impact the course can have for the learners. Framing the disciplining tendencies of standards within a dialogue helps to open the horizon within which they function and the language educators use to discuss and implement them. The use of tools like rubrics can help turn a standard and set of indicators from a high-stakes outcome into a decision aid for instruction.

Instructional Decision Aid

Decision aids are used throughout medical and information systems to guide diagnostics and workflow decisions. Building upon and formalizing routine decisions, as experienced and analyzed at critical points within a process, helps to build expertise and clarify disciplinary processes that are identified as foundational competencies by participants in the field. The utility of well-designed decision aids is provided in the explicit patterns of cues, and relationships between cues, identified in the guide. Learners can structure their existing knowledge and newly acquired knowledge to mimic these patterns with little or no explanatory feedback. As the learner acquires more experience implementing the structures and decision sequences recommended within the decision aid, their knowledge becomes more complex, their understanding of the relationships becomes deeper, and they are more able to respond to authentic events (Day, Authur, & Gettman, 2001; Glasser & Chi, 1988; Goldsmith, Johnson, & Acton, 1991; Trumpower & Goldsmith, 2004).

Foucault's (1988) discussion of "caring for the self" typology of technologies provides instructors with a language for discussing these decision aid structures and sequences. Foucault's typology includes

> (1) technologies of production, which permit us to produce, transform, or manipulate things; (2) technologies of sign systems, which permit us to use signs, meanings, symbols, or signification; (3) technologies of power, which determine the conduct of individuals and submit them to certain ends or domination, an objectivizing of the subject; (4) technologies of the self, which permit individuals to effect by their own means or with the help of others a certain number of operations on their own bodies and souls, thoughts, conduct and way of being, so as to transform themselves in order to attain a certain state of happiness, purity, wisdom, perfection, or immortality. (1988, p. 18)

How the instructor perceives the content and, importantly, the purpose of the decision aid structures and sequences related to agreed-upon standards influence the technology for the care of self that the standard develops. As Foucault's typology indicates, efficacy with the technologies of power is necessary in order to develop efficacy with the technologies of self that enable the individual to have agency within a particular context—to move beyond compliance (Foucault, 1988).

Within teacher preparation programs, candidates are required to create lesson plans. Many times these plans take the form of templates to be filled in by the candidate—something in every box to comply with the required performance. These templates represent hegemonic technologies of production that are recipes handed down by the powerful. Alternatively, some programs simply list a set of essential components: learning objective, required material, assessment strategy, instructional performance, accommodation, and so on. Level of detail and differentiation of content, process, and product are left to the candidate to determine for themselves. Performances vary by candidate and provide indication of the candidate's proficiency (position with regard to desired competency) and attention (candidate focal concern within the assigned task). This format remains a technology of production but does not dictate final product, leaving space for the candidate to develop technologies of self, and their performance will be authentic and reflect their proficiency.

Within education, the rubric can play the role of the decision aid. Utilizing decision aid structures and sequences to map standard outcomes can help facilitate instruction and learning. Rubrics directed toward the development of technologies of self are not without structure. The expertise of the instructor with regard to the technology of production allows for the anticipation of a learning sequences. Drawing on the standards of the Association for Childhood Education International (ACEI), the following rubric as decision aid will serve as an example (Table 4.1).

TABLE 4.1 ACEI Standard 3 Rubric

Desired Learning Outcome	Basic Proficiency	Developing Proficiency	Target Proficiency	Exemplary Proficiency
3.1 Integrating and applying knowledge for instruction	Candidate: • Explains biological development • Explains brain and cognitive development • Explains identity development	Candidate plans and implements instruction-based knowledge of students, learning theory, and their connections	Candidate plans and implements instruction based on knowledge of students, learning theory, connections across the curriculum, curricular goals, and community	Candidate sequences multiple learning experiences to meet learning and developmental needs
3.3 Development of critical thinking and problem solving	Candidate: • Understands a variety of teaching strategies • Understands critical thinking • Understands problem solving	Candidate: • Demonstrates teaching strategies for critical thinking • Demonstrates teaching strategies for problem solving	Candidate understands and uses a variety of teaching strategies that encourage elementary students' development of critical thinking and problem solving.	Candidate: • Sequences multiple learning experiences to meet critical thinking development • Sequences multiple learning experiences to meet problem-solving development

Source: University of Evansville School of Education, 2013

The decision aid presented in Table 4.1 provides guidance to both the instructor and learner. By making explicit the required competencies the learner will need to demonstrate, the decision aid provides some guidance regarding the instruction and learning experiences that should occur. For example, to demonstrate proficiency in the development of critical thinking and problem solving, the learner will need to

- Understand a variety of teaching strategies: Summarize syntax for multiple instructional practices.
- Understand critical thinking: Define and summarize what critical thinking represents and means.
- Understand problem solving: Define and summarize what problem solving represents and means.
- Demonstrate teaching strategies for critical thinking: Apply guided instructional strategies designed to facilitate critical thinking. And
- Demonstrate teaching strategies for problem solving: Apply guided instructional strategies designed to facilitate problem solving.

If learners are to demonstrate the target proficiency, then the instructor will need to provide the learner with the opportunity to acquire the constituent competencies. Arguably, each of these proficiencies is necessary in order to understand and use a variety of teaching strategies that encourage elementary students' development of critical thinking and problem solving. As learners are developing their competencies through various guided performances, the decision aid offers the instructor a guide for just-in-time feedback and prompting for further learning. It also serves as a scaffolded presentation of the complexity of learning to be accomplished. In a concise manner, a process-driven rubric expresses the complexity of both content and process to be developed.

Consider the "Integrating and Applying Knowledge for Instruction" criterion. When a student successfully explains biological development during a learning experience (Basic Proficiency), the instructor can prompt the learner to explain the instructional process they would use given that explanation. When a learner provides a rationale for an instructional event based upon their understanding of biological development (Developing Proficiency), the instructor can prompt the learner to consider the connections between biology, cognition, and identity development within the context of the curricular goals. And finally, when the learner plans and implements instruction based on knowledge of students (Target Proficiency), they can be challenged to sequence multiple learning experiences to meet learning and developmental needs. At the metacognitive level, the learner is presented with a progress-monitoring advance organizer that can be utilized to inform their learning experience and to structure future learning experiences. Rubrics provide this guidance in a concise manner.

An integral part of the reframing of rubrics processes involves bringing students into the dialogue about the criteria represented in the rubric (Andrade, 2000, 2005). Acknowledging that these criteria are contingent and not definitive will be a risk for some instructors. Allowing students to participate in the determination of the standards by which they will be evaluated creates a climate in which fairness, understanding of expectations, and personalized learning goals come together to create intrinsic motivation. This is a difficult adjustment for all the stakeholders. Again, standards and established learning outcomes provide the horizon for this process. Each learning objective is matched to a set of indicator activities that address a variety of proficiency levels. Using self-assessment based upon the rubric criteria (advance organizer utilized to inform learning experiences and to structure future learning experiences), the students are enabled to identify the types of performance indicators that they prefer (Andrade, 2000, 2005). Their preferences can be integrated into the learning performance tasks (Parkison, 2010; Riggs & Gholar, 2009).

Self-evaluation includes student reflection upon previous learning activities. As part of self-assessment, students are asked to consider what helps them succeed and what limits their performance. They are also encouraged to assess the degree to which they were able to accomplish the learning goal. As the students become acquainted with the collaborative methodology, they demonstrate greater awareness of their responsibility in the successes and limitations they experience within the classroom. (Parkison, 2010, 2014)

By indicating a contingent proficiency beyond the minimum competency expressed in the target proficiency, the decision aid implicitly recognizes that the development of the learner's understanding is ongoing. Continued development of expertise should be one of the desired goals. Helping learners understand the disciplinary processes that exist is critical, but it is equally valuable to promote the deconstruction and deautomatization of these processes so that the opportunities instructors provide for learners continue to expand (Vygotsky, 1978).

It is important to recognize that the decision aid is not used to generate a grade or evaluation of the learner's performance. Decisions regarding the next instructional step or prompt to continued learning or proficiency development are guided by the rubric. By not linking the proficiency levels to points or grade equivalents, the rubric remains a decision aid that aligns to a technology of power but does not force compliance. By detaching the points or grade alignment from the rubric, students are enabled to see the next level of proficiency within the rubric as a goal. It provides a structure for them to frame reflective inquiries to the instructor for guidance

(Parkison, 2010; Riggs & Gholar, 2009). The learner is able to take ownership of the process and utilize the instructor as the expert-learner who can provide guidance. Once a learner becomes confident in the process or expert knowledge structure represented in the rubric, they will be able to turn this process toward a technology of self that enables creativity and authentic instructional decision-making.

Rubrics and Evaluation

As asserted above, the distinction between assessment and evaluation is critical. Though these processes are highly related, they are distinct and fulfill different roles within the learning and schooling context. Assessment is a vital process that occurs through the use of decision aids and planning guides during the learning experience. Assessment involves making just-in-time decisions about learner proficiencies and appropriate next steps in the learner's progression toward the desired learning outcome. Evaluation, on the other hand, is the process of making judgments about the quality of a learning performance (Airasian, 2005). Confusion about the relationship between these distinct processes has resulted in the misappropriation of rubrics as tools for evaluation, grading, and accountability.

When the necessity arises for the evaluation of learner proficiency in relation to the desired learning outcome, the rubric is a tool for the instructor only. This is not in line with current practice. Rubrics are typically shared with the learner at the time of the evaluation performance due to a sense of fairness to the learner and, in some cases, a desire to maximize the end performance as a means to demonstrate the instructor's proficiency as an educator; this rests on the assumption that there is a causal relationship between instruction, student learning, and student performance that does not relate to the internalization of the desired learning or proficiency. By providing the rubric at the time of the evaluation, the instructor is taking away the learner's opportunity to demonstrate their internalization of the desired understanding or competency by providing a recipe or script for their performance. The learner is no longer doing the thinking (Boostrom, 2005). They are following the directions provided in the rubric. Rubric criteria cease being an advance organizer utilized to inform learning and to structure future learning experiences and become hoops to jump through to receive a grade.

If assessment and instruction have been linked throughout the learning experience, then the learner will have been prompted to develop the constituent components of the desired learning. They will have been given the opportunity to internalize and habituate the disciplining technologies of power that are represented by the desired learning outcomes. The instructional decision aids (rubrics) will have been used to intentionally scaffold instruction and provide learning prompts and feedback. The evaluation is meant to determine the degree to which the learner has developed the desired understanding or proficiency. The evaluator can only make a valid and reliable evaluation of the learner's proficiency if there is not a script or recipe that is being followed.

In the end, a scoring guide can be developed that aligns to the decision aid rubric that was used during instruction. The alignment of the assessment framework and the evaluation instrument is not a complicated process (see Table 4.2).

The rating scale presented in Table 4.2 illustrates the alignment. Each aspect of the disciplinary proficiencies that makes up the desired learning outcome is represented in the scale. In order to perform the target-level proficiency, the learner must provide evidence of the "Basic Proficiency," "Developing Proficiency," and the "Target Proficiency." There should also be anticipation that a learner could outperform the expectation and provide an exemplary performance. In Table 4.2, each factor is equally

TABLE 4.2   Standard 3 Rating Scale

Desired Outcome	Check	Possible/Received
3.1 Integrating and Applying Knowledge for Instruction		8 pts.
• Explains biological development	_____	
• Explains brain and cognitive development	_____	
• Explains identity development	_____	
• Candidate plans and implements instruction based on knowledge of students, connections across the curriculum, curricular goals, and community	_____	
• Candidate sequences multiple learning experiences to meet learning and developmental needs	_____	
3.3 Development of Critical Thinking and Problem Solving		7 pts.
• Understands a variety of teaching strategies	_____	
• Understands critical thinking	_____	
• Understands problem solving	_____	
• Demonstrates teaching strategies for critical thinking	_____	
• Demonstrates teaching strategies for problem solving	_____	
• Understands and uses a variety of teaching strategies that encourage elementary students	_____	
• Sequences multiple learning experiences to meet thinking development needs	_____	
Total		

weighted in the determination of the final evaluation. A grade could be calculated based on the percentage of factors present in the performance, or the instructor could determine a points-to-grade metric for the overall performance. What is critical within the framework presented here is the desire to see all of the component parts of the desired learning outcome and not just the target description. This rating scale is a tool for the instructor or evaluator and not a guide or script for the learner's performance. Learners are made aware of the criteria and expectations throughout the instructional process. What is being evaluated is the learner's internalization and habituation of these criteria.

Role of the Instructor

By reframing rubrics within the learning process, instructors-as-expert-learners are encouraged to consider the experiences that are helpful in leading students toward desired or disciplinary understanding. Dialogues that deconstruct standards or desired learning outcomes based upon cognitive behavior or complexity of the content to be learned and that guide feedback and student self-assessment provide a process for reframing rubrics. By focusing on the tools used to construct and manage the learning horizon, rubrics can encourage reflection and intentional learning. A "process-driven" rubric emphasizes that individuals need a toolkit of technologies that enable them to negotiate diverse contexts. Instructors-as-expert-learners utilizing this type of reframed rubric facilitate students' independence. Instructors-as-expert-learners, through process-driven rubrics, help students develop their toolkit of technologies so that they enter the world prepared to be successful, authentic individuals.

Learning requires public dialogue regarding the desired outcomes and the options available for the learner to develop more complex understandings and proficiencies. What could be a more appropriate topic of discussion within the public sphere of the classroom than the content and meaning of the learning experiences that will be engaged? The role of the instructor in this process is that of the more expert learner (Parkison, 2010). It is common to focus on content expertise within education; however, the framework presented here relies upon an understanding of the instructor as an expert learner. This process depends upon expertise in the competencies that are being developed in the learning context. In many instances within a compliance paradigm, the instructor is not acknowledged as the expert they have become through experience and study.

The expertise of the instructor allows for the anticipation of learning sequences that will likely be experienced within a class. By structuring rubrics as decision aids, instructors can simultaneously plan for a course's learning sequence and remain responsive to the learner needs within the class. Rubrics reframed in this manner become tools for learning and responsive guides to instruction rather than mechanisms of accountability and compliance.

REFERENCES

Airasian, P. W. (2005). *Classroom assessment: Concepts and applications* (5th ed.). Boston, MA: McGraw-Hill.

Andrade, H. (2005). Teaching with rubrics: The good, the bad, and the ugly. *College Teaching, 53*(1), 27–30.

Andrade, H. (2000). Using rubrics to promote thinking and learning. *Educational leadership, 57*(5), 13, 18.

Apple, M. W. (2006). *Educating the "right" way: Markets, standards, God, and inequality* (2nd ed.). New York, NY: Routledge.

Archbald, D. A., & Newmann, F. M. (1988). *Beyond standardized testing: Assessing authentic academic achievement in the secondary school.* Reston, VA: National Association of Secondary School Principals.

Arends, R. I., & Kilcher, A. (2010). *Teaching for student learning: Becoming an accomplished teacher.* New York, NY: Routledge.

Bandura, A. (1986). *Social foundations of thought and action: A social cognition theory.* Englewood Cliffs, NJ: Prentice Hall.

Beane, J. A. (2005). *A reason to teach: Creating classrooms of dignity and hope.* Portsmouth, NH: Heinemann.

Black, P., & Wiliam, D. (2006). Assessment for learning in the classroom. In J. Gardner (Ed.), *Assessment and learning: An introduction* (pp. 9–25). London, UK: Sage.

Boostrom, R. (2005). *Thinking: The foundation of critical and creative learning in the classroom.* New York, NY: Teachers College Press.

Cornelius-White, J. H., & Harbaugh, A. P. (2010). *Learner-centered instruction: Building relationships for student success.* Thousand Oaks, CA: Sage.

Costa, A. L. (2008). *The school as a home for the mind: Creating mindful curriculum, instruction, and dialogue.* Thousand Oaks, CA: Corwin.

Council for the Accreditation of Educator Preparation (CAEP). (2013). *CAEP accreditation standards.*Washington, DC: Council for the Accreditation of Educator Preparation.

Day, E., Authur, W., & Gettman, D. (2001). Knowledge structures and the acquisition of a complex skill. *Journal of applied psychology, 86*(5), 1022–1033.

Foucault, M. (1988). Technologies of the self. In L. H. Martin, H. Gutman, & P. Hutton (Eds.), *Technologies of the self: A Seminar with Michel Foucault.* Amherst: University of Massachusetts Press.

Gardner, H. (2000). *Intelligence reframed: Multiple intelligences for the 21st century.* New York, NY: Basic.

Giroux, H. A. (2012). *Education and the crisis of public values: Challenging the assault on teachers, students, & public education.* New York, NY: Peter Lang.

Glasser, R., & Chi, M. (1988). *The nature of expertise.* Hillsdale, NJ: Erlbaum.

Glasser, W. (1986). *Control theory in the classroom.* New York, NY: Harper & Row.

Goldsmith, T., Johnson, P., & Acton, W. (1991). Assessing stuctural knowledge. *Journal of Educational Psychology, 83*(1), 88–96.

Gonzalez, N., Moll, L. C., & Amanti, C. (Eds.). (2005). *Funds of knowledge: Theorizing practices in households, communities, and classrooms.* Mahwah, NJ: Erlbaum.

Habermas, J. (1994). Three normative models of democracy. *Constellations: An International Journal of Critical & Democratic Theory, 1*(1), 1–10.

Interstate Teacher Assessment and Support Consortium (InTASC). (2013). *InTASC model core teaching standards and learning progressions for teachers 1.0.* Washington, DC: Council of Chief State School Officers.

Jackson, P. W., Boostrom, R. E., & Hansen, D. T. (1993). *The moral life of schools.* San Francisco, CA: Jossey-Bass.

Kleijnen, J., Dolmans, D., Willems, J., & Hout, H. (2013). Teachers' conceptions of quality and organizational values in higher education: Compliance or enhancement? *Assessment & Evaluation in Higher Education, 38*(2), 152–166.

Kohn, A. (1996). *Beyond discipline from compliance to community.* Alexandria, VA: Association for Supervision and Curriculum Development.

Langer, J. A. (2011). *Envisioning knowledge: Building literacy in the academic disciplines.* New York, NY: Teachers College Press.

Lawy, R., & Tedder, M. (2012). Beyond compliance: Teacher education practice in a performative framework. *Reseach Papers in Education, 27*(3), 303–318.

Mandinach, E. B., & Jackson, S. S. (2012). *Transforming teaching and learning through data-driven decision making.* Thousand Oaks, CA: Corwin.

Mehrens, W. A. (1992). Using performance assessment for accountability purposes. *Educational measurement: Issues and Practice, 1,* 3–20.

Myford, C., & Mislevey, R. J. (1995). *Monitoring and improving a portfolio assessment system.* Princeton, NJ: Educational Testing Services.

Parkison, P. (2010). The changing role of instructors as both leaders and learners. In M. A. Fallon & S. C. Brown (Eds.), *Teaching inclusively in higher education* (pp. 77–94). Charlotte, NC: Information Age.

Parkison, P. (2013). Teacher identity and curriculum: Space for dissent. *Curriculum and Teaching Dialogue, 15*(1), 13–26.

Parkison, P. (2014). Collaborative assessment: Middle school case study. *Current Issues in Middle Level Education, 19*(1).

Peck, C. A., Gallucci, C., & Sloan, T. (2010). Negotiating implementation of high-stakes performance assessment policies in teacher education: From compliance to inquiry. *Journal of Teacher Education, 61*(5), 451–463.

Popkewitz, T. S. (1987). *The formation of school subjects: The struggle for creating an American institution.* London, UK: Falmer.

Popkewitz, T. S. (1997). The production of reason and power: Curriculum history and intellectual tradition. *Journal of Curriculum Studies, 29*(2), 131–164.

Riggs, E. G., & Gholar, C. R. (2009). *Strategies that promote student engagement: Unleashing the desire to learn* (2nd ed.). Thousand Oaks, CA: Corwin.

Spring, J. (2011). *The politics of American education.* New York, NY: Routledge.

Tomlinson, C. A., Kaplan, S. N., Renzulli, J. S., Purcell, J. H., Leppien, J. H., Burns, D. E., et al. (2009). *The parallel curriculum: A design to develop learner potential and challenge advanced learners.* Thousand Oaks, CA: Corwin.

Trumpower, D., & Goldsmith, T. (2004). Structural enhancement of learning. *Contemporary Educational Psychology, 29*(4), 426–446.

University of Evansville School of Education. (2013). Preparing profession, skilled, and caring teachers for all learners. *Student and Candidate Handbook.* Evansville, IN: University of Evansville.

Vygotsky, L. (1978). *Mind in society.* Cambridge, MA: MIT Press.

Wiggins, G. P. (1993). *Assessing student performance: Exploring the purpose and limits of testing.* San Francisco, CA: Jossey-Bass.

Wittgenstein, L. (1958). *Philosophical Investigations* (3rd ed., G. Anscombe, Trans.) New York, NY: Macmillan.

CHAPTER 5

THE SANCTITY OF SOFTWARE AND RUBRICS AS HOLY INTERFACES

A Critical Software Analysis of Rubrics as Vehicles of Education Reform

Tom Liam Lynch

Between 2009 and 2013, Secretary of Education Arne Duncan delivered nearly 200 speeches totaling about half a million words. During this time, Duncan uses the word rubric only once. In a speech entitled "Lessons from High-Performing Countries" (Duncan, 2011) he said, "Teachers are entitled to a review by trained observers against a clear rubric of what effective teaching looks like—and to feedback about their practice" (para. 79). The use of the word here suggests that rubrics should be used by supervisors to support teachers in developing their craft by receiving "feedback" in a professional context. This picture, however, is not wholly accurate. The feedback the teacher receives does not remain a private conversation used to improve his or her practice. There is more to it. Rather, the secretary's reform agenda

Rubric Nation, pages 67–83

requires that the evaluation of the teacher be shared with others, often with the district, state, and a national consortium of public and private entities. This sharing occurs through an assemblage of software-powered technologies (Lynch, 2014), especially information systems. That suggests a reason why Duncan's Race to the Top competition, which offered states hundreds of millions of dollars to propose and implement education reform plans that align with federal priorities, includes "building data systems that measure student growth and success, and inform teachers and principals about how they can improve instruction" (U.S. Department of Education, 2010). To say that data systems measure success or inform educators about how to improve practice is inaccurate. While related, measurement does not occur through data systems per se; it occurs via other devices like rubrics, the results of which are entered into data systems. In fact, both rubrics and software are necessary to implementing the secretary's plans. Nevertheless, despite the importance of this connection, the way in which they interrelate has received very little attention. In a reform climate as technophilic and data-lusting as the one in which we exist, it is vital to examine the relationship between rubrics and the ontology of software, asking, How do the use of rubrics and software-powered information systems shape the ways we view and discuss pedagogy?

The Interrelation of Rubrics, Interfaces, and Software

The word *rubric* emerges in the English language in the 1400s, stemming from a French word meaning *red*. In this early usage, rubric refers to the topical headings and marginal instructions to clerics in their liturgical books specifying how to conduct church services, both of which appeared in red ink. Not until the mid-18th century do we see the more familiar definition we know today, which refers to a general set of guidelines one uses to shape one's judgment, decisions, and actions. In its original usage, rubrics act as a kind of interface through which individual human beings interact with authoritative institutions, specifically the church. Rubrics attempt to limit variations in individuals' thinking and actions as a way to preserve that which is deemed sacred. In contrast, the use of rubric that emerges later conveys a sense of fairness and equity in judgment. That is, the work of the rubric is to reflect fairness back to those individuals who use it.

When we consider how rubrics are used in teacher preparation and evaluation, it is worth questioning what we mean: rubrics as *holy interfaces* to a sacred world or rubrics as *earthly interfaces* in a social attempt at fairness? I use the word *interface* intentionally. In software studies, interfaces serve as a precise space of study where the worlds of human users and software converge. Interfaces are not passive visual representations, but rather are dynamic spaces that direct users' actions even as they appear to be passive receptors for users' wishes. When we use software-powered technologies, a transaction occurs between the worlds of users and the worlds of "software" that is facilitated through interfaces.

Media theorist Lev Manovich (2001, 2013) argues that in our increasingly digital age, software drives much of human creativity, productivity, and consumption. Unlike previous technologies, software is not a neutral extension of human beings' natural abilities (McLuhan, 1964; Ong, 1982) as the pencil is to our hands or the bicycle is to our legs. Rather, software has an active quality. It pushes into our worlds in ways that we often don't recognize until it makes a mistake: it autocorrects our text messages, crashes our stock markets, or misdirects a missile (Lynch, 2013a). In education, though we seldom hear the word *software* used, save in the context of preparing the future workforce of coders, software is in fact the hidden enabler of the current reforms. Software powers the new assessments students will be taking on computers. Software powers the information systems through which performance data is shared across states and with private companies. Software powers the new teacher certification systems being rolled out in many states. And software powers teacher evaluation systems. While some have expressed fears that technology will replace teachers (Ravitch, 2013), I believe it isn't replacement we have to fear, nor is it technology per se. The real fear is that as we continue to interact with software in certain ways, we will slowly defer to computational logic and the pedagogies it encourages. Teachers won't be replaced by software; they'll be seduced to think and teach like it. Rubrics are one of the ways in which this seduction begins, especially when they are used to feed data into information systems.

A Call for Critical Software Studies

The idea that software acts in our world in troubling ways is not a new idea, though the systematic application of such ideas to educational theory and practice is rare (see Adams, 2010 for a notable exception). Elsewhere, I attempt to build a conceptual bridge between a field known as software studies and educational research (Lynch, 2013a). I construct this bridge by combining concepts from three fields: critical educational studies, multimodal and text analysis, and software studies. Below, I introduce key concepts from these three fields and attempt to synthesize them under the name *critical software studies* in order to examine the way rubrics are being used to prepare pedagogy for information systems.

Critical Educational Studies

Critical educational studies is a term used by Michael Apple (1993, 1996) to refer to the examination of the ways in which institutional forces infringe upon the educational freedom, dignity, and rights of individuals. One of his key critiques focuses on the way in which the conservative apparatus, which he defines as neoliberal and neoconservative politicians, officials, and associates, works to dismantle public education. In place of public schools that truly prepare the young to participate in our democracy, the conservative apparatus seeks to control the content of curriculum to align with conservative ideologies while increasing the role of private companies and capitalistic logic to education. In addition to the creation of "official knowledge" (Apple, 1993), we are also witnessing what I call the *commercialization of pedagogy* as neoconservatives and neoliberals agree upon the strategic and ubiquitous use of software-powered technologies (Lynch, 2013a, 2013b, 2014). Other more recent voices (Picciano & Spring, 2013; Ravitch, 2013) echo these criticisms, though they use different terms.

Multimodal and Text Analysis

Both multimodal studies and text analysis focus on theorizing and implementing approaches to unpacking multimodal texts, which can refer to written texts as well as video, pictures, sounds, and even furniture (Jewitt, 2009). I rely heavily on Kress's (2003, 2011) notions of modal logic and epistemological commitments. Kress argues that each mode of communication we consider has certain logics that compose its nature and makes certain kinds of expression possible while limiting others. Consider, for instance, the difference between hearing a friend give you directions on the phone as compared to being able to look at a map. In the former instance, you rely on a spoken mode of communication; the latter relies on a visual mode. The kinds of meaning you are able to make through these two modes are different. With regard to education, Kress argues that the modes through which we both communicate content to students as well as the modes we allow students to use to communicate what they have learned greatly impact our perception of learning. To extend the example above, your friend whom you've asked for directions might be able to convey what she knows clearly to you by drawing you a map while appearing unknowledgeable if forced to rely on spoken modes of communication. The kinds of epistemological commitments she could make—what it is she can demonstrate knowing—would be directly affected by modal logic.

Software Studies

Software has become an essential component of society. It powers the phones in our pockets, computers on our desks, trains we ride to work, cars we use, markets we invest in, wars we wage, and much more. In addition, the media we consume is increasingly created, edited, and shared via software. This chapter was written using cloud word processing applications on multiple computers and my phone, downloaded to a desktop computer for final formatting and citations, emailed to the editors who used their own software to make edits and comments, shared with the publishers who then used more sophisticated publishing software to organize multiple chapters and layout, graphic designers created the cover you see in separate software applications, the final manuscript compiled and published in both paper and digital form. For those of you reading this on e-readers, it's worth noting that you are reading this chapter on the kind of device I composed it with, albeit we use different software applications for our different purposes. In short, software is everywhere. Or, to put it differently, we live in an age of "everyware" (Kitchin & Dodge, 2011).

Software studies seeks to unpack the interplay between the ontology of software—the nature of it—with the effects it has in our world. The creation process of software is not neutral. Software is developed by teams of individuals for different purposes, many of which are profit-seeking. The decisions made by software development teams and their corporate sponsors have direct impacts on our lives. These impacts range from inconvenient to deadly. On the lighter end of the continuum, many of us have experienced the frustration or humor of our mobile phones' autocorrect feature. Companies choose to program their autocorrect algorithms in ways that serve their interests, which is why on an iPhone you might notice that the word *googel* will not be automatically corrected, whereas on the Chromebook *Google* comes ready to be inserted upon mistyping.

It is vital that we build theories to better understand software and develop methodologies to examine its effects. Scholars in software studies have put forth examinations of both complex networks of software like airports (Kitchin & Dodge, 2011) to user interfaces we encounter (Murray, 2011) to the use of buttons in Web applications (Pold, 2008). Further, Manovich has thoroughly theorized the role of software in the production of media (2001, 2013). In his work, Manovich argues that there are certain characteristics of new media—by which he means media created, edited, and shared via software—that are distinct from previous technologies. For our purposes, we'll focus on the following:

- *Database Logic:* Software relies fundamentally on databases and algorithms to work. Databases demand that information be clearly identifiable in preordained ways so it can be stored unambiguously and retrieved rapidly.
- *Quantification:* Software requires inputs to be quantifiable in order for them to be acted upon by algorithms. For instance, any color

you see on a picture you take has an alphanumeric code that can be algorithmically altered instantly (which we experience as "effects" and "filters" in popular photo sharing applications).

- *Automation:* Software can be programmed to anticipate inputs and automatically apply rules (i.e., algorithms, functions, scripts) to such inputs without further human intervention. For example, smartphones often check for email and other data feeds even when the phone appears to be off.
- *Transcoding:* For Manovich, transcoding technically means to translate new media into different formats, but can be extended to refer to "the computerization of culture" wherein "cultural categories and concepts are substituted, on the level of meaning and/or language, by new ones that derive from the computer's ontology, epistemology, and pragmatics." (2001, p. 47)

Critical Software Studies

Each of the three fields above have both affordances and limitations that are worth briefly noting. Critical educational studies offers thoroughly developed concepts and methods for analyzing institutional and high-level discursive moves used to further the ideologies of the conservative apparatus. It offers little with regard to actionable methods for analyzing multimodal texts like those that are being used in the current education reforms. Multimodal and text analysis provide rigorous methods for both transcribing and theorizing a wide array of texts, but they do not account for the nature of software itself. Software studies, which is still relatively new, offers helpful theoretical frameworks but offers less in terms of social criticism and methodologies. It also says precious little about the use of software in education. What I am calling critical software studies (CSS) refers to the layering of critical educational studies, multimodal and text analysis, and software studies to create a composite framework that seeks to examine the ways in which software is used by the conservative apparatus to disempower educators, students, and families in an effort to privatize our public schools. I have explored the interplay of these fields in previous studies without naming it CSS. When it comes to the current education reforms, software is being used ubiquitously. This is especially the case when we consider the way in which the complexity of teaching and learning is transcoded to align with database logic. We are being required to quantify pedagogy in numerous ways so it can be fed into information systems and acted upon automatically. Rubrics are, in fact, instrumental in this process and merit critical inspection.

On the Nature of Software and Rubrics as Holy Interfaces

In order to consider the ways in which rubrics can be regarded as a vehicle of computational logic, we have to first examine the ontology of software. Though the history of software dates back many decades, its ubiquity in society is a more recent occurrence. Whereas we once talked about technology and computers, it would be more accurate to talk about software today. Software is what increasingly enables our social lives—the World Wide Web, hospitals, transportation systems, automobiles, wartime weaponry, peacetime surveillance, and our education system—to function. "While various systems of modern society speak in different languages and have different goals," Manovich (2013) writes, "they all share the syntaxes of software: control statements 'if then' and 'while do,' operators and data types (such as characters and floating point numbers), data structures such as lists, and interface conventions encompassing menus and dialog boxes" (p. 8).

Users encounter these syntaxes in different ways, most explicitly through interfaces. Consider the degree to which our interaction with a web page is dictated by links, buttons, and menus. Seldom is it the case that users can freely navigate a website. Their actions are tightly controlled, their choices carefully limited. The interface is designed to ensure software and information systems get the inputs that are needed. As Manovich suggests, when we engage in the world through software, we engage (at least in part) on its terms. We twist our desires and expressions, for example, to conform to the options provided on a menu of a web page. In addition, we help *transcode* our experiences so software can process them.

> In new media lingo, to "transcode" something is to translate it into another format. The computerization of culture gradually accomplishes similar transcoding in relation to all cultural categories and concepts. That is, cultural categories and concepts are substituted, on the level of meaning and/or language, by new ones that derive from the computer's ontology, epistemology, and pragmatics. (Manovich, 2001, p. 47)

Here, Manovich extends a technical definition of transcoding, which applies originally to media, to apply to the way in which software-powered technologies (Lynch, 2013a, 2014) transcode lived experience. An example helps.

When we take pictures with our phones, light sensors in the camera lens convert our world into data that software understands, that can be stored in specific data structures, and can be acted upon via algorithms. The logic that undergirds software and transcoding is that of the database. Manovich (2001) argues that database logic seeps into our lives as software becomes increasingly omnipresent. Database logic demands unambiguous information to be filed into clearly defined folders. Together, concepts like interfaces, transcoding, and database logic offer some explanation for the role that rubrics play when used to evaluate teachers: rubrics might be said to transcode human activity into computational data that can be stored and retrieved according to preordained categories and labels. Who determines the parameters of such preordination and for what purpose? Examining this question requires that we begin with reformers' end goal in mind, which the conservative apparatus envisions as building sophisticated data systems that make student and teacher data more widely available.

Though the language of Race to the Top above does not call attention to the role of private entities, it is worth noting that as these reforms gained traction—in no small part due to the ideological and financial support of the federal government and philanthropic groups—the presence of non-educational entities grew. In direct response to federal priorities, an elaborate data system called the Shared Learning Collaborative (SLC) emerged, a consortium of state agencies and private advisors enticed by federal and private funding, who collaborated to integrate their data systems to make national-level education reporting possible. Any state or district that took Race to the Top funding was "encouraged" to participate in the SLC. The board of the SLC includes members of the conservative apparatus like former governor of West Virginia Bob Wise, whose crossing of public-educational and private industry priorities has been the subject of criticism (Fang, 2011). After gaining enough cooperation and momentum for a pilot, the SLC was transitioned into a nonprofit called InBloom. Though InBloom was eventually forced to close its doors due to public and parent outcry, it still serves as an educative case in point. InBloom's stated mission reads,

> To succeed in today's global economy, students need learning experiences that meet their individual needs, engage them deeply and let them learn at their own pace. This requires teachers to have an up-to-date picture of a student's progress; an understanding of where he or she needs extra attention; and access to materials that will help progress their students' learning. inBloom is a nonprofit organization helping to make this possible by providing efficient and cost-effective means for school districts to give teachers the information and tools necessary to strengthen their connection with each student. (inBloom, n.d.)

There are implications to public entities like states and districts engaging so deeply with inBloom, despite its nonprofit status. First, educators are not the ones making the decisions about the value of generating, sharing, and analyzing the data. Administrative and executive members of state and district educational agencies required schools' participation because of the strings attached to the funding they received, in many cases from nonpublic sources. Second, inBloom seeks not simply to use data internally to improve teaching and learning in schools, but rather the student and teacher data made available to inBloom is also made available to companies hawking curricular products, prompting parent groups to cry foul (Singer, 2013) and many states pulling out of the partnership. In the reformers' end state, a teacher will log into an online portal, be presented with their strengths and weaknesses based on student testing and teacher evaluation data, and an algorithm will make recommendations of products they or their school district can purchase from a for-profit company.

A Critical Software Analysis

Above, I outline the final system into which teacher preparation and evaluation results feed. I posit that there are two aspects to the way in which rubrics act as holy interfaces: (a) rubrics transcode the complexity of lived experience into discrete data in preparation for (b) entry into information systems that represent pedagogy as data structures. If the purpose of the current teacher preparation and evaluation systems are to feed into a data system created by the conservative apparatus to profit from student and teaching data, rubrics are being used to transcode learning experiences into data for computer processing as well as for sale at market. In what follows, let us examine two cases. The first is a rubric used in the preparation of new teacher candidates in New York State. Like inBloom's system described above, the data generated from the rubric's use is intended to be shared with other information systems, in part to serve as a public evaluation of the quality of schools of education. The second rubric is one used in New York City public schools to evaluate current teachers.

Teacher Preparation Rubric: New York State

New York State had plans to reform the process for teaching certification for many years. However, it was only after winning $700 million in Race to the Top money that the funding and motivation were sufficient for implementation. The final reform initiative is called the edTPA (Teacher Performance Assessment). The edTPA consists of two main components: (a) three new or revised sit-down exams and (b) a performance assessment portfolio in which students write dozens of pages of reflections in response to artifacts of their planning, teaching, and assessment, all of which candidates upload to Pearson Education's servers for a fee. In New York, the total fee to students approaches $1,000. Teacher educators received various materials to help prepare their candidates for the edTPA, which include the rubrics through which teachers' performance assessments would be scored.

Rubric 9 of the English/Language Arts edTPA handbook (Stanford Center for Assessment, Learning and Equity, 2013) provides a site of study. It contains elements of at least two logics: visual logic and written logic. Visual logic privileges spatial thinking rather than narrative sequence. Written logic, on the other hand, privileges narrative and sequential thinking. Our rubric integrates writing in the form of the labels and descriptors it provides. The rubric identifies a topic of focus ("Subject-Specific Pedagogy") and guiding question ("How does the candidate use textual references to help students understand how to construct meaning from and interpret a complex text?"). It then integrates a powerful visual logic in the form of a grid with five levels of achievement, each containing distinct language articulating what constitutes each of the levels. Some words in the rubric are in bold typeface. Let us look more closely at two levels to better understand how the visual logic of the grid and the written logic of the descriptors create tension. Level 3 reads, "Candidate uses *textual references in ways that help students understand* strategies to construct meaning from and interpret complex text." Level 4 reads, "Candidate uses textual references *in ways that deepen student understanding* of strategies to construct meaning from and interpret complex text." Between each of these levels are lines which visually create a sense of unambiguous delineation between not only the numerical levels (i.e., 3 and 4) but also the language represented within the levels. The result of these two logics is a dangerous tension that manifests itself in the kinds of epistemological commitments users of the rubric are ultimately able to make about the nature of teaching and learning.

The person using this rubric to assess a video clip of a teaching candidate's classroom instruction has to determine if the candidate has "[helped] students understand strategies" or "[deepened] student understanding of strategies" to construct meaning from and interpret complex texts. The key difference in language is the rubric's use of the phrases "help students understand" as opposed to "deepen student understanding." It is important to consider two things here: (a) whether these two concepts—helping and deepening—are, as the rubric demands, mutually exclusive, as well as (b) whether a candidate could differentiate instruction in a way that helps some students while deepening other students' understanding. In fact, the two qualifiers used in the rubric are not contradictory but complementary. It should also be clear that not only is it possible for a candidate to demonstrate the ability to both help some students understand while deepening other students' understanding but it is a highly desirable form of differentiation. The rubric, however, is not designed to permit this kind of nuance. The visual logic invoked by the grid forces upon written logic something that is not inherent unto it. That is, written logic permits ambiguity, ambivalence, metaphor, double-meaning, and other communicative devices. The visual logic invoked by the use of a grid, however, does not permit such devices. The rubric does not tolerate the notion that a candidate could demonstrate elements of levels 3 and 4 at once. The unique tension between visual and written logics that the rubric creates results in the treatment of pedagogy that is prepared for a third logic, that of the database.

The rubric, despite its analog form, forces database logic on those who use it. Database logic requires that clearly defined data be stored in compartmentalized folders and await being acted upon by computational functions. These functions take the form of either/or, if/then, and many other such binary commands. In this case, the nature of the rubric forces the user to make a series of false choices in order to prepare the complexity of pedagogy for information systems. She must choose one level or the other. *Either* the candidate is helping students *or* she is deepening their understanding. *If* the candidate is determined (however falsely such a determination is reached) to be merely helping students understand, *then* she will be evaluated as level 3 in this rubric. Rubrics act as software insofar as they transcode teaching by both falsifying and forcing the quantification of pedagogy.

This labeling of the candidate's teaching as "a 3" marks the end of the first part of how rubrics transcode pedagogy. The second phase of this transcoding occurs when we ask ourselves what happens to "a 3" and other evaluation data. In the case of New York's edTPA, human scorers of the candidate's performance portfolio will enter "a 3" and similar data into information systems (which are as likely to belong to Pearson as they are the state) where eventually they will be combined with testing data of the students the candidate teaches. The idea is that the government should be able to trace the performance of teachers (by which they mean test scores more than classroom observations by principals) to their performance on the edTPA, which will then be interpreted as a reflection of the quality of the teacher preparation program the teacher attended. The rubric used to evaluate the teacher candidate does not simply represent but rather *is* the necessary and crucial transcoding event that makes the officiating of knowledge and commercialization of pedagogy possible.

I have argued that rubrics force us to transcode candidates' pedagogy into data. Candidates' data is created, manipulated, and likely stored on the servers of private companies like Pearson, upon whose services New York State and the architects of the edTPA rely. When the candidate becomes a fully certified teacher, her students will take exams aligned to the Common Core Standards—exams that are likely to come from Pearson or a comparably large company with computerized assessments—and those test scores will be traced back to the edTPA data on the teacher in databases and used to determine the effectiveness of the teacher preparation program the teacher attended as a candidate. This long-term process represents a concerted effort by the conservative apparatus to control both the knowledge students and teachers learn as well as the pedagogy used in our schools.

Teacher Evaluation Systems in New York City

New York City created a repository of resources to support schools in implementing reforms like teacher evaluations and new standards. One video featured on the repository website shows how one school's administrators conduct teacher evaluations (NYC DOE, 2011). It features a middle school principal, assistant principal, and several teachers. Footage of classroom activity is interspersed with interviews. In the video, the assistant principal visits a teacher's classroom with the evaluation rubric in hand. The rubric evaluates teachers on a scale from low to high (Unsatisfactory, Basic, Proficient, and Distinguished). After the observation, the assistant principal meets with the principal to determine the appropriate scoring. During their meeting, they have the following exchange:

> **P:** You have for all of pretty much Domain 1 *proficient*, so when he came to his lesson with his lesson plan, you felt like those elements were proficient, or did they become proficient through your conversation with him?
>
> **AP:** There were some minor details that we worked through where he would go from basic to proficient.
>
> **P:** If you feel like he didn't come to the observation with it narrowed and specific than in Domain 1 rather than giving him a *proficient* that he has a *basic*... um ... because he didn't come with that. He's doing that now that you coached him on how to change that.
>
> **AP:** OK.

The assistant principal agrees in the end that his original evaluation of Proficient is more accurately Basic because the teacher required "coaching" to strengthen the "minor details" that were missing.

The rubric used by the city at the time of the video clip focuses on Domain 1 and more specifically "designing coherent instruction (1e)." In this clip, the focus of the discussion is whether to evaluate the teacher as Basic or Proficient. The rubric (Danielson, 2013) articulates the following:

- *Basic:* Some of the learning activities and materials are suitable to the instructional outcomes and represent a moderate cognitive challenge but with no differentiation for different students. Instructional groups partially support the instructional outcomes, with an effort by the teacher at providing some variety. / The lesson or unit has a recognizable structure; the progression of activities is uneven, with most time allocations reasonable.

- *Proficient:* Teacher coordinates knowledge of content, of students, and of resources, to design a series of learning experiences aligned to instructional outcomes and suitable to groups of students. / The learning activities have reasonable time allocations; they represent significant cognitive challenge, with some differentiation for different groups of students. / The lesson or unit has a clear structure, with appropriate and varied use of instructional groups.

Both evaluation categories refer to "instructional outcomes" and differentiation, lesson plans that have clear structure and logic, as well as awareness of "time allocations." Differences between Basic and Proficient include the degree to which "suitable" instructional outcomes are differentiated for students (including the teacher's use of "variety") and the "reasonable[ness]" of time allocation.

When the principal and the assistant principal discuss how to evaluate the teacher, it is notable that their discussion does not hinge on instructional outcomes, suitableness of those outcomes with regard to differentiation, or offering reasonable time allocations. While it is possible that these terms were used in moments that were not featured in the video, what is shown is what is publicized as a model of evaluation. It is also notable that the conversation between the administrators focuses on the degree to which the teacher "came to his lesson with his lesson plan" already "narrowed" or if that occurred through the in-the-moment coaching of the assistant principal. There is no reference to this distinction—whether or not a teacher's performance is evaluated more highly if admittedly "minor details" are not addressed by a coach. Whereas in the examination of the teacher preparation rubric we see how the tension between visual and written modes of communication work to transcode pedagogy, here, what moves the administrators' decision to select one category over another is something that is not explicated in the rubric section itself. If the point of the rubric is to limit the degree to which individual human beings impose their own subjectivity on a learning experience, in this case we see the imperfection of such intentions. Here, after negotiation between the assistant principal's observations, the rubric, and the principal's insights, the process of transcoding pedagogy begins with a word: it is Basic.

The result of using the rubric now enters into its second phase. Because New York State and City have committed to reporting teacher evaluation data to nationwide entities, including inBloom, then a transcoded (i.e., quantitative) representation of a teacher's pedagogy must be entered into a database and fed to other information systems. This might occur by the assistant principal accessing the city's evaluation system online, called Advance, looking up the teacher's employee ID number, and selecting "Basic" from a dropdown menu next to "Domain 1(e)." After these selections are made, the administrator commits to his evaluation by clicking a submission button. When the submission button is clicked, software works to send the quantitative representation of the teacher's identity and pedagogy to a city database that is integrated with comparable information systems at the state. In order for the state to have useful data, all districts have to have agreed upon a schema to name, store, and feed their data in precisely the same ways. These schema that are agreed upon by multiple parties, referred to broadly as metadata, are another way in which the needs of database logic shape education, if not pedagogy directly, certainly the discourse about pedagogy. When the data feeds arrive in the state's databases, they are packaged to be fed with other information systems around the country, including inBloom. inBloom systems read this kind of data feed, apply algorithms intended to assess teachers' professional learning needs, and identify where the teacher needs development. In this case, algorithms might quickly determine that the teacher in our video clip needs support in "designing coherent instruction." When the teacher logs into inBloom's system, he might find, in addition to visualizations of his students' test scores, a recommendation of professional resources aimed at improving his instructional design abilities, including for-purchase options from private companies. He can click on a link and be led to an online marketplace awaiting his purchase.

DISCUSSION

The use of rubrics in both the teacher preparation and the teacher evaluation video above demonstrate that rubrics themselves are devices that are used to convert pedagogy into data for information systems. That is, they are used to translate the complexity of lived experience into a format that is ready for processing by computers. The categories in rubrics, the tension between visual and written modal logics, and the lines between Basic and Proficient on the grid the administrator sees when evaluating the teacher serve the same computational purpose as the drop-down menus and buttons he encounters in Advance, which is to say that in order for software-powered technologies to work, it is necessary to limit the ways in which human beings interact with them. Our experiences in online environments and with digital technologies consist of clicking links, tapping buttons, selecting from menus, and typing into text boxes precisely, because without these points of control, computer environments would be unable to "understand" what it is human users intend. Rubrics in these examples serve a comparable purpose as the user interfaces we encounter when using computers: to funnel human perception into actions and languages ready for software. To be clear, rubrics can be used in ways that do otherwise. For instance, users of the teacher preparation rubrics could take their findings and meet with each teaching candidates to improve their practice—no computer system, no data feeds, no profiteering companies, and no public reporting. In fact, one could argue that if the end goal truly is to impact individual teacher practice, this approach would be both more befitting and effective. The same can be said for teacher evaluation systems. While the principal in the video discusses her school's evaluation practice as "honing the craft," the fact is that eventually the final evaluation has to be entered into the city's information system. In both cases, the use of rubrics is not as earthly interfaces—their use does not feed back into a social setting with the purpose of improving some immediate phenomenon. Rather, the use of rubrics in these cases is one of holy interfaces, where the sacred world with which they interface is that of software. The holiness of the rubric interface in question, then, refers not to the institutional nature of the church but rather the conservative apparatus' education reform agend, which applies the logic of the market to schools: competition, choice, transparency of data, and an increasing reliance on the private sector. And software facilitates their agenda.

While I noted above that the secretary used the word *rubric* only once (Duncan, 2011), it is worth reiterating that in the sentence in which he refers explicitly to rubrics, he does so in a misleading way. His use of the word focuses on "trained observers," yet he makes no mention of the sophisticated network of information systems into which the human beings will input evaluation scores, to say nothing of the role that private companies play. Rather, he only says that teachers will receive "feedback about their practice." To say "feedback" is insufficient, if not inaccurate. It suggests that the primary purpose of rubrics is that of earthly interfaces, that is, to reflect back to teachers insight about pedagogy. In fact, the purpose of the rubrics is to begin the process of transcoding pedagogy into data that can be entered into a database via a series of menus, check boxes, links, and buttons the administrator will encounter via software like Advance. Teachers might receive feedback from their administrators, but their data is transcoded in the ways described above so software can generate "feedback" as well. Software's feedback, however qualitatively it might read, is necessarily merely the result of preordained categories, canned responses, if/then statements, and the pedagogical assumptions of those who promote it.

CLOSING THOUGHTS

Software is being used by reformers to systematically transcode pedagogy into something from which companies can most easily profit. It can be difficult to see this, I admit, in part because much of our society is becoming reliant on software: information systems, data structures, algorithms, mobile phone applications, and much more. Some of these uses of software are clear. Some are not. The kinds of software-powered technologies used to realize the current education reforms—rubrics fed into data systems, testing software, reporting applications, to name a few—are being injected into education in quiet and required ways that are slowly twisting pedagogy to align with database logic. The logic of databases, as Manovich (2001) notes, drives our software culture and, as I have demonstrated, it is also the logic of rubrics. In many ways, rubrics *are* software. We must acknowledge this if we are to resist the officiating of knowledge and the commercialization of pedagogy. Each time we uncritically check a box, select a menu option, and click a button in order to report on teaching and learning, we contribute to the sanctification of software. It is a submission we make not on our knees before an altar, but seated at our computers with genuflecting fingers.

REFERENCES

Adams, C. (2010). Learning management systems as sites of surveillance, control, and corporatization: A Review of the critical literature. In D. Gibson & B. Dodge (Eds.), *Proceedings of society for information technology and teacher education international conference 2010* (pp. 252–257). Chesapeake, VA: AACE.

Apple, M. W. (1993). *Official knowledge: Democratic education in a conservative age.* New York, NY: Routledge.

Apple, M. W. (1996). *Cultural politics and education.* New York, NY: Teachers College Press.

Danielson, C. (2013). The framework for teaching evaluation instrument. *The Danielson Group.* Retrieved from http://www.danielsongroup.org/userfiles/files/downloads/2013EvaluationInstrument.pdf

Duncan, A. (2011, May 24). Lessons from high-performing countries. *U.S. Department of Education.* Retrieved December 30, 2013, from http://www.ed.gov/news/speeches/lessons-high-performing-countries

Fang, L. (2011, December 5). How online learning companies bought America's schools. *The Nation.* Retrieved from http://www.thenation.com/article/164651/how-online-learning-companies-bought-americas-schools

inBloom. (n.d.). *About inBloom.* Retrieved from https://www.inbloom.org/about-inbloom (Please note this web site has been removed since the publication of this chapter.)

Jewitt, C. (Ed.). (2009). *The Routledge handbook of multimodal analysis.* New York, NY: Routledge.

Kitchin, R., & Dodge, M. (2011). *Code/space: Software and everyday life.* Cambridge, MA: MIT Press.

Kress, G. (2003). *Literacy in the new media age.* New York, NY: Routledge.

Kress, G. (2011). Discourse analysis and education: A multimodal social semiotic approach. In R. Rogers (Ed.), *An introduction to critical discourse analysis in education* (2nd ed.). New York, NY: Routledge.

Lynch, T. L. (2013a). Pecs Soviet and the Red underscore: Raising awareness of software's role in our schools. *English Journal, 103*(1), 128–130.

Lynch, T. L. (2013b). The secretary and the software: On the need for integrating software analysis into educational spaces. In J. Gorlewski & B. Porfilio (Eds.), *Left behind in the race to the top.* Charlotte, NC: Information Age.

Lynch, T. L. (2014). The imponderable bloom: A multimodal social semiotic study of the role of software in teaching literature in a secondary online English course. *Changing English, 21*(1), 42–52.

Manovich, L. (2001). *The language of new media.* Cambridge, MA/London, UK: MIT Press.

Manovich, L. (2013). *Software takes command.* New York, NY: Bloomsbury Academic.

McLuhan, M. (1964). *Understanding media: The extensions of man.* New York, NY: McGraw-Hill.

Murray, J. H. (2011). *Inventing the medium: Principles of interaction design as a cultural practice.* Cambridge, MA: MIT Press.

NYC DOE Promising Practices. (2011). *Classroom observation cycle: Structures and supports at MS 331* [Video]. Retrieved from http://vimeo.com/26737635#

Ong, W. (1982). *Orality and literacy: The technologizing of the word.* New York, NY: Methuen.

Picciano, A. G., & Spring, J. (2013). *The great American education-industrial complex: Ideology, technology, and profit.* New York, NY: Routledge.

Pold, S. (2008). Button. In M. Fuller (Ed.), *Software studies: A lexicon.* Cambridge, MA: MIT Press.

Ravitch, D. (2013). *Reign of error: The hoax of the privatization movement and the danger to America's public schools.* New York, NY: Knopf.

Singer, N. (2013, October 5). Deciding who sees students' data. *The New York Times.* Retrieved from http://www.nytimes.com/2013/10/06/business/deciding-who-sees-students-data.html?_r=0

Stanford Center for Assessment, Learning and Equity. (2013, January). *Secondary English-language arts: Assessment handbook.* Board of Trustees of the Leland Stanford Junior University.

U.S. Department of Education. (2010). *Race to the Top.* Retrieved from http://www2.ed.gov/programs/racetothetop/index.html

CHAPTER 6

STANDARDS, RIGOR, AND RUBRICS

Prefabricated Critical Thinking

Robert Boostrom

The professed goal of the accountability-through-assessment movement is a fully aligned curriculum all the way down the chain, from legislative mandates to core standards to district curriculum maps to school curriculum guides to teacher's daily lesson plans to students' brains. Rubrics are the linchpin of this alignment. Without common assessments derived from common rubrics, the chain breaks down at critical junctures, and in turn reformers are unable to label some teachers (and schools) successful and others failures.

The price of this rhetorically coherent system is the surrender of any hope for a transformative education that encourages openness of mind and creativity of thought. This is because rubrics are used as a way to specify, prior to the educative encounter, the educationally significant outcomes. Everything students bring to the encounter (as well as everything they elicit from it that is not measured by the rubric) is irrelevant. Ironically, even some of those who most fervently espouse accountability-through-assessment and

Rubric Nation, pages 85–99
Copyright © 2015 by Information Age Publishing
All rights of reproduction in any form reserved.

a "standards-based, grade- and content-level-aligned curriculum" (Indiana Department of Education, 2011) admit that these reforms cripple children's capacity for creative and critical thinking. This chapter analyzes one such admission—a state document offering teachers advice for the use of curriculum maps—and argues that the epistemological naïveté embodied in this document is endemic within the rubric movement. If we wish to promote transformative education characterized by thoughtfulness and informed rationality, we need unpredictable classrooms that value the delight of recognition and the surprise of uncertainty rather than prefabricated, rubric-bound classrooms.

Curriculum Mapping in Indiana

In July 2011, the Indiana Department of Education posted some online assistance for teachers regarding how to use the state curriculum maps (Indiana Department of Education, 2011). In addition to links to all the subject-area curriculum maps, the Common Core State Standards, and help for navigating the software, the posting included a short paper titled, "The Importance of Quality Curriculum to Prepare Students for College, Careers, and Citizenship."

The paper argues "that a rigorous, standards-based, grade- and content-level-aligned curriculum is one of the key components of high-performing schools" and that the maps created in Indiana by "teachers, content specialists, curriculum mapping experts, and university professors" (Indiana Department of Education, 2011) represent the essential skills that students need. The Indiana document is a straightforward exposition of the standards-based, accountability-through-assessment school reform that has been common in the United States for some years now. What makes this paper remarkably revealing is something it says about how curriculum alignment practices bear upon the experiences that students need. First, here is how the document describes those experiences:

> The best way to ensure students are prepared for college and careers and any assessments they will encounter is to ensure that they are prepared with Conley's four intellectual standards:
>
> 1. Read to infer/interpret/draw conclusions. 2. Support arguments with evidence. 3. Resolve conflicting views encountered in source documents. 4. Solve complex problems with no obvious answer. (Indiana Department of Education, 2011)

The document does not refer to these "intellectual standards" as elements of reasoning or critical thinking, but goals like these can be found in most lists of critical thinking skills (e.g., Boise State University, 2010–2011, p. 48; Bowell & Kemp, 2010; Paul & Elder, 2007; Wagner, 2010). The revealing part of the paper comes next:

> If curriculum design begins with the content and skills identified from the standards, it is quite possible and very likely that schools will develop curriculum that will address the skills. However, this can mean that students learn these skills in isolated, low level, skills-based lessons with short, contrived passages, which build limited content knowledge and which rarely if ever provide the kinds of experiences described above. (Indiana Department of Education, 2011)

This is an astonishing admission. Consider what is being said: According to the Indiana Department of Education, if teachers design curriculum by following the standards it is "very likely" their students will "rarely if ever" engage in any critical thinking.

The document does not, of course, leave this flaw in the curriculum hanging. The solution, says the document, is for all curriculum units developed by schools to be uniformly constructed:

> The precise amount of text and the number of books, including titles to be taught in common by all teachers for a given course; The number and length of papers to be written; Common rubrics by which students will be graded; and . . . The type and frequency of research and current events to be included. (Indiana Department of Education, 2011)

This solution is, in its own way, as astonishing and revealing as the admission that standards-based curricula inhibit critical thinking. It says, in effect, that, because regimenting lessons by aligning them with standards does not encourage students to think deeply and carefully, we should increase the regimentation of lessons. Because specifying lesson content inhibits student thinking, we should specify lesson content more thoroughly.

Now, there are plenty of situations in which the rule of thumb makes sense: if a little bit doesn't work, use more. But I think the state of Indiana is misapplying the rule here. Just because a little bit of regimentation in the curriculum fails to encourage student thinking doesn't mean that a lot of regimentation will get those students to begin supporting their arguments with evidence and solving complex problems.

This chapter will examine the nature of this regimentation, and in particular the central element of Indiana's suggestion for remediating the problem of nonthinking students: the "common rubrics by which students will be graded" (Indiana Department of Education, 2011) This is where the hopes for turning students into thinkers are pinned. Without the common rubrics, the fully aligned curriculum comes unhinged, but the use of them very nearly guarantees that students will not need to think and will not profit by it. The mistake the Indiana Department of Education is making is twofold: it first involves a misunderstanding of the nature of interpretation, and second a too-narrow conception of what makes curriculum "common."

Rubrics and the Nature of Interpretation

An insidious assumption is at work in the argument of Indiana's "Quality Curriculum" document—that school resources (and especially texts) are univocal, that texts and content are the same thing. At first, the assumption is explicit: "Curriculum developers must also decide which instructional resources they will use. The resources largely define the content knowledge students will learn." Later on in the document, the assumption is simply taken for granted, without the modifier "largely": "Once the content for each course has been selected by determining the texts that will be used" (Indiana Department of Education, 2011).

But this assertion that "determining the texts" is the same thing as "selecting the content for each course" should not be embraced so easily. The processes may sometimes be identical, but they don't have to be, and almost certainly shouldn't be, a point that becomes obvious when we recognize that embedded in this assertion is yet another assumption (this one unstated) about the nature of texts and about how they should be used in classrooms. While it is possible to view a text as a repository of the content for each student to master, this is far from the only way to view a text, and it is a way peculiarly inimical to any sort of thinking and reflection.

I often see the educational outcome of this way of viewing texts demonstrated by students in my History of American Schooling course. One of the course textbooks is a collection of educational essays, legislative and judicial documents, readings from schoolbooks, and aubiographical excerpts. In a section called "The Cold War Era," there is an excerpt from a 1950s Scott Foresman reader. This excerpt includes a story about Abraham Lincoln growing up in a cabin in Indiana. Here is part of what it says:

> Pigeon Creek was a lonely place when the pioneers began to settle Indiana. But as young Abraham Lincoln tramped across a field, he was thinking how much he loved his new home in the Indiana wilderness.
>
> The Lincoln cabin was roughly built. At night from his bed in the loft, the lad could see the sky through the cracks between the logs. Great white stars shone down on him. Sometimes the yellow moon lighted his room like a bright candle. Sometimes on warm summer nights, cooling raindrops fell gently over his face. In winter, feathery flakes of snow fell on his pillow. (Fraser, 2010, p. 260)

Many of my students are inclined to view this excerpt as nothing more than a genteel depiction of the happy life of young Abe in frontier Indiana, even though there is no reason for an early 19th century pastoral scene to be included among the readings about education during "the Cold War Era" in America. Read as a straightforward biographical item, the excerpt, in the context of 1950s schooling, makes no sense. So how can so many of my students read the passage this way? What do they think they're doing?

Asked about the passage and the reason for its being in "the Cold War Era" section of the book, these students say they see the excerpt as no more problematic than any other document in the book. For them, the book is a textbook in a history class. That is to say, it is (by definition) a collection of bits of information about "the past," some of which are to be stored in short-term memory for retrieval at test time.

We might want to ask how, with an excerpt that makes no sense to the student (like the Lincoln piece in the Cold War Era section of the book), does a student know which are the bits to be stored, which are the facts they're supposed to remember? Does it matter that the "cooling raindrops" only fell on "warm summer nights"? Or that the "feathery flakes of snow" fell not on his freezing ears but "on his pillow?"

The problem with such questions is that they assume that students typically engage in interpretive work on class-assigned readings, that they make decisions about how to make meaning from a text, and that these decisions vary with the text and their response to it. But this assumption of individual, interpretive meaning-making is not what is reported by those students who see the Lincoln excerpt as simply a biographical item. These students— mostly college freshmen, mostly raised in the U.S. Midwest, mostly studying U.S. history for the fourth time in their school career—apparently see all of the readings as equally incoherent. For them, the Lincoln reading is not about the sentimental deification of American heroes during the 1950s or about the forging of a middle-class morality; it's simply facts about the youth of Abraham Lincoln, even though these facts have nothing to do with the ostensible topic, education during the Cold War Era. For these students, determining the text *is* the same thing as selecting the content.

Ironically, these same students have probably heard (in Language Arts, not History) that there are different ways to read a text. They have probably heard that, as Joseph Schwab (1969) put it,

> Novels can be read, for example, as bearers of wisdom, insights into vicissitudes of human life and ways of enduring them. Novels can also be read as moral instructors, as sources of vicarious experience, as occasions for aesthetic experience. They can be read as models of human creativity, as displays of social problems, as political propaganda, as revelations of diversities of manners and morals among different cultures and classes of people, or as symptoms of their age. (p. 19)

In other words, my students almost certainly at some point in their school career have been asked to read a passage of text as a symptom of its age or as political propaganda (both potentially ways of reading the Lincoln passage). They may even, in some classes, have been judged to be skilled at what Schwab called "arts of recovery of meaning in the act of reading"— skilled, that is, provided that they have been directed as to which particular art is to be employed on a given passage. But in my class, where I don't tell them how to read the passage, many students simply revert to the default setting for reading history: seeing the text as a repository of content, they look for the information they're supposed to remember. They engage in what has been called "efferent" reading, rather than "aesthetic" reading (Rosenblatt, 1994). When we read efferently, we focus on something—a name, a date, a recipe, an algorithm—that can be taken away from the text for future use. When we read aesthetically, we approach the text holistically, attending to the author's purposes and rhetorical devices, the context of the writing, and our responses as we read.

Advocates for the use of rubrics (like the authors of the Indiana document I'm focusing on) will say at this point that the problem that arises when there is a lack of certainty about the mode of reading to be employed is precisely the reason for using rubrics. If we want students to read a text the way we think it's supposed to be read (or write an essay the way we think it's supposed to be written, or solve an equation the way we think it's supposed to be solved), we have to tell them how to do it. We have to guide them as to which particular "art of recovery of meaning" we want them to use. That's what rubrics are for. They tell the student which of the "arts of recovery of meaning" is to be deployed on a given text. The establishment of rubrics that assess the student's interaction with a text determines the purpose for the reading; that is the instructional function of a rubric.

Of course, if we begin to see that the meaning of a text—the content— does not lie on the surface—that in fact to speak of "the meaning" as if there is only one thing a text could mean is to misunderstand how readers interact with texts, is to confuse efferent reading and aesthetic reading, is to misunderstand interpretation itself—if we begin to see that, then we recognize that when we embrace rubric-driven instruction and embrace the idea that "determining the texts" is the same thing as "selecting the content," we dispense with interpretation. The only way that "texts = content" is if texts are univocal repositories of previously identified information, so that the meaning students find in texts has been determined *prior to their opening the books.* The "close, annotated reading, discussion, and writing" (Indiana Department of Education, 2011) that the Indiana document insists students need to do is intended to lead only to their discovery of the "big ideas and essential questions" that curriculum developers have already selected to "guide students' inquiry." Thus, this "close, annotated reading" is only a recapitulation of the prepared material, not a fresh interaction between a thoughtful reader and a provocative text.

If we see the meaning or message of a text as the *result* of the interaction of reader and text, rather than as a prelude to or preparation for that interaction, the meaning remains somewhat open, not fully defined, dependent on the ability and willingness of readers to bring their background and experience to bear on the text. Slavoj Zizek (2006) provides a striking example:

> At the top of Gellert Hill in the Buda part of Budapest, there is a monument to the liberation of the city by the Red Army in 1945: the gigantic statue of a woman waving an outstretched flag. This statue, usually perceived as an exemplary case of socialist-realist baroque kitsch, was actually made in 1943 on the orders of the Fascist dictator Admiral Horthy to honor his son, who fell on the Russian front fighting the Red Army; in 1945, when Marshall Kliment Voroshilov, the Soviet commander, was shown the statue, he thought it could serve as the monument of liberation ... does this anecdote not say a lot about the openness of the "message" of a work of art? (p. 147)

Just as "the gigantic statue of a woman waving an outstretched flag" may be seen as a patriotic emblem of the German side or the Soviet side of the same World War II battle, it may also be seen as simply a woman waving a flag. Those who want to be sure that viewers of the statue get the "right" message can instruct them as to who commissioned the statue, on what occasion, and its subsequent history. Viewers can in effect be told what to see when they look at the statue, but this futile attempt at "aligning a curriculum" can neither guarantee that deferential viewers will experience the supposedly "right" message when they encounter the statue nor prevent independent viewers from experiencing an entirely different message.

In the same way, I can tell my students that in the Scott Foresman passage about Lincoln's boyhood I see messages about patriotism and middle-class values, but this doesn't mean that my students will see these same messages. The effect of my telling, even when supported by a rubric that defines what students will get out of the reading, cannot coerce my students into finding the text meaningful to themselves, nor does it prevent them from experiencing a message I do not intend.

However, telling my students what I think the message of the passage is supposed to be, especially when supported by a rubric defining what students should get out of the reading, inevitably encourages students to believe that every text carries a defined, fixed message and that it is their job as students to find out from me what that message is and be able to reproduce it. Rubrics encourage this sort of epistemological naïveté, as if everything in the world comes with a meaning attached, like a label on a Christmas present. For example, according to the Indiana Language Arts standards for high school literature, students demonstrate their literary analysis skill by such tasks as these:

> Read and evaluate the short story, "The Celebrated Jumping Frog of Calaveras County," by Mark Twain, as an example of Twain's gentle satirizing of human behavior. Listen to the audio version of *The Hitchhiker's Guide to the Galaxy* by Douglas Adams as an example of satirizing culture. Read and evaluate the allegorical aspects of the novel *Animal Farm* by George Orwell. Read *Zorro: The Novel* by Isabel Allende to analyze how this novel is an allegory. (Indiana Department of Education, 2009)

I'm entirely in favor of students reading Twain, Adams, Orwell, and Allende, and I agree that Twain's story can be read as a satire of human behavior (perhaps even a "gentle" one), that Adams' story can be read as a satire of "culture," and that allegory can be found in both Orwell and Allende. But all of these readings are one-dimensional and prescriptive. More importantly, when we call even a legitimate interpretation of a text "the message" of the text, when we tell students, "This is what it means," or "This is what you should get out of this reading," and assess them using a rubric that defines and brackets this meaning or purpose, we convert reading itself from a dynamic act of thinking into passive mimesis. As a society, we pay the cost of this conversion in the dismal quality of our public discourse with its ubiquitous dependency on rubric-like talking points that provide the public with "the message" of events.

RUBRICS AND THE NATURE OF A COMMON CURRICULUM

While the first mistake the Indiana Department of Education (2011) makes in its reliance on the educational efficacy of rubrics involves a misunderstanding of the nature of interpretation; the second mistake arises from a too-narrow conception of what makes curriculum "common." The word *common* appears 22 times in Indiana's 2,300-word "Curriculum Mapping" paper (Indiana Department of Education, 2011). It is used to describe the curriculum, assessments, standards, assignments, and rubrics that will become "common" as the result of curriculum alignment. In addition, there are references to the "agreed-upon curriculum," "shared . . . content knowledge," and other versions of the goal of making sure that all students are being taught and assessed the same things in the same ways. In an attempt to reach the understandable and laudable goal of equity—"that ALL students must be provided a coherent, content-rich curriculum"—the state of Indiana assumes that this means the curriculum must be the same for all.

The error in this view should be obvious: it is the arrogant assumption that what students learn is what we intend to teach them. The document explicitly expresses this modern form of hubris: "Students are guaranteed curriculum when teachers ensure that what they teach is an agreed upon curriculum." Of course, the state of Indiana isn't so naïve as to believe that students' brains can be so easily manipulated; so the distraction of inevitable unintended learning is compensated for by "common assessments": "data from common assessments become the primary tools for monitoring implementation and promoting improvement and should be the basis for team discussions" (Indiana Department of Education, 2011). This is where rubrics play their essential role. As long as teachers focus on assessments aligned with standards (we do this with rubrics), what students learn can be satisfactorily measured on the scale of what we intend to teach them. The fully aligned curriculum is thus supposedly common all the way down the chain, from legislative mandates to core standards to district curriculum maps to school curriculum guides to teacher's daily lesson plans to students' brains. This is why the final section of the document is titled, "What is the role of assessment?" and why that section opens with this reminder: "Formative assessments aligned to curriculum are a critical component of successful schools." Without assessments that smooth over the messiness of learning by forcing us to look only at outcomes directly linked to standards, we couldn't be quite so smugly doctrinaire about which ones are the "successful teachers" or the "successful schools."

The stance in this document reminds me of a presentation I did some years ago in which I asked the participants (university instructors) to work in groups, listing things they would consider when constructing a curriculum for a general education class. Collectively, we reviewed the lists, and when we discussed them, I noted that none of the lists mentioned students. One of the participants responded to my comment, asking, "What do *they* have to do with the curriculum?"

I don't say that the Indiana Department of Education is quite so oblivious to the role of students in curriculum development, but this document does imply that curriculum exists external to students and is something to which students must be fitted. The "content, skills, and learning targets" against which all students are measured are common to all; they exist on their own; they can be identified even before children have been born into this world and become "students."

This is not how curriculum has always been conceived. In the mid-1920s, Harold Rugg wrote about ongoing school surveys, looking into what children were being taught in schools. He said, "As these investigations accumulate, it will be increasingly possible to fit the content of school textbooks to the mental abilities and attainments of pupils" (Rugg, 1927/1975, p. 299). For Rugg, the given, fixed material in the educational equation was the pupil, not the curriculum or texts or assessments: these tools of schooling were to be fitted to the pupil, not the other way round, as the state of Indiana would have it in 2013.

The essence of this current stance toward a common curriculum is captured in the directive that teachers should specify the same "precise amount of text and the number of books" for all students, and the "number and length of papers to be written" by all students, and the "common rubrics" to be used to assess the work of all students (Indiana Department of Education, 2011).

Now, I confess that I hesitate in my criticism of this directive. After all, in my own classes I typically assign the same books to be read by all students and the same number of papers to be written by all students. Isn't Indiana calling for P–12 teachers to do exactly what I am doing in my undergraduate and graduate classes?

The answer to this question is not obvious. Everything hinges on those "common rubrics." How narrowly do they define what students should think and do? How narrowly do they define what a text might mean? How much emphasis do they put on formatting at the expense of content? How much emphasis do they put on procedure at the expense of originality? The problem that the directive is intended to solve is that without specifications regarding readings and assignments "students learn…skills in isolated, low level, skills-based lessons with short, contrived passages, which build limited content knowledge and which rarely if ever provide the kinds of experiences [associated with creative and critical thinking]" (Indiana Department of Education, 2011). But making the readings longer and less "contrived" won't solve the problem if student responses are still as narrowly defined (by rubrics) as they were with the "short, contrived passages." The problem doesn't lie in the length of the readings or the length of the papers students write: it lies in the thinking students are encouraged and enabled to do. It's possible for them to think deeply and originally about a sonnet, a haiku, or a television commercial as it is a full-length drama or article.

When the focus shifts from the number and names of books to be read and the number and formats of papers to be written to the creative and critical thinking that students do, we see the problem with Indiana's insistence on a *common* curriculum. Thinking can never be "common"—at least, not in the sense of "same." One of the essential qualities of thinking is its individuality, a quality not assessable by a rubric used identically on every student's work. This clash between the individuality of thinking and the universality of rubric-based assessment reveals a deep problem in Indiana's "Curriculum Mapping" document (and in the rubric movement generally): the notion of curriculum at the heart of rubric-based assessment treats "common" in the trivial sense of sameness, like a 6-year-old's notion of equality.

But there is a different meaning of "common"—a meaning inaccessible to rubric-based assessments—that provides a different rationale for common readings and assignments. This is the idea of the "common" as that which is "shared." When I have graduate students in my course on the moral life of schools watch a movie—say, *Friendly Persuasion* in connection with reading the William James essay, "The Moral Equivalent of War"—I don't expect them to have the same response to the movie. In fact, I would be unable to state in rubric form exactly why I want them to watch that particular movie in that particular class—other than the shallow observation that I expect them to see that *Friendly Persuasion* deals (as does the James essay) with the "martial virtues" (heroism, strength, persistence, loyalty, pugnacity). The really important (but not clearly definable) reason for viewing this movie and reading this essay is to hear the students share the details of what they think the movie and essay say about the martial virtues. Are they persuaded? Do they feel a case has been made for (or against) aggression and pugnacity? What is it about the movie or the essay that persuades or amuses or repels them? What do they learn about their own attitudes toward the martial virtues?

Now, some of this is surely assessable. I have the students write a response to the essay and film, in which they answer the question, "Do we need the martial virtues?" As I evaluate these responses I ask myself these questions:

- Does the student essay deal accurately with the reading (or movie)?
- Does the student essay address the question?
- Does the student essay use the reading (or movie) to make its case?
- Is the student essay convincing (logical and coherent)?

The questions function as rudimentary rubrics, but they would be—rightly!—criticized by rubric enthusiasts for lacking the precise description of the differences between, say, an "exceptional" level of accuracy (or pertinence or groundedness or persuasiveness) and an "inadequate" one. I've provided the categories for a system of rubrics but left out (says the rubric enthusiast) the specifics needed to make the assessment fully transparent. Most importantly, the rubric enthusiast asks, "How can students be sure that you are grading the responses the same way? How can students be sure that this is a *common* assessment?"

My response to these concerns is that while I could define the assignment more narrowly by spelling out in rubrics exactly what I expect students to learn from watching *Friendly Persuasion* and reading "The Moral Equivalent of War," and could by this spelling out, make the activity more "common" in the sense of "same," I would at the same time diminish the potential for the activity to lead to the sharing that is a deeper and more educative sense of "common." The most recent time I did this activity with students provides an example of what I mean by "sharing." As we discussed in class what students had written, one of the students said that he found battle scenes in movies to be "inspiring" and "thrilling." He mentioned the Little Round Top scene from the movie *Gettysburg* as an example of what he meant. Another student said that he too experienced the same emotions when viewing such scenes.

I had not, when planning this class, thought to ask students about their emotional response to battle scenes, although the topic is certainly pertinent, given the climactic battle scene in *Friendly Persuasion* and James's discussion of the "higher aspects of militaristic sentiment." But because I wasn't thinking along these lines, even if I had spelled out my rudimentary rubrics, I would not have thought to include a rubric that would assess how students investigate their emotional response to battle scenes. But confronted with these students' sharing, I pursued the topic. I asked each male in the class if he too experienced similar emotions when watching battle scenes in movies. All but one said his experience was the same.

I then asked each female in the class if she experienced the same emotions. Each of them said no. Several said that when they saw such things, their thoughts went to the wives and children who would suffer when a husband or father was killed. Others talked about feeling the pain that those in the battle felt or about feeling pity for them. Their feelings when viewing the battle scene in *Friendly Persuasion*—which highlights the pain, ambiguity, and horror of war—were (they said) the same as their feelings when watching scenes (like the one from *Gettysburg*) that emphasize the heroism of war and the "higher aspects of militaristic sentiment."

Later during the same discussion, I asked each female in the class if she would prefer that the males in her life did not feel thrilled and inspired by battle scenes. Would she rather that they felt what she felt about such things? Each woman said no. One even said that she would not love her husband so well if he did not feel those male responses.

Through this unexpected discussion, fueled by the written responses to an assignment without clear rubrics, the students in this class shared the *common* experience of watching *Friendly Persuasion* and reading "The Moral Equivalent of War." It was common not because the same learning objectives were defined in advance for all students and achieved in class. It was common because all of the students contributed something to the stew of discussion. I would like also to think that all of the students came away with a reading of the essay (and of the movie) that was enriched and challenged by what they had shared in common with the others, but I cannot know this is so. And it may be that this inevitable agnosticism about learning outcomes when classroom activities are not rubric-driven is one reason for the popularity of rubrics. Rubrics provide an evident learning outcome to believe in, even if that outcome is, as the 2011 Indiana document says, "isolated, low level, skills-based lessons," rather than a transformative exploration of texts that challenge our understanding of the values of ourselves and our society.

The Quest for Certainty

"Man who lives in a world of hazards," says John Dewey in his opening line of *The Quest for Certainty* (1929/2008, p. 3), "is compelled to seek for security." One of the ways humanity has historically sought to do this, says Dewey, is expressed "in supplication, sacrifice, ceremonial rite, and magical cult" (p. 3). These have been our ways of allying ourselves "on the side of the powers which dispense fortune" (p. 3).

Our current love affair with rubrics seems to me to be an example of this sort of seeking for security, one heavily freighted with "ceremonial rite and magical cult." So desperate are the authors of Indiana's "Quality Curriculum" document to believe in the magical efficacy of rubrics within a "standards-based, grade-, and content-level-aligned curriculum" (Indiana Department of Education, 2011), that even their own recognition that rubric-driven teaching undermines creative and critical thinking fails to shake their faith in the ultimate importance of "data from common assessments." (Indiana Department of Education, 2011).

And they are not alone.

CONCLUSION

This Indiana document is not unique or groundbreaking; it is commonplace. It intones the same ritualistic language that might be found in any U.S. state's education policy statements, for we are all searching for certainty while engaged in the always-uncertain activity of teaching and learning, and according to the tenets of our current faith, certainty lies in rubric-driven instruction.

The benefits of rubrics are clear: they tell students how we want them to read a text, or write a paper, or solve a problem. They tell students what we want them to think. Without this guidance, some students seem almost blind in their encounters with the paraphernalia of instruction (texts, assignments, assessments). We teachers lay the curriculum before them, but without rubrics, students don't know what to think about the curriculum.

The costs of rubrics are equally clear: they tell students what we want them to think. Limiting students to what we can conceive a text or a theorem or an experiment to mean, we steal the opportunity for them to be surprised by what they do not know and to be delighted by what they teach themselves to see. In most of my courses, I leave the form of the final assignment entirely open. I'll ask students, for example, in a course about the moral life of schools, to provide a response to the prompt, "How are you a moral educator?" They can write a paper if they wish, but they can also paint a picture, compose a song, write a poem, or respond in any other way that allows them to deal with the question. Some students come up with predictable results. A poster filled with the stuff shaping classroom life—classroom rules, daily schedule, inspirational messages; a paper that examines situations involving moral dilemmas and choices; a poem describing those times the children challenge the teacher's patience. But other students turn in responses I could never have imagined: a wood carving of a cat encountering a hedgehog; a recording of the student's rock band playing an original song about the nature of morality; a three-course meal prepared for the class; a bound volume of calligraphy and sketches called, *The Book of "Wa,"* depicting usage of the Japanese morpheme meaning "harmony." I cannot know all the possible responses of my students to the curriculum we explore together. The more I use rubrics to support or structure their responses, the more I limit their ability to find a genuine, individual, creative response. The more I use rubrics to reduce the painful surprise of being confounded by ignorance, the more I rob them of their chance of being delighted by recognition.

If we behave as if assessments aligned with standards tell us all we need to know about learning, if we treat a text as a container in which facts are kept, if we try to tell students how they will interpret a text before they read it, if we suppose that the virtue of a common curriculum is that all students do the same thing at the same time in the same way, if we think and act in these ways, we will—as even the Indiana Department of Education agrees—create classrooms and schools in which students are never encouraged to think. The question, then, is can we bear the uncertainty that comes with abandoning our faith in the magic of rubrics to link curriculum mandates to student brains? Can we instead come to believe in the incomplete, unpredictable, imperfect ability and desire of students to encounter curriculum in the only genuine way any of us can—by finding out how it touches our lives, by each finding out what it means to our own self?

REFERENCES

Boise State University. (2010-2011). *Undergraduate catalog.* Retrieved from http://registrar.boisestate.edu/undergraduate/files/2011/08/catalog-8.pdf

Bowell, T., & Kemp, G. (2010.) *Critical thinking: A concise guide* (3rd ed.). New York, NY: Routledge.

Dewey, J. (2008). *The later works, 1925–1953, Volume 4: 1929.* (J. A. Boydston & H. F. Simon, Eds.). Carbondale: Southern Illinois University Press. (Original work published 1929)

Fraser, J. (2010). *The school in the United States: A documentary history* (2nd ed.). New York, NY: Routledge.

Indiana Department of Education. (2009). *Learning connection. EL.LIT.3 2006–literary analysis and criticism of fiction.* Formerly posted at https://learningconnection.doe.in.gov/Standards/About.aspx?art=11. Retrieved February 26, 2013.

Indiana Department of Education. (2011). *Learning connection.* Formerly posted at http://pod.doe.in.gov/groups/learningconnectionhelp/revisions/8bd1c/4/. Retrieved May 21, 2012.

Paul, R., & Elder, L. (2007). *The miniature guide to critical thinking concepts and tools* (4th ed.). Dillon Beach, CA: Foundation for Critical Thinking.

Rosenblatt, L. M. (1994). *The reader, the text, the poem: The transactional theory of the literary work.* Carbondale: Southern Illinois University Press.

Rugg, H. O. (1975). Curriculum-making and the scientific study of education since 1910. *JSTOR.* Retrieved May 19, 2012, from http://www.jstor.org/stable/1179267 (Original work published 1927)

Schwab, J. (1969). The practical: A language for curriculum. *The School Review, 78*(1), 1–23.

Wagner, T. (2010.) *The global achievement gap: Why even our best schools don't teach the survival skills our children need—and what we can do about it.* New York, NY: Basic.

Zizek, S. (2006.) *The parallax view.* Cambridge, MA: MIT Press.

CHAPTER 7

EMPLOYING
A TECHNOLOGY OF POWER

An Orientation Analysis
of a Teacher Task Rubric

Conra D. Gist

Michelle held her frame together as if she were going places. There was a look of certainty in her shoulders and an intense curiosity in her eyes. During her interview event, she taught a coherent and creative poetry lesson and it was obvious she had a flare for the art of words. She also spoke of the challenges she faced in her youth as a sluggish uninterested student until a middle school teacher sparked a thirst for literature in her spirit. In her essay, the Ivy League teacher of color expressed a belief in the capacity of a critical mind to transform an individual's life circumstances and cultivate a better world. She appeared to be committed to becoming a strong teacher even if the alternative certification program to which she was applying only offered 6 weeks of training. From the view of a panel selector for the 6-week program, what is not to like?

Rubric Nation, pages 101–117
Copyright © 2015 by Information Age Publishing
All rights of reproduction in any form reserved.

The answer to that question depends on one's conceptual orientation of teaching and learning. Regardless of the teacher education model (e.g., 6-week training, traditional coursework and internship, or year-long residency), faculty often utilize rubrics to evaluate particular teaching and learning orientations. This chapter spotlights a piloted teacher task rubric used at the end of a 6-week institute to explore how orientations can be evidenced in a rubric and consider the type of teacher the program aims to produce. To achieve this objective, the chapter begins with a brief overview of how rubrics are currently being utilized as a technique of power in the teacher development field, and then briefly examines the types of conceptual orientations that commonly anchor the teaching and learning vision of teacher preparation programs. Foucault (1977) is utilized to ground the claim that rubrics are currently being positioned in the teacher development field as a technique of power; however, similar to Foucaultian logic, this chapter frames power as neither a positive or negative force. I do not make claims about the value of rubrics, the necessity of rubrics for making decisions about teaching and learning, or the misuse of power associated with rubrics. Feiman-Nemser's (2012) typologies of teacher preparation program orientations are also applied as a conceptual tool to help make sense of how a teacher education program's views of teaching and learning are evidenced in the content and practices described in a rubric. Subsequently, as a point of analysis, I explore the intersection between rubrics as a technique of power (Foucault, 1977) and the conceptual orientations of teaching and learning (Feiman-Nemser, 2012) revealed in the piloted rubric, and speculate the type of teacher likely produced.

This is critical intellectual work because a program's ideological commitments can go unchecked without close analysis. The evaluator may appear to simply be examining "good teaching" or reading "strong writing" as defined in a rubric, but there are often ideological stances about teaching and learning embedded in the rubric to mold a particular type of teacher. This analytical process has implications for understanding how rubrics, which can be steeped in a plethora of understandings of teaching and learning, are used as a technique of power to determine who becomes a teacher and ultimately who can teach our children.

Rubrics and Control in Teacher Development

Tomlinson (2003) describes a rubric as a tool that assists users to determine quality work in a progression from exemplary to less distinguished levels of work. Such rubrics can be task specific (i.e., rubrics that allow the user to plan or assess a particular piece of work) or generic (i.e., rubrics that can be used across a variety of scenarios and subjects). McMillian (2007) assigns five criteria for the design of quality rubrics: (a) focus on important aspects of performance; (b) match the type of rating with the purposes of the assessment; (c) describes criteria that are directly observable; (d) includes criteria that parents, students, and others can understand; and (e) clearly and specifically defines characteristics and traits. Particular to teacher preparation, rubrics are commonly applied to determine a teacher's learning progression, effectiveness, and/or overall fitness to enter schools as a teacher of record (Pecheone & Chung, 2006). Similar to gatekeepers who police subjects through restriction or access, the rubric, as a technique of power, describes what are acceptable behaviors and dispositions for teachers to embody in order to enter the teaching profession.

Foucault (1977) describes disciplinary power as the coordination of individuals through technical strategies of space (e.g., limiting teaching and learning activities to a common ground), labor (e.g., controlling the number of hours and activities that must be completed), and training (e.g., a series of courses necessary to complete preparation program or professional development requirements) to continuously establish and maintain control (McHoul & Grace, 1993). These techniques often work in tandem with the development of knowledge systems that are committed to pursuing scientific truths to validate mechanisms of power. This theoretical perspective is illuminating when examining the teacher development movement's focus on developing an extensive and credible research base to operationalize and assert understandings of effective teaching. Research is replete with teacher education scholars critiquing the profession and challenging their colleagues to more carefully ensure and monitor the quality of their programs through rigorous research (Ball & Forzani, 2009; Grossman, 2008; Zeichner, 2012). Certainly, neoliberal educational policies have increased competition among teacher preparation programs (Kumashiro, 2010), which has placed pressure on educational researchers and teacher educators to ensure the professional integrity of the field (Darling-Hammond, 2006). Regardless of the political motive, however, rubrics are frequently asserted to develop and control knowledge production about teachers by an array of teacher development entities.

For instance, stakeholders use rubrics at critical junctions on the teacher development pipeline, including alternative certification selection models (e.g., The New Teacher Project Teaching Fellows Program), teacher learning progressions (e.g., Interstate Teacher Assessment and Support Consortium [InTASC]), teacher candidate assessment portfolios (e.g., edTPA), teacher evaluation systems (e.g., Danielson Framework for Teaching [2013]), and novice teacher development models (e.g., New Teacher Center Induction Program). Each of these rubrics is used to assert particular views about teaching and learning, and use various research-based frameworks and rationales to legitimize the content and practices stipulated.

Rubrics can provide the evaluator with the power to ask questions about a teacher candidate's potential (i.e., when recruiting and selecting teachers for programs), a teacher candidate's competence (i.e., when teacher candidates exit programs), and a teacher's performance (i.e., when teachers seek tenure in the profession). From this perspective, the rubric can be viewed as a high-leverage technique of power by the very fact that the content and practices outlined in its structure determine whether or not candidates are, for example, admitted to the teacher education program or allowed entry in to the profession. Furthermore, in the cases of its evaluative uses in teacher education programs, the rubric is often grounded in conceptual orientations that prioritize certain views about teaching and learning.

Conceptual Orientations of Teaching and Learning

Feiman-Nemser (2012) describes a particular set of orientations (i.e., technological, practical, personal, critical, and academic) that commonly anchor the teaching and learning vision of teacher education programs. These orientations are not necessarily separate from one another in application, but certain orientations can more strongly inform and determine a teacher education program's design, curriculum, mission, and support structures than other orientations. These orientations are relevant to the use of rubrics in teacher education because they relate to current research in teacher development. The academic orientation places a particular emphasis on the pedagogical content knowledge (Shulman, 1986) teachers need, which are often evidenced in discipline-specific rubrics such as the Protocol for Language Arts Teaching Observation (PLATO) and Mathematical Quality of Instruction (MQI) observation rubrics (Kane & Staiger, 2012). More specifically, the academic preparation orientation relates to a tendency to view learning as the transmission of particular sets of knowledge and deep understanding of the discipline. There is a higher value placed on academic training and disciplinary knowledge, which requires teacher candidates to blend content and pedagogy into an understanding of how particular aspects of subject matter are organized, adapted, and represented for instruction (Borko & Putnam, 1996).

Also, the practical and personal orientations stress the processes (e.g., one-to-one feedback and coaching, study groups, course modules [Danielson, 2009; Hattie & Timperley, 2007]) through which teachers can grow as teacher-learners, and this view of teaching and learning is apparent in commonly utilized learning progression rubrics (e.g., InTASC) and new teacher mentor rubrics (e.g., The New Teacher Center Induction Program). The personal orientation views learning to teach as a process of "learning to understand, develop, and use oneself [*sic*] efficiently" (Feiman-Nemser,

2012, p. 85). Teacher learners' ideas and interests are prioritized in this stance and teacher educators often assume the role of facilitative guide. In contrast, the practical orientation emphasizes situated learning experiences in which a teacher's instruction is strengthened by the repetition of practice and feedback over time. Mentors are commonly cited as a key source of support for novice teachers as this teacher preparation orientation, similar to an apprenticeship orientation model, creates opportunities to interact regularly with pedagogical experts while teaching in classrooms (Moir, Barlin, Gless, & Miles, 2009).

Additionally, the technological orientation is commonly associated with the assessing and evaluation of teacher products (e.g., unit and lesson plans, videos of classroom instruction, tracking of professional learning goals, reflection logs) that represent competency performance at optimal levels (Lampert, 2009), which is evidenced in teacher education assessment (e.g., EdTPA) and teacher evaluation (e.g., Danielson, 2013) rubrics. The technological orientation of teaching and learning prioritizes a teacher's ability to proficiently master particular competencies through performance. For instance, the *Measures of Effective Teaching Project* (Kane & Staiger, 2012) is one of the largest-scale research studies to have investigated the validity and reliability of observation rubrics created to operationalize effective instructional practices. Through the scientific study of teachers, the research project worked to establish correlations between rubric competency ratings and student growth measures to more precisely identify proficient instructional practices that effective teachers regularly enact. Finally, the critical orientation is related to nondominant approaches to teaching and learning to address the opportunity gap (Gay, 2010), and can be evidenced in diversity pedagogy rubrics (Sheets, 2005). The critical orientation reflects a set of commitments that challenge students to read the world in critical ways and question the role of education in transforming their lives and the lives of others. The teacher educator in this preparation model is committed to helping novices enact culturally responsive practices and democratic principles for social justice in their future classrooms.

In her synthesis of the five preparation orientations, Feiman-Nemser (2012) draws the following conclusion:

> While some of the orientations focus on the essential tasks of teacher preparation, collectively they [orientations] do not represent a set of equally valid alternatives from which to choose. Rather they constitute a source of ideas and practices to draw on in deliberating about how to prepare teachers in a particular context. Each orientation highlights different issues that must be considered but none offers a fully developed framework to guide program development. (p. 91)

Given the time and resource constraints all programs face, however, they must grapple with decisions to determine which teaching and learning orientation should be prioritized. I argue the highly valued orientations guiding the teacher education programs are often crystalized (in subtle and at other times in explicit ways) in a rubric that acts as a technique of power to affirm program views of teaching and learning associated with teacher quality. Feiman-Nemser (2012) does not address rubrics in her discussion of program orientations, but rather sets out to map the historical context that gave birth to each orientation and how they are currently framed in the teacher education literature. Still, her conceptual orientation framework is a useful heuristic because it provides a set of lenses for analyzing how different views of teaching and learning can shape performance expectations in rubrics and as a result work to control the type of teachers produced in the program.

METHODOLOGY

To dissect the intersection at which the rubric as a technique of power and conceptual orientations meet, four strands of a piloted rubric are analyzed through an orientation analysis of the task rubric. Each strand of the rubric is closely analyzed to address the question: How does the rubric, as a technique of power, espouse particular conceptual orientations of teaching and learning? This particular piloted teacher task rubric was asserted as a technique of power in a couple of ways. First, the training and development took place in a limited time frame and specific location that required candidates to meet and assume compulsory roles as student teachers in school classrooms in order to begin the learning process required by the piloted teacher task rubric. Candidates also had to adhere to all the required program hours in the 6-week program in order to complete the various stages of learning described in the rubric, and the institute culminated by requiring candidates to successfully demonstrate their learning by adhering to the performance task requirements in the rubric. Failure to demonstrate overall proficiency, according to the evaluative descriptors in the rubric, would cause the teacher candidate not to gain entry in to the teaching profession.

The new alternative certification program was in the first year of development and sought to address research on effective teaching by incorporating elements from Danielson (2013) and mirroring the development of products (e.g., presentation, unit plans, reflection papers) commonly required when teacher candidates complete traditional Master of Arts in Teaching (MAT) programs (Zeichner, 2010). To protect the anonymity of the program and participants, limited situational and contextual information is provided about the program and pseudonyms are used in the findings description.

Teacher Task Rubric

To determine the candidates' learning at the end of the institute, the task rubric was used to assess the quality of teacher performance as distinguished, proficient, or basic. The differences between the quality tiers are evidenced by descriptors such as extensive, thorough, and comprehensive (distinguished level); in comparison to sufficient, acceptable, and complete (proficient level); and approaching, inconsistent, lacking, and incomplete (basic level).

Specifically, the task rubric examines four strands of teacher work: (a) Classroom Environment Plan, (b) Understanding by Design (UbD) Unit, (c) Student and Teacher Assessments, and (d) Effective Instruction Reflection. The entire rubric is not provided in this chapter but rather a description of the rubric's four task strands. In order to successfully complete the summer institute, the candidates had to score proficient on all four strands. The four rubric strands describe products the candidate developed working with mentor teachers and students at a summer school placement site during a 6-week period. The first week candidates received a general orientation before being placed in summer school sites. Over the next 4 weeks, they practiced the work of teaching in schools while implementing the tasks outlined in the rubric. The candidates then spent the final week of the institute refining their artifacts for presentation and review. Candidates met on a weekly basis to receive feedback from mentors and also in daily content-specific professional learning communities.

Classroom Environment Plan Strand

The classroom environment plan strand asks candidates to develop the following four components: (a) a vision statement; (b) establish plans for building relationships with students, families, and stakeholders; (c) create class rules/norms, outline classroom expectations and procedures (beginning, middle, and end of class); and (d) develop a behavior management plan based on their summer school classroom. According to the rubric, the distinguished classroom environment plan is described based on two features:

- An extensive, creative, and appropriate list of strategies, tools, and approaches for addressing each component of the classroom environment plan is included.

- There is a detailed and well-reasoned explanation of why specific strategies, tools, and approaches were chosen during the implementation of the unit.

Understanding by Design (UbD) Unit Strand

The UbD unit strand asks the candidates to develop a narrative that explains the 2-week unit rationale, the desired results (stage one), evidence of learning (stage two), learning plan (stage three), and the lesson plans candidates used with students in their summer school session. According to the rubric, the distinguished UbD unit is operationalized based on three features:

- All three UbD stages are accurately aligned and thoroughly completed. The reader is able to easily discern the key ideas communicated in each stage of the UbD plan.
- Seven detailed and coherent lesson plans are included addressing each component of the lesson plan template.
- There is also an in-depth explanation of why the designer chose the unit focus, a description of learners and the appropriateness for learners, and an overview of the unit of study.

Student and Teacher Assessments Strand

The student and teacher assessments strand requires that the candidate develop student assessments (i.e., assessments designed for the UbD unit) to track student learning as well as complete teacher self-assessments (i.e., video-based reflections on candidates' teaching during different parts of their unit). The distinguished description addressing student assessments is explained based on the following four features:

- There is a comprehensive description of the performance task, explanation of how it aligns (accurately) to the learning goals in stage one, and the rationale for the specific evaluation criteria used.
- A descriptive analysis of preassessments, formative assessments, and student work from the unit is included. Samples of assessment and student work are included and referenced to explain how assessment was used during the implementation of the unit.
- There are seven comprehensive and reflective self-assessments (e.g., identifying glows and grows, ratings on each spotlight competence, and crafting next steps) based on a daily review of video recorded lessons.
- There are seven instructional videos included, each representing a lesson taught from the unit of study.

The following spotlight competencies were identified from Danielson's Framework for Teaching (FfT; 2013) for candidates' self-assessments on daily video recording and lesson plans: 1e, Designing Coherent Instruction; 2b, Establishing a Culture for Learning; 2d, Managing Student Behavior; 3b, Engaging Students in Learning; 3c, Questioning and Discussion Techniques; and 3d, Using Assessment in Instruction. The candidates received training on each spotlight component prior to beginning their self-assessments.

Effective Instruction Reflection Strand

The effective instruction reflection strand of the rubric asks candidates to reflect on their learning experience over the course of the institute and contemplate how their institute experiences will shape their work as future teachers. According to the rubric, a distinguished set of effective instruction reflections is described as follows: An evaluative and in-depth reflection that explains the effectiveness of the unit and classroom environment plan, synthesizes areas of strength and growth in the spotlight competencies, and identifies specific changes and adjustments in preparation for teaching in the fall.

FINDINGS

In this section, I discuss two key initial findings that emerged from the analysis: (a) the rubric espouses a strong valuing of practical and personal views of teaching and learning. While the critical and academic orientations are entirely omitted, the technological orientation is acknowledged in the language of the rubric, yet when pitted against a practical view of teaching and learning, is clearly inferior; and (b) the piloted teacher task rubric provides a vague description of specific knowledge and skill practices required by teacher candidates and thus offers a significant amount of freedom for teacher candidates to make meaning of their teaching and learning experiences. At the same time, this freedom is juxtaposed by an ambiguity afforded to the evaluator to interpret the rubric from a variety of teaching and learning perspectives.

Prioritizing Practical and Personal Orientations

A close analysis of the piloted rubric across the four task strands reveals that the practical orientation dominates, with the technological orientation relegated to a lesser role, and the academic and critical orientations being completely ignored. The personal orientation is often present, in some form, when the practical orientation is emphasized, but the personal is frequently dependent on the practical opposed to operating as a distinct view of teaching and learning in the piloted rubric. For instance, the language of the classroom environment rubric strand emphasizes a practical orientation to learning because the rubric expectations (i.e., an extensive, creative, and appropriate list of strategies, tools, and approaches for addressing each component of the classroom environment plan are included) are focused on the candidate evidencing, through a list of approaches they practiced and implemented, direct learning applications in the context of the summer school classroom. As a result of this practice, the rubric requires (i.e., a detailed and well-reasoned explanation of why specific strategies, tools, and approaches were chosen during the implementation of the unit) that the teacher candidate personally reflect on and explain the implementation. The same trend is apparent in the language of the UbD rubric strand description (i.e., all three UbD stages are accurately aligned and thoroughly completed) because the candidate is asked to apply UbD ideas learned early in the summer institute to practically design and implement a unit and then personally reflect on the unit rationale and decisions made while teaching the unit. In the classroom environment and UbD strands there is no reference to disciplinary knowledge expectations (e.g., common disciplinary misconceptions to consider in the design of the unit) or an expectation that candidates explicitly demonstrate knowledge of the sociopolitical context of the classroom, school, or community.

Additionally, one component of the student and teacher assessment strand asks candidates to complete self-assessments of their instructional practice by viewing their videotaped lessons from the UbD unit (i.e., 20-minute snapshot of each lesson they taught in the unit) and rating their performance on spotlight competencies. Although the task conveys a technological orientation because the characteristics of proficient practice are clearly defined, the language in the rubric more heavily emphasizes a personal orientation (e.g., comprehensive and reflective self-assessments) since there are no expectations described about the quality of candidates' performance on the spotlight competencies in the videos except that candidates craft a reflection on their instructional practices and describe how they plan to improve in the future. There is no language indicating an expectation of candidates' rating accuracy (i.e., accurately identifying the appropriate level of performance) on videos of their instructional practices or an expectation that candidates perform at a proficient level on the competencies in their videos of classroom instruction.

For example, one of the teacher candidates in the program rated himself as developing in all the spotlight competencies and listed the following next steps in a self-assessment of his classroom practice in the video: (a) establish clear procedures/norms/expectations for class discussions from the beginning. Model and enforce respectful discussion techniques. Build up to more complex/difficult/sensitive discussions; (b) be attentive to the class (notice when students have hands up; instead of pressing on when the class atmosphere feels tense, make efforts to let students take a step back from the discussion or redirect the discussion to make students more comfortable); and (c) use more formative assessments (fist to fives, etc.) to gauge understanding/engagement/comfort. In this instance, the personal, practical, and technological orientations are intertwined in that the teacher candidate's next steps are connected to his practical teaching experiences based on competency understandings of what effective instruction entails. Although there are not competency-based performance expectations outlined in the rubric, the candidates did receive weekly feedback from a mentor trained on the Danielson framework and also shared video clips of their instructional practice in professional learning communities to receive feedback, which is steeped in practical and personal orientations of teaching and learning.

Similar to the student and teacher self-assessment strand, the effective instruction reflection strand stresses the relationship between the personal and practical orientation because candidates are asked to personally synthesize their learning experiences from instructional practice in summer school and consider future implications for pedagogy when they begin teaching in the fall. The following is an excerpt from a teacher candidate's effective instruction reflection:

> 3c (engaging students in learning) is probably the competency I struggled with the most, and it is also a competency I wish to prioritize when I start teaching in the fall. Too many of my lessons were concerned with teaching my students skills through direct instruction. And while I still think that many concepts and skills can be taught effectively through lectures, slideshows, and note-taking, taking a more varied approach may have been more beneficial for my students.

In this case, the ELA teacher is framing her personal reflection through the lens of a spotlight competency and identifies her need to incorporate varied instructional approaches in the future. She is not expected to perform at a proficient level on the spotlight competency. Instead, she is required to understand what that level of performance requires and to continuously aspire to exhibit that level of performance in her future instructional practice. The candidate has freedom to perform at novice and developing levels as long as the candidate supplies a well-reasoned explanation as to why, which is evidenced by the absence of the competency-based performance expectations. Taken as a whole, in each rubric strand, the practical and personal orientations are prioritized over other orientations.

Ambiguous Knowledge and Skill Requirements

The emphasis on practical and personal orientations highlights an omission of specific content and instructional practices candidates are required to learn. In other words, given the void of academic and critical orientations in the rubric, the knowledge and skills candidates are required to exhibit are ambiguous. For instance, there are no explicit expectations in the classroom environment rubric requiring that the candidates identify specific strategies, tools, and approaches that should be used; the candidate just needs to "include" the list. The rubric strand does require that candidates defend their decisions (e.g., there is a detailed and well-reasoned explanation of why), but the expectations for quality are not precise or extensive, which allows the evaluator to determine what is appropriate. For example, an ELA teacher submitted a vision statement for his classroom environment plan that opened by stating, "Students in my class will be encouraged to grow both academically and personally, both as individuals and as global citizens. Throughout the session, students will be encouraged to engage in continual, honest, and probing self-reflection." The candidate then proceeds to describe the self-reflection steps he would take with the class. From reading this opening, how is the evaluator to make sense of the candidate's statement separate from asserting his or her on viewpoint given the ambiguity in the rubric? If the evaluator has a strong academic orientation of teaching and learning, he or she may look for the candidate to apply classroom learning theories related to the effective design of their classroom environment plan and to reference the theories in the remainder of the classroom environment rationale. From the view of the evaluator, if the candidate failed to include such information, the response could be viewed as not well reasoned. Or, if the evaluator has a preference for a strong critical orientation, the evaluator may expect the candidate to discuss critical parent partnership ideas or possible alliances with community organizations.

In the UbD strand, the knowledge and skill expectations are more straightforward because accurate alignment requires that the teacher candidate's performance task (stage 2 of UbD) be established to assess the overall learning goals (stage 1 of UbD). Additionally, the learning events (stage 3 of UbD) must be delineated in such a way that students are prepared to master the performance task (stage 2 of UbD). However, the UbD strand is still curious because there is no language addressing pedagogical content knowledge for teaching middle school language arts as referenced in more discipline specific rubrics (e.g., PLATO). The teacher candidate is asked to develop an in-depth explanation of why the designer (candidate) chose the unit focus, a description of learners and the appropriateness for learners, and defend his or her decisions. In the absence of an academic orientation that emphasizes pedagogical content knowledge, the candidate has the leeway to make a wide range of claims about effective ways to design high-leverage learning experiences for students.

Furthermore, an evaluator can assert a preference or a particular expectation and challenge the candidate to address discipline specific or critical mindsets that are not explicitly stated given the vague nature of the rubric strand. The language in the UbD strand asks candidates to provide a description of the learners, but according to what views of learning? From a critical perspective, this may mean addressing cultural and linguistic diversity, race, class, sexual orientation, and gender characteristics of learners. But from an academic perspective, this may mean describing the reading and writing levels of all the learners, or in the case of the technological perspective, describing the proficiency scores on the end of year ELA exam. Given the rubric strand's ambiguity, the evaluator has to determine what exactly "in-depth explanation" means, although the teacher candidate may interpret the strand to mean any assortment of responses are acceptable. In sum, the classroom environment plan and UbD rubric strands are unclear about knowledge and skill requirements for candidates, which gives the evaluator leeway to evaluate the quality of the candidate's work from various perspectives and stances.

DISCUSSION AND IMPLICATIONS

Rubrics, as techniques of power, offer evaluative descriptions of how teachers' bodies and minds fit in boxes. A close analysis of the piloted rubric revealed that the practical and personal orientations were clearly packed in each strand. As explained from the onset, this chapter did not intend to make any claims about the abuse or misuse of rubrics as a technique of power, but rather attempted to illustrate how the orientations may be embedded in the rubric and contemplate how the rubric impacts the type of teacher generated by the program. Therefore, based on these findings, the question still remains: what type of teacher does the piloted rubric likely produce? The prominence of the practical and personal orientations suggests a desire to manufacture a teacher with habits of mind that exhibit a personal accountability for pedagogical growth, a commitment to engage in critical thinking, and a practice of constant refinement through inquiry, reflection, and adjustment. In this sense, these habits of mind are not discipline specific but rather transdisciplinary cognitive routines that prepare teacher learners to meet challenges across knowledge and pedagogical boundaries in the classroom. If this is the type of teacher likely produced by the rubric, then it is reasonable to consider that this view of teaching and learning, when separated from the other orientations, may not be a good fit for other types of teacher learners. Although the rubric does not reject particular types of teacher learners, the candidate trained in a liberal arts background may be well suited to fit the requirements stipulated in the rubric. However, candidates with other learning preferences or educational experiences may find the rubric expectations lacking substantive learning opportunities. Teacher candidates with a deep appreciation for academic knowledge and the primary concerns of a specific discipline may be disenchanted with this type of transdisciplinary approach if it is not married to pedagogical content knowledge. Moreover, teacher candidates who are performance driven and motivated to achieve proficiency may find the rubric's performance expectations unchallenging or inferior given the lack of a strong technological orientation. Lastly, candidates who may be interested in joining the program to address social justice issues through education would not find a framework or set of pedagogies to hang their hats own and might easily become frustrated with the lack of attention given to addressing oppressive schooling conditions for students commonly marginalized in the education system.

The preparation sequence also can play a critical role in determining the type of teacher produced by the piloted teacher task rubric. Given the abbreviated nature of the training institute, the recruitment of candidates to teach across a variety of content areas and the limited amount of time to prepare the teachers, a practical and personal approach can be viewed as a high-leverage entry point to scaffold and evaluate teacher learning at the end of a 6-week institute. In other words, the timing and location of preparation will shape which orientations teacher education programs more heavily rely on in end-of-program evaluation rubrics. For example, perhaps residency-preparation models would more strongly intertwine the technological, academic, practical, and personal orientations since teacher educators are able to consistently assess and support candidates in schools by housing their courses, mentors, and professional learning communities all at the same site over the course of a year prior to the candidates becoming teachers of record in their classrooms. On the other hand, grow-your-own programs that require teachers to complete a degree before becoming certified to teach can afford to spend time emphasizing more of an academic component as well as a critical orientation of teacher learning given the teacher development community mission of the program.

Another important perspective is to consider what is lost when programs prioritize particular orientations at the expense of others. If only the practical and personal orientations are emphasized in an end-of-institute teacher task rubric, what are teacher candidates not prepared to do when they begin teaching in the fall? In this case, the critical orientation is important for cultivating and continuing to reimagine democratic life in the United States. If teachers are only prepared to address the variables they can control in the four corners of the classroom, then they learn to operate with a limited dataset and overlook social, cultural, and community data points that may be key for helping students succeed. Furthermore, in the absence of a solid academic orientation, how will teachers be prepared to deal with common disciplinary misconceptions that are significant hurdles to student learning? In the case of the piloted rubric, the practically prepared teacher candidate would be committed to critically thinking about instructional solutions, but it may take them some time before they discover, through practice and refinement, efficient pathways for ensuring student learning. This may result in students' academic growth suffering in the meantime. And while the teacher effectiveness movement is not without critique, especially as it relates to teacher evaluation and dismissal policies, a teacher candidate's ability to develop proficient instructional practices is fundamental to the learning process. Although all learning can be argued to be a product of practice, without an expectation of proficient instructional practices, how can we rely on candidates to foster student learning in the context of their future classrooms?

CONCLUSION

The analysis of the piloted rubric suggests that rubrics can assert a vision of teaching and learning through the presence or absence of conceptual orientations toward teaching and learning. Given the recent reform efforts to centralize teaching and learning in teacher education as a common core for learning to teach (Ball & Forzani, 2011) and the ongoing implementation of common teacher certification assessments nationwide (e.g., EdTPA), ruminations on the conceptual positionality of rubrics may seem pointless. Yet quick acceptance of these common understandings should be explored with caution. In a pluralist and collective democracy, reifying one dominant view of education, regardless of the global superiority a particular education standpoint enables our nation to maintain and advance, constrains our creative vision and dulls the activist's sensitivity to real everyday educational struggles. Also, because certain orientations are inevitably prioritized, and contradictions between orientations have to be resolved, common frameworks, in the pursuit of universal understandings, can often obscure the distinct and arguably important differences in views of teaching and learning.

In light of these concerns, the orientation analysis of the piloted rubric suggests a critical set of questions scholars and researchers who employ rubrics in a high-stakes fashion should consider: Who created the rubric and what do their backgrounds reveal about their commitments and interests? What views of teaching and learning are prominent? What views of teaching and learning are missing? If certain views of teaching and learning are absent, what type of teachers may lose the opportunity for representation or participation in the teaching profession? How will teachers impact diverse student populations when they are only evaluated for certain orientations? Are views of teaching and learning in the rubric asserted in an authoritative manner or positioned as one of many perspectives on teacher development? Finally, when framing the preparation orientation of teacher education programs, leaders who apply rubrics to determine the professional fate of a candidate should wrestle responsibly, democratically, and critically with the question, what does this rubric say about who can teach our children?

REFERENCES

Ball, D. L., & Forzani, F. M. (2009). The work of teaching and the challenge for teacher education. *Journal of teacher education, 60*(5), 497–511.

Ball, D. L., & Forzani, F. M. (2011). Building a common core for learning to teach and connecting professional learning to practice. *American Educator, 35*(2) 17–21, 38–39.

Borko, H., & Putnam, T. (1996). Learning to teach. In D. C. Berliner & R. C. Calfee (Eds.), *Handbook of educational psychology* (pp. 673–708). New York, NY: Simon & Schuster/Macmillan.

Danielson, C. (2009). *Implementing the framework for teaching in enhancing professional practice* Alexandria, VA: ASCD.

Danielson, C. (2013). The framework for teaching evaluation instrument. Princeton, NJ: *Danielson Group.* Retrieved from http://danielsongroup.org/framework

Darling-Hammond, L. (2006). Assessing teacher education: The usefulness of multiple measures for assessing program outcomes. *Journal of Teacher Education, 57*(2), 120–138.

Feiman-Nemser, S. (2012). *Teachers as learners.* Cambridge, MA: Harvard Education Press.

Foucault, M. (1977). *Discipline and punish: The birth of the prison.* New York, NY: Random House.

Gay, G. (2010). *Culturally responsive teaching: Theory, research, & practice.* New York, NY: Teachers College Press.

Grossman, P. (2008). Responding to our critics: From crisis to opportunity in research on teacher education. *Journal of Teacher Education, 59*(1), 10–23.

Hattie, J., & Timperley, H. (2007). The power of feedback. *Review of Educational Research, 71*(1), 81–112.

Kane, T., & Staiger, D. O. (2012). *Gathering feedback for teaching: Combining high-quality observations with student surveys and achievement gains.* Seattle, WA: Bill and Melinda Gates Foundation.

Kumashiro, K. (2010). Seeing the bigger picture: Troubling movements to end teacher education. *Journal of Teacher Education, 61*(1/2), 56–65.

Lampert, M. (2009). Learning teaching in, from, and for practice: What do we mean? *Journal of Teacher Education, 61*(1/2), 21–34.

McHoul, A., & Grace, W. (1993). *A Foucault primer: Discourse, power, and the subject.* Washington Square: New York University Press.

McMillan, J. H. (2007). *Classroom assessment: Principles and practice for effective standard-based instruction* (4th ed.). Boston, MA: Pearson.

Moir, E., Barlin, D., Gless, J., & Miles, J. (2009). *New teacher mentoring: Hopes and promise form improving teacher effectiveness.* Cambridge, MA: Harvard Education Press.

Pecheone, R. L., & Chung, R. R. (2006). Evidence in teacher education: The performance assessment for California teachers. *Journal of Teacher Education, 57*(1), 22–26.

Sheets, R. (2005). *Diversity pedagogy: Examining the role of culture in the teaching and learning process.* Upper Saddle River, NJ: Pearson.

Shulman, L. S. (1986). Those who understand: Knowledge growth in teaching. *Educational Researcher, 15*(2), 4–14.

Tomlinson, C. A. (2003). *Fulfilling the promise of the differentiated classroom: Tools and strategies for responsive teaching.* Alexandria, VA: Association for Supervision and Curriculum Development.

Zeichner, K. (2010). Rethinking the connections between campus courses and field experiences in college- and university-based teacher education. *Journal of Teacher education, 61*(1/2), 89–99.

Zeichner, K. (2012). The turn once again toward practice-based teacher education. *Journal of Teacher Education, 63*(5), 376–382.

CHAPTER 8

RUBRICS IN CONTEXT

Dana Haraway
David Flinders

This chapter examines the challenges of using rubrics in relation to the particular norms and structures of schooling. Our thesis is that the value and utility of rubrics cannot be judged outside their context of use. We develop this thesis in three parts. First, we argue that rubrics significantly overlap with fundamental curriculum questions, and that curriculum theory serves to highlight the potential challenges and unintended outcomes of rubrics. We also argue that classroom relationships are integral to context. Second, we provide a case-study to illustrate how rubrics function within a particular teacher education program. Finally, we analyze this case in order to identify contextual factors that, for better or worse, shape how rubrics are used and to what ends.

RUBRICS AND CURRICULUM

Teachers and educational scholars most often view rubrics as more closely aligned with evaluation and assessment rather than the content of what is taught. Cooper and Gargan (2009) offer a partial definition: "Today's

---

Rubric Nation, pages 119–134
Copyright © 2015 by Information Age Publishing
All rights of reproduction in any form reserved.

rubrics involve creating a standard and a descriptive statement that illustrates how the standard is to be achieved" (p. 55). This view concurs with Evan's (2013) definition of assessment feedback as a way to identify "...the gap between the actual level of performance and the desired learning goals" (p. 70). Although somewhat technical, these assessment-based definitions still allow rubrics to serve a wide range of proposes. For example, Cooper and Gargan (2009) highlight three functions:

1. A rubric can help teachers think carefully and critically about what they are teaching and what *students need to learn.*
2. Rubrics can make expectations and *standards of performance* clear to the students, parents, teachers, educators, and others.
3. Rubrics provide *opportunities for reflection, feedback, and continued learning* (emphasis added) (p. 55).

What students need to learn, standards for performance, and creating opportunities for continued learning—all of these functions are central to issues of curriculum theory and development. Put another way, the separation of rubrics and curriculum is largely artificial.

For this reason, it is not surprising to find curriculum scholars interested in assessment and its influence on other components of educational programs. Ralph Tyler (1949), for example, identified evaluation as one of the "four fundamental questions which must be answered in developing any curriculum and plan of instruction" (p. 1). Elliot W. Eisner (1991), another noted curriculum theorist, included evaluation as one of the five primary components of what he called "the ecology of schooling" (pp. 79–81). Michael Apple (1986) sees assessment as implicated in processes such as de-skilling, re-skilling, and work intensification. We will return to these concepts shortly, but mention them here to represent the ubiquitous links between curriculum and assessment.

ON CURRICULUM THEORY

We are suggesting that rubrics and curriculum can be viewed as two sides of the same coin. Doing so is useful because curriculum scholarship introduces complications into an otherwise hyper-rationalized activity. First, Cooper and Gargan's three uses of rubrics describe explicit and intentional forms of learning. We want teachers to think carefully about what they teach; we want students to understand expectations; and we want them to have opportunities for continued learning. Yet, curriculum theory has drawn considerable attention to unanticipated, implicit, and/or hidden outcomes of learning. Michael Apple (1986), Andrew Hargreaves (1994), and Philip

Jackson (1968), for example, have long been concerned that schools may unintentionally de-skill students by reducing the cognitive demands of what they learn. When curriculum is broken down into smaller and smaller steps, it threatens to remove opportunities for critical thinking and personal judgment; learning is made formulistic. In the case of re-skilling, students learn "to work the system" for better grades. Their aim is no longer to learn, but to satisfy the requirements for a particular grade. Sometimes well-intentioned advice, such as suggesting examples be provided to accompany rubrics (Wiggins, 1998), can have the unanticipated consequence of students "working to the rubric" rather than using the rubric as a framework or jumping off point for creative performance and products. In this context, de-skilling and re-skilling raise important questions: Do rubrics encourage "grade grubbing?" And if so, can such an outcome be avoided?

Conceptualizing rubrics as "tools" brings up still other questions. Are rubrics "neutral" in the sense that most tools can be used for good or ill? For example, hammers may be used to help people or to harm them. We still value such tools because they welcome a variety of positive and constructive uses. We will have more to say about what counts as positive and constructive in the context of education. At this point, we wish to note that rubrics (like so many tools) may be used mindlessly or intelligently. Again we face another complication: namely, tools often entail unavoidable tradeoffs. They enhance one ability but at the expense of another. Here the question becomes what is gained, what is lost, and the value of each. Early humans learned to use sticks as tools to knock down fruit from the high branches of trees. Sticks extended their reach, but not without a tradeoff. Sticks could not "feel" the fruit for ripeness resulting in the premature selection of fruit. We find a similar situation today with the tools of social media, such as texting. Is texting convenient? Absolutely. Often it is much more convenient than face-to-face communication or even a phone call. Yet by comparison, this tool is not without its sacrifices in terms of opportunities for intimacy and gaining nuanced understandings conveyed through tone of voice, pitch, proxemics, and body language.

Because tools present practical trade-offs, they are neither neutral nor simply at the service of those who use them (e.g., Eisner, 1994; Bowers & Flinders, 1990). We like to think that we use our professional tools—that we control them and not that they control us. When tools begin to exert their own influence, we have the adage: *If all you have is a hammer, everything begins to look like a nail.* On this point, we want to ask further questions: By the way tools are designed, what do they—rubrics—imply about ways of defining a problem? What do rubrics imply about our values and assumptions? Are values such as equity and self-knowledge reflected in the ways rubrics are being used? Whose beliefs are privileged in the process? These questions are asking about the hidden, implicit, and/or assumed curriculum of rubrics.

Curriculum theory may complicate the use of rubrics in still another way. We have been using terms such as "learning outcomes" and "learning opportunities" as values that should be promoted through the use of rubrics. Yet "learning" may reference both positive and negative outcomes. John Dewey (1938) viewed learning as a biological fact. His point was that humans (like many nonhuman animals) would find it difficult to negotiate daily life without learning a wide range of beliefs and habits. Dewey sought to differentiate learning from education by pointing out that we often learn "lessons" or habits that are mis-educational. Some individuals and groups learn to be racist, sexist, intolerant, close-minded, hateful, or self-deprecating. Dewey believed that such learning was mis-educational because it closes off future learning. For our purposes, we will simply note that racism, sexism, intolerance, and the like are rarely embraced as educational goals. Again, we are arguing that the value of rubrics depends on the contexts and ends to which they are used. As rubrics are used to promote learning, they privilege certain learning outcomes over others by design. The reasons we have for choosing particular outcomes are significant.

RUBRICS AND CURRICULUM IDEOLOGIES

How we decide what to teach may seem obvious. Can't we just take it for granted that children should learn to read, to write, and be able to do basic math? Don't we have shared values around (culturally defined) notions of honesty, respect, civility and so on? While perhaps we do, we still find vigorous public and private debates over what children should learn (e.g., Hirsch, 1987; Greene, 1995; Ravitch, 2010) Thus far we have argued that rubrics have both intended and unintended consequences depending on why, how, and with whom they are used. By noting that we privilege certain types of learning, we want to suggest that educators should not take for granted the explicit values that education seeks to promote.

For example, the essentialist movement gained notoriety in the 1980's that was heralded as the "back to basics" decade in education. Essentialists believe that there are critical bodies of information that all students should learn. While this curriculum includes basic content, it also embraces information "to produce a literate and skilled workforce able to compete in a technological society" (Eggen & Kauchak, 2011, p. 203). From this view, new content is added to the realm of essential knowledge and skills in response to changes in society and resulting identified needs. Essentialists' beliefs can be found in No Child Left Behind (NCLB), and the standards-based reform movement and these trends have likely increased the contemporary use of rubrics. In the essentialist's view, the teacher's role is to ensure that all students successfully master identified skills. With the Internet now at our fingertips, we have ready access to detailed standards and rubrics for teaching just about anything anyone would want to teach. Rubrics are a rational tool, and if used well, they can provide structure and organization for teachers and students. Misuse occurs from this perspective when rubrics are either too general to be useful or too specific to a task or a manner of assessment (Popham, 1997). These unintended phenomena sometimes occur when teachers become understandably muddled in all things "essential." For despite the variety of input and efforts to guide (some would say control) curriculum decision-making, teachers remain a central player as they make judgments regarding what and how they teach as well as what and how they assess their students.

We briefly mentioned that Dewey (1938) suggested his own criteria for distinguishing an educational experience from a mis-educational one. Progressive teachers and curriculum scholars who follow Dewey look to the quality of an experience and where that experience leads. They seek to provide opportunities for engagement and continued growth—moral as well as intellectual. The teachers' role is to encourage interests and the students' ability to develop their interests through their own inquiry. This is neither a didactic nor passive role, but rather one of facilitation, consultation, and assistance. The teachers' wider experience makes them active and responsible members of the classroom community.

Dewey's criteria are appealing, but they are not the only criteria available by which to evaluate educational worth. Educators might recognize the importance of student interest and personal growth, but choose (like present-day essentialists) to emphasize the school's contributions to society. Two other approaches that take this stance are known as social adaptation and social reconstruction. Those in the former group may focus on preparing students for the world of work through vocational programs or career education, thus allowing youth to more readily become productive members of our economy. Even more generally, adaptationists believe that schools should help students navigate other adult roles, including parenting, citizenship, or homemaking (Bobbitt, 1918). The teacher in this view represents the interests of society and his/her job is to help students contribute to society needs. Because most parents today expect their sons and daughters to go to college (Bushaw & Lopes, 2012), it follows that secondary teachers should help prepare adolescents to succeed in a rigorous academic environment. The point of such preparation is not that students will benefit, but to produce engineers, doctors, scientists, and the like to benefit society. In the wake of the first Sputnik launch, the United States Congress passed the National Defense Education Act to motivate a generation of college students to pursue studies in fields deemed vital to national security, primarily in science and mathematics.

Social reconstructionists such as Freire (1970), Apple (1986) and Eisner (1994) have argued that the purpose of schools is to help others become what we are not. Their point is to call attention to social problems that our society has failed to resolve. For example, in the 1960s and 1970s, the United States failed to achieve racial integration, turning to the schools as a means of desegregation through busing, Affirmative Action policies, and ethnic studies programs (Banks, 2014). Many parents today are reluctant to talk with their teenage children about safe sex, and so it falls to schools to teach about HIV and AIDS (Silin, 1995). As social inequities grow, schools are called on to provide equal opportunities for all. Reconstructionists call on schools not to support political institutions, but to change them. Whenever public schools are put in the role of "first responders" or whenever they are expected to produce social benefits, the question becomes which benefits, and specifically what in our society needs fixing.

Still another way to define educational learning is in terms of cognition. Neurological researchers today suggest that the human brain is more "plastic" and more generative than it was once believed (Posner & Rothbart, 2007). Like many scientific advances, these findings hold explicit educational implications. If the brain can be nurtured, do schools have a role to play in strengthening what at the turn of the 20th century were called "mental faculties" (Dewey, 1910, p. 45)? Can the mind be strengthened though the study of formal logic, higher mathematics, and other rigorous subjects? And if so, shouldn't we expose all students to a curriculum that promotes intellectual development? The teachers' role in this view is one of coaching students to help identify, explicate, and promote "higher" levels of cognitive performance. Some, like Mortimer Adler (1982), suggest that this be accomplished by passing on the heritage or cannon of established knowledge represented in common academic disciplines. In this context, rubrics would seek to strengthen cognitive processes and opportunities for liberal education.

The many examples we have cited underscore the range of values that people expect schools to support. As a result, we often find ongoing and sometimes acrimonious debates over school curricula. Moreover, the extent to which rubrics are implicated in these ongoing debates suggests that they are not simply "tools of learning" that can be removed from the intellectual and structural contexts in which they are used. Neither can they be removed from the relational contexts of schools. We recognize that teachers have perhaps the most difficult job in this context because they are called on to bear responsibilities for thoughtful planning and complex decision-making while engaging in relationships with their students.

RUBRICS AND RELATIONSHIPS

The day to day decisions about what and how to teach remains in the hands of teachers, and we, as a society, trust that teachers have the best interests of students at heart. Good instruction begins with a general goal or aim and then moves to consideration of what and how a student will demonstrate, in some measureable, assessable way, that which they know and understand. Likewise, good assessment involves establishing criteria by which this performance will be evaluated that "highlights the most revealing and important aspects of the work" (Wiggins & McTighe, 2005, p. 173). When criteria are organized into a rubric, they become a descriptive framework to discriminate between degrees of successful performance and provide "qualitative distinctions in students' responses" (Popham, 2014, p. 214). The goals for rubric development are to devise a tool which aids in consistency in evaluation, can be clearly communicated to learners, and guide instruction (Wiggins & McTighe, 2005; Popham, 2014). We want the criteria to be understood by students so that they can "confidently and competently evaluate their own and each other's work" (Stiggins & Chappuis, 2012, p. 20).

The wisdom of these experts sounds clear and comprehensible. Yet despite guidance and mandates about what students should learn and how rubrics should function, in practice it is not uncommon to find that what teachers are hoping students will think about and demonstrate remains a hidden agenda. Whether due to inexperience or intent, many teachers fail to effectively communicate their focus and/or their expectations. What results at best may be rubrics that serve little value to teachers or students and at worst may be an arbitrary or capricious use of rubrics that leads to anger and frustration for students who are unsuccessful yet confused about where they went wrong. Stiggins & Chappuis (2012) advocate sound assessment principles to avoid such a scenario described as follows:

> Some unfortunate students may be mired in classrooms in which they are left on their own to guess the meaning of academic success. Their teachers may lack a vision of success, focus on an incorrect one, or intentionally choose to keep the secrets of success a mystery to retain power and control in the classroom. When their students guess at the valued target and guess wrong, they fail. Under these circumstances, they fail not from lack of motivation, but from lack of insight as to what they are supposed to achieve. This can be very discouraging. It destroys confidence. Besides, it can be very unfair. (p. 11)

As applied to our specific focus on rubrics, we contend that teachers should have, or take the time to develop, a clear picture in their minds of desirable performance and be transparent in their communication of what success looks like to students. To this end, performance expectations encompassed in the rubric would match or align with explicit directions or instructions for relevant tasks. Students can play an active role in helping to identify the most critical aspects and in helping teachers refine their "pictures" of successful performance (Wiggins & McTighe, 2005). In this way, teachers become accountable to their students while students are held and hold themselves accountable for their own learning.

The setting and purpose of the task assessed will largely determine the flexibility and level of rigidity of rubrics. In general, the larger scale and more standardized the task, the less frequently changes to rubrics are likely to be made. Rubrics vary in quality and effectiveness for a plethora of reasons that are beyond the scope of this chapter. The point we are making here is that while good rubrics more easily lend themselves to trusting relationships with students even flawed rubrics can result in productive learning environments if they are used within the context of positive relationships between teachers and students. We hope that rubric use will be less about a contract for a grade and more about a transaction within the relationship where individuals have the freedom to explore and create within a flexible framework that protects and reduces fear of negative consequences. Thus, the trust within the relationship and the context of how the process of learning is presented may reduce rather than increase the risk of de-skilling, getting by with as little as possible, or re-skilling, expending energy and developing skills to avoid intended learning tasks. We will return to re-skilling later in noting the dangers of students whose goal is simply to "play the system." This notion is also related to "busy work" and "grade grubbing."

Those who like absolutes and linear thinking may groan when rubrics are conceptualized in this way. Where others seek to standardize and script, we contend that rubrics can be used to ensure skill development while still encouraging critical thinking and helping to develop negotiation skills. In situations where rubrics are generated outside the immediate teacher-student environment such as in the case of standardized or external assessment mandates, the evaluative criteria is essentially removed from interpersonal relationships and can potentially further student-teacher trust. An *esprit de corps* may result in which students and teachers face a common task—to meet rubric expectations.

Next, we turn to a specific case-study illustration. With respect to the curriculum theories described above, this case represents a progressive education tradition in higher education. It is offered as an opportunity to reflect on how rubrics are used within a particular cohort-model learning environment where relationships are developed over time.

RUBRICS IN TEACHER EDUCATION

The following case describes a secondary teacher education program including events that led to the program's adoption of rubrics to assist in portfolio development and evaluation. This case could be considered the result of "teacher-research" spanning ten years —from 2003 to 2013.

The program described below is known as CoT, short for Community of Teachers. CoT was founded 21 years ago by two School of Education faculty and a small group of local secondary teachers. Their aim was to design a performance-based route to teacher certification in a range of subject areas. The program has grown somewhat with the addition of students seeking licensure in special education, but it still remains small compared to the institution's primary teacher education program. CoT is referred to as a "boutique" program among other alternatives. While not an honors program, admission to CoT requires a separate application and an in-person interview with faculty and current students. In this respect, CoT students have a hand in selecting their "colleagues."

The structure of the program includes three components. First, students attend an ongoing, three-hour seminar each week. Each seminar includes a faculty leader and about 15 graduate and undergraduate students representing the subject areas of English, math, science, art, social studies, and special education. Seminar members decide as a group on common readings and discussion topics. Each semester is jointly planned in the first two weeks of that semester and seminar members rotate responsibilities for planning and conducting each weekly session. Typically, much of the seminar time is devoted to discussion of the program's second component—a professional teaching portfolio. Faculty recommendations for licensure of individual CoT students are based on the completion of the portfolio and a successful student teaching experience. In this sense, the portfolio is a "high stakes" requirement.

The third program component is an apprenticeship in a local school. New CoT students spend their first semester in the program visiting a range of local schools. In program parlance, this is called "shopping for a mentor." The mentor that a student selects (by mutual consent) will serve as that student's cooperating teacher when that student reaches his or her student teaching semester. Prior to that time, students are required to spend the equivalent of one day a week working in their mentor's classroom. In some cases, CoT students have been present in the same local school and working with the same cooperating teacher for two or three years before they begin their student teaching.

The apprenticeship is directly linked to the portfolio in that a student's apprenticeship experience provides the primary evidence for meeting portfolio expectations. Students must complete 16 program expectations in areas such as: subject area knowledge, multicultural understandings, teaching reading and writing, curriculum development, and professional growth. Each expectation is described in the program's 116-page handbook (Indiana University School of Education, 2012) and each description includes: an explanation of the expectation (consisting of a rationale, elaboration of "what the expectation is" and "what the expectation is not"); outcomes of what CoT students should know, value, and be able to do; possible strategies for gathering evidence; examples of evidence; suggested readings and (as of 2003) an expectation rubric (Indiana University School of Education, 2012). All of the 16 expectations require a critical reflection (a type of self-evaluation). While students may use university course work as evidence, it would be difficult, and in most cases impossible, to complete any of the expectations without some artifacts from the candidate's classroom teaching experience in a middle or high school.

Rubrics are described in the program handbook as follows:

> **CoT**'s rubrics have been developed to enable **CoT** faculty, Mentor Teachers, and **CoT** Seminar colleagues to provide constructive feedback and ultimately to determine a teacher candidate's readiness to enter the profession (and apply for licensure). Rubrics represent a framework for evaluating a teacher candidate's evidence as it is presented in a Portfolio. Equally important, they become a useful mechanism for communicating the standards of the program to those outside the **CoT** community, including the Indiana Professional Standards Board, which determines whether we should be allowed to grant teaching licenses in Indiana, and the National Association of Colleges of Teacher Education, the national accrediting body which must approve our programs. (p. 17)

The handbook also contains a chronology of "community decisions" that comprise additions and changes to program policy. The process for making changes or additions begins with a program governance committee of CoT students responding to a particular concern. This committee drafts a proposal and distributes it to all CoT members asking for comments or suggestions. The proposal is revised and the committee calls a program-wide meeting. An electronic vote is then taken usually one or two weeks after the meeting. The decision to adopt expectation rubrics followed this process. A proposal was designed, distributed, and discussed using the program's websites. As a result, CoT members were familiar with the issues prior to the program-wide meeting. At this meeting, some spoke against adopting the rubrics, worried that they would increase the standardization of the portfolios and reduce opportunities for individuals to put their particular "fingerprints" on their work. Others argued that rubrics could be used flexibly and that they could motivate students to "reach higher" in developing their own teaching skills and dispositions.

The rubrics were subsequently adopted. Regardless of the outcome, the process of governance had been educational in its own right. The students were asked to express and argue for their beliefs in a professional milieu. Moreover, students had been given input that may have increased their individual investment in the program; and the decision had been made as a group, thus promoting a sense of community. Finally, dissent was tolerated by the others. Put another way, no one felt compelled to change his or her mind or fear significant conflict between specific concerns about rubrics in general and use of the program rubrics in particular. Pro and con perspectives were respected.

We want to mention several other points about CoT before moving on. First, seminars are structured as "rolling cohorts." Most students return each semester, but a few finish and leave, while a few new students join. Second, the seminar, portfolio, and student teaching are graded pass/fail. Third, as we have implied in our description, CoT is probably more student-centered and democratic that other teacher education programs at large. Students stay in the program over multiple semesters (typically four semesters for graduate students and up to three years for undergraduates). Moreover, the seminars, program governance, and admissions are student run. Students select their mentor teachers rather than being assigned to them, and students work on their portfolios largely at their own pace.

THE ABSENT PRESENCE OF RUBRICS

At this point, the plot of the case study is most notable for its lack of drama. The years subsequent to adopting the rubrics can only describe as "business as usual." On the one hand, some continued to worry about standardization, de-skilling, re-skilling, and the potential narrowing of values that informed their teaching. On the other hand, we did not witness in subsequent years any detriment (intended or unintended) to the program that could be attributed to the program rubrics. The heavens did not open and no disembodied voice pronounced that we had embarked on the road to either damnation or sainthood.

However, the story that continues below is still newsworthy. Seminar sessions and school placements included countless discussions among CoT students about portfolio expectations. These discussions raised pertinent queries: What counts as evidence? How much is needed? Why might some evidence be considered stronger than other evidence? What does a particular artifact mean and how should it be interpreted? How much context is needed for others to make similar interpretations and does that matter? What makes evidence from others reliable? How much stock should be put in samples of student work or a cooperating teacher's feedback? Should you trust your own limited experience, and if so, why? We reveled in these discussions and were hesitant to point students in the direction of the rubrics for fear that doing so would end their deliberations. Yet, after some time, we began to worry that the students were not even reading the rubrics as not a single CoT student had raised a question about a specific rubric in or outside of seminar. So we asked them. Had they read the rubrics as instructed? New students told us they had referred to the rubrics and that the rubrics were useful, albeit we suspected the latter claim was partly born of politeness. Students wanted to appear cooperative. Veteran students were more sheepish, hesitantly admitting that they had not read the rubrics for the particular expectations on which they were currently working. Here we asked students if they found the rubrics limiting, and they responded with a nonchalant "no."

The difference between new and returning seminar members is worth repeating. Below is how much of our dialogue played out:

Act I, Scene I

> **Instructor:** Did you read the rubric for this expectation?
> **Newbie:** Yes.
> **Instructor:** Was it helpful? Do you have any questions?
> **Newbie:** It was helpful, but most of my ideas came from Philip (a veteran member). He has already done this expectation and he let me read his. I felt I needed to see a finished one before I got too far on my own.

Act I, Scene II

> **Instructor:** Did you read the rubric for this expectation?
> **Veteran:** Not really.
> **Instructor:** Why not?
> **Veteran:** I forgot.
> **Instructor:** You forgot?
> **Veteran:** I just didn't think of it. I already knew what evidence I was going to include. I read the rubric for the first expectation I worked on. Do we really need to read them all?

Our students' use of rubrics has always remained a one-act play. But even a short play can be significant. Most faculty members who have taught in a cohort or rolling-cohort program like CoT know that it may be difficult for new students to 'break in." Communities, after all, are both inclusive and exclusive. Over the years, CoT seminars have addressed this problem in a number of ways. Some seminars assign new members a "seminar buddy." Our seminar begins each semester with a ritual "convocation" that is specifically designed to welcome new members. Rubrics seem to have taken on a similar initiating function. As others have suggested (e.g., Arter &

McTighe, (2001); Cooper& Gargan, 2009; Popham, 1997; Tierney & Mari-elle, 2004), rubrics are designed to clarify expectations. In this respect, they are akin to rule books. But once you have learned the game, you don't need to keep referring to the rule book at the beginning and end of every play.

Rubrics were important on one front because they underscored the in-tentional bias of the faculty in favor of evidence derived from the students actual teaching; that is, their apprenticeship. The rubrics helped to clarify program values. On the other hand, assessment feedback was largely forma-tive. Here again the structure and norms of the program come into play. Students typically turn in expectations multiple times before the expecta-tion is "checked off;" thus, unless we are reading a "final" version of a port-folio, our feedback is specifically geared to how to improve a specific set of evidence, its organization, and the particulars of the students' reflections.

LESSONS LEARNED

Overall, the role of rubrics has been limited in the case at hand for several possible reasons. Perhaps the students did not perceive a need for the ru-brics or perhaps the instructor failed to adequately support positive uses of the rubrics. A third consideration is whether the expectations had become so ingrained in the culture that explicit use of the actual rubrics was unnec-essary. Finally, drawing again on curriculum theory, perhaps the students shied away from the rubrics because they were resisting the hyper-rational-ization (i.e., de-skilling) of their work. Critical theory suggests that indus-trial workers faced with deskilling will "fight back" by refusing to engage in adopted procedures. Rationalization in this case came through the use of rubrics. Forms of resistance are seen positively as an expression of agency. Still again, however, educators must be cautious. "The lads" in Paul Willis' study, *Learning to Labor* (1977) offer an example of how bucking the system restricted working class British youth to working class, industrial jobs. Were our students disadvantaging themselves by not playing the system?

We would argue the contrary. "Playing the system" does not benefit stu-dents in the long run if students become dependent on others to tell them what to do. The sociologist Erving Goffman (1961) argued that whenever we create a system, we also create an "underlife." This underlife can take the form or jumping through hoops or what Powell, Farrar, and Cohen (1985) called classroom treaties. Such treaties represent unspoken agree-ments between teachers and students that minimize the demands that in-struction places on both groups. The extent to which students develop an underlife or treaties that allow them to "game the system" is the extent to which life in classrooms become a matter of superficial compliance.

How, then, do teachers avoid having rubrics contribute to this outcome? Our thesis has been that questions of this sort depend significantly on context and relationships. There are several protective factors in the CoT scenario that help avoid the dark side of rubric use. The CoT program structure and curriculum largely follows progressive ideals. One related advantage common to professional preparation is the relevance of goals. In this case, students seek specific preparation to be successful in educational settings, and the program is designed to match these goals. This alignment is important because students are less likely to game the system when they view the program as a path to career aspirations rather than as a hurdle to jump.

Perhaps most importantly, the CoT program is based on a sense of community where extensive efforts are made to create and maintain cooperative relationships. It is possible that the inaugural group of students who participated in the development and adoption of the rubrics engaged in a type of transaction where they had voice and influence. If so, this group likely proceeded confidently and with a sense of unity with faculty. In this scenario, their experiences and interpretations of expectations became part of the organizational history or lore which was subsequently passed down to future cohorts. As the culture deepens, rubric expectations are met and exceeded without overt dependence on the formal documents. As cohorts and instructors become more removed in time from the initial adoption of rubrics, successful navigation of completing the program may become viewed as a common goal, imposed by an outside source, that students and instructors are dedicated to meeting (and beating) together. Nevertheless, as practices become internalized and taken for granted, forms of "re-invention" that question these practices may become increasingly important to students' investment in their learning.

Teachers face a delicate balance between providing enough structure without creating over dependence on rubrics with merely a passing grade as the goal. While many students meet or exceed expectations seemingly without reliance on the formal documents, struggling or novice students can be guided to "follow the rubrics" as a way to provide a supportive, if only temporary framework. This course of action is typically based on the students and instructor's judgment in individual cases. Again, both the structure and culture of CoT encouraged such judgments.

In the absence of trusted relationships, we fall back on James Madison's saying that: "If men were angels, no government would be necessary. If angels were to govern men, neither external nor internal controls on government would be necessary." Because we are not governed by angels, rubrics may serve as a shield to protect both students and teachers from the arbitrary use of power.

CONCLUSION

In this chapter we have asserted that rubrics can be used to achieve both educational and mis-educational aims. We explore these uses of rubrics from two perspectives. The perspective of curriculum theory helps contextualize the use of rubrics and highlights the dangers of the over-reliance resulting from unreflective implementation. The perspective of practice is explored through the description and analysis of the CoT case study. This case study points to the importance of balancing the need for structure with flexibility, and illustrates the benefits of trust in classroom relationships. In some cases, within or outside of the program we have considered, certain students simply may not need rubrics while others may find them useful in their particular circumstances. For this reason, much is lost when we decide to require all teachers or all students to use the same rubrics in the same way.

REFERENCES

Adler, M. J. (1982). *The Paideia proposal: An educational manifesto.* New York, NY: Simon & Schuster.

Apple, M. W. (1986). *Teachers and texts.* New York, NY: Routledge.

Arter, J. & McTighe, J. (2001). *Scoring rubrics in the classroom: Using performance criteria for assessing and improving student performance.* Thousand Oaks, CA: Corwin Press/Sage Publications.

Banks, J. A. 2014. *An introduction to multicultural education* (5th ed.). Boston, MA: Pearson, Allyn & Bacon.

Bobbitt, F. (1918). *The Curriculum.* Cambridge, MA: Riverside Press.

Bowers & Flinders, D. J. (1990). *Responsive teaching: An ecological approach to classroom patterns of language, culture, and thought.* New York, NY: Teacher's College Press.

Bushaw, W. J. & Lopes S. J. (2012). The 44th annual Phi Delta Kappa/Gallup poll, *Phi Delta Kappan, 94*(1), 9–25.

Community of teachers' handbook (2012). http://portal.education.indiana.edu/Portals/174/CoT%20Handbook%20v4.pdf

Cooper, B. S. & Gargan A. (2009). Rubrics in education: Old term, new meanings. *The Phi Delta Kappan, 91*(1), 54–55.

Dewey, J. (1910). *How we think.* Boston, MA: D.C. Heath and Company.

Dewey, J. (1938). *Experience and education.* New York, NY: MacMillan.

Eggen, D. & Kauchak, P. (2011). *Introduction to teaching* (4th ed.). Upper Saddle River, NJ: Merrill/Prentice Hall.

Eisner, E. W. (1991). *The enlightened eye.* New York, NY: Macmillan.

Eisner, E. W. (1994). *The educational imagination,* (3rd ed.). New York, NY: Macmillan.

Evans, C. (2013). Making sense of assessment feedback in higher education. *Review of Educational Research, 83*(1), 70–120.

Freire, P. (1970). *Pedagogy of the oppressed.* New York, NY: Continuum.

Goffman, E. (1961). *Asylums: Essays on the social situation of mental patients and other inmates.* New York, Doubleday.

Greene, M. (1995). *Releasing the imagination: Essays on education, the arts, and social change.* San Francisco, CA: Jossey-Bass Inc.

Hargreaves (1994). Changing teachers, changing times. New York, NY: Teachers College Press.

Hirsch, E. D. (1987). *Cultural literacy: What every American needs to know.* New York, NY: Random House.

Jackson, P. (1968). *Life in classrooms.* New York, NY: Holt, Rinehart and Winston.

Madison, J. (1788), The structure of the government must furnish the proper checks and balances between the different departments. *The Federalist,* 51.

Popham, W.J. (1997). What's wrong—and what's right—with rubrics. *Educational Leadership, 55,* 72–75.

Popham, W. J. (2014). *Classroom assessment: What teachers need to know,* (7th ed.). Upper Saddle River, NJ: Pearson.

Posner, M. I. & Rothbart, M. K. (2007). *Educating the human brain.* Washington, DC, US: American Psychological Association.

Powell A. G., Farrar E., & Cohen, D. K. (1985). *The shopping mall high school: Winners and losers in the educational marketplace.* Boston, MA: Houghton Mifflin.

Ravitch, D. (2010). *The Death and life of the great American school system: How testing and choice are undermining education.* New York, NY: Basic Books.

Silin, J. (1995). *Sex, death, and the education of our children.* New York, NY: Teachers College Press.

Stiggins, R. J. & Chappuis, J. (2012). *An Introduction to student-involved assessment for learning.* Boston, MA: Pearson Education, Inc.

Tierney, R. & Marielle, S. (2004). What's still wrong with rubrics: focusing on the consistency of performance criteria across scale levels. *Practical Assessment, Research & Evaluation, 9*(2).

Tyler, R. W. (1949). *Basic principles of curriculum and instruction.* Chicago: University of Chicago Press.

Wiggins, G. (1998). *Educative assessment: Designing assessments to inform and improve student performance.* San Francisco, CA: Jossey-Bass Publishers.

Wiggins, G. & McTighe, J. (2005). *Understanding by design.* Alexandria, VA: Association for Supervision and Curriculum Development.

Willis, P. (1977). *Learning to labor. How working class kids get working class jobs.* New York, NY: Columbia University Press.

CHAPTER 9

(DIS)POSITIONING LEARNERS
Rubrics and Identity in Teacher Education

Catherine Lalonde, David Gorlewski, and Julie Gorlewski

Teaching, rightfully, carries the title professional. Its foundational core has been rendered problematic by federal and state policies and practices that frame teaching as "less than" a profession and teachers as "less than" professional. To counter this, teacher certification programs, more and more, are being required to use rubrics to assess the professionalism of candidates. Rubrics are mandated by certification agencies, as well as edTPA (the newly developed "Teacher Performance Assessment for Education," which will be used to certify teacher candidates in most states beginning in 2014) and are purported to measure such features as academic language, critical reflection, advocacy and caring for students, and democratic citizenship. As part of accreditation processes across higher education, rubrics are becoming a mandated aspect of assessment and therefore have a tremendous influence on instruction and learning. Curriculum committees, state agencies, and accreditors frequently require samples of assignments accompanied by scoring rubrics, as well as common rubrics across course sections—and even across programs. For example, a program may require all instructors

Rubric Nation, pages 135–147

to use the same set of guidelines and associated rubrics every time a lesson plan is assigned. Furthermore, instructors may be compelled to participate in a calibration process designed to ensure that rubric-generated scores are consistent across scorers. These factors exemplify the contemporary movement to standardize the field of education, a move based on a resurgent positivism (Lees, 2007) that privileges easily quantifiable forms of evaluation over human interaction and engagement.

Teacher dispositions are a complex, nuanced aspect of professional identity; they are difficult to instill and even more challenging to assess. Moreover, when working with teacher candidates, teacher educators must consider interrelationships among programs, individuals, and professional expectations. Should we expect students to enter our programs with particular dispositions, or do we intend to cultivate dispositions as part of the program? Are we claiming to be able to imagine ideal dispositional characteristics, or are our rubrics open-ended enough to allow for new imaginings? And, perhaps most importantly, is it possible (or even desirable) to disentangle the performance of dispositional behaviors from the internalization of these behaviors? That is, how can we (or should we) separate a candidate who *is* caring from one who *acts* caring?

In this chapter, we will examine rubrics currently used in a teacher education program in New York State and consider how these rubrics connect to the following questions. Key questions related to the development and assessment of dispositions include How are rubrics used with respect to professional dispositions of teacher candidates? How can we balance the obsession with the mechanisms of accountability, often accompanied by rubrics, with the need for authentic education? That is, how does the creation and implementation of a clearly established scoring plan potentially limit educators' ability to foster educational experiences that extend beyond the limits of our imaginations? Does the use of specific criteria focused on easily defined, described, observed, and measured characteristics restrict educational aims to superficial targets rather than more meaningful, humanistic aspirations? How do the uses of rubrics define and delimit how we imagine the teaching profession? Finally, what does this mean for teacher education and for the future of the profession?

In order to explore both the textual and anecdotal aspects of this process of building a professional dispositions assessment form for our candidates, we employed case study and document analysis methodologies. The narrative aspects of case study methodology can help unpack teaching and learning interactions in ways that allow for self-reflection, critical analysis of complex educational issues, and the impacts of "insider researcher" roles of faculty members (Corcoran, Walker, & Wals, 2004; Petty, Thomson, & Stew, 2012; Shulman, 2002; Unluer, 2012). It is our hope that constructing this case study about rubric development and critically analyzing it with pertinent theories will encourage other institutions involved in similar assessment development efforts to enter this important conversation in order to effect productive changes to these accreditation-related processes.

Document or content analysis of the Dispositions Assessment Form's various iterations, and faculty revisions involved therein, complement the narrative qualities of the case study well. The form itself becomes both a starting point and a point for continuously revisiting three key aspects: (a) expected/performed professional dispositions (for both faculty and candidates), (b) reflective teaching and learning, and (c) tensions between accreditation- and program-related expectations for candidates. Through the use of this qualitative research method, we were able to engage in critical, in-depth analysis of what we were asked to do by accrediting bodies, what we produced as a "measure of evidence," how our candidates and colleagues responded to the initial form's iteration, and how we approached the "re-visioning" process (Petty et al., 2012).

Teacher Identity, Professional Dispositions, and Rubrics

Dispositions are a complex aspect of teaching and teacher preparation. While certain characteristics seem unassailable (e.g., demonstrating a "strong work ethic"), others are arguable, at least in terms of priority (Is it more important to appreciate diversity or to have high expectations? To be kind or to think critically?). Furthermore, even if educators could agree on a set of dispositions, the question of how to foster and assess them is another matter. Helm (2006) provides a clear statement of the issue at hand: "But how can dispositions be assessed, not only if they are present, but present to what degree? If certain dispositions are deemed essential in order to be successful in the classroom, how are these dispositions identified and assessed?" (p. 237).

Dispositions are often understood as a "summary of actions observed" using "employment of skills" and "manifested by behaviors" (Katz & Raths, 1985, 1986; Raths, 2001). Huber-Warring and Warring's (2006) definition, on the other hand, helps to explain why dispositions are so difficult to address and assess:

> Dispositions are often thought of as goals that describe a person's desired behaviors and attitudes. Typically, dispositions in the educational setting are large ideas that, when examined, encompass many areas and skills, address individual development as a whole, and relate to how students function in class and society. (pp. 38–39)

Like learning standards, professional dispositions are, by necessity, general statements of aspirations, not prescriptive statements of outcomes.

Moreover, as Hodkinson (2005) explains, teaching is a multifaceted, complicated, social, embodied profession. Dispositions cannot be simply separated and assessed as though they are not enacted in particular contexts. People are integrated in social contexts, and thoughts and actions are not easily predicted, identified, replicated, or assessed.

> No single person is synonymous with their learning or teaching context, even though they are part of it. Each of us has lives outside our current site of learning. We had lives before it, we have lives in other contexts alongside education, and most of us will have lives after we have left that particular place of learning. Furthermore, the ways in which one person is part of a learning context may be very different from the ways in which another person is part of even the same learning context. (p. 107)

Because dispositions are socially derived and socially constructed, and people are perpetually positioned within social structures, dispositions are not static or divisible. They cannot be detached from the circumstances in which they manifest. Characteristics described as "dispositions" purport to be concrete representations of thoughts—transformations of beliefs into actions.

In an effort to clarify disposition in ways that facilitate teacher candidate development and assessment, Jung and Rhodes (2008) distinguish between dispositions as dimensions of personality, dispositions as patterns of behavior, and dispositions as cultivatable human qualities. Furthermore, they note the importance of differentiating between predispositions and dispositions, arguing that "Extensive review of the literature suggests that we separate the two terms since dispositions include behaviors or actions while predispositions may not" (p. 651).

Ripski, LoCasale-Crouch, and Decker (2011) emphasize the importance of dispositions in teaching, a profession that is essentially interactive. Dispositions, they note, can be linked to beliefs and attitudes about student learning which is associated with student achievement. Their findings indicate that an exploration of the existence and stability of traits and emotional states might be useful in identifying promising teacher candidates.

Phelps (2006), a teacher educator who is determined to influence her students to develop dispositions that will enhance their classroom practice, suggests the adoption of Drake and Burns (2004) know/do/be framework. This framework is built around the idea that the shift from being to becoming can be scaffolded by focusing first on knowing, then doing, and ultimately becoming fully part of one's conscious and unconscious self. Guided by the question, "How do I want teacher candidates to be at the end of the course?" (p. 174), Phelps (2006) decided to explicitly state the expectation that her students would be "collaborative, creative, and reflective," thus revealing what might otherwise remain a "hidden curriculum" and increasing the likelihood that students will exhibit these qualities.

Using rubrics to identify and assess critical dispositions is inherently contradictory. Rubrics potentially represent a temporal perspective that is static; however, a critical approach, in theory and practice, is fluid, ever-evolving, and reflective. A critical disposition involves beliefs that are continually analyzed, reconsidered, and transformed. Such a disposition is not static; it intentionally defies reproduction or replication. Huber-Warring and Warring (2006), however, describe a method for developing critical dispositions using a rubric as an authentic tool for self-assessment. Teacher candidates reflect on dimensions of growth linked to culturally conscious reflection, with the ultimate aim of privileging process, fostering social justice, and embracing diversity. With flexibility and transformation modeled as intentional components, possibilities exist for rubrics and dispositions to coexist and, when used thoughtfully, to be mutually beneficial. Ultimately, this chapter explores the complexities of an attempt to implement rubrics related to dispositions using a critically reflective approach, thus providing an example of just such a process.

NCATE, Their Rubrics, and Assessment of Professional Dispositions

The primary impetus for developing a tool for measuring our teacher candidates' professional dispositions is associated with our department's pursuit of the National Council for Accreditation of Teacher Education (NCATE) accreditation. Whereas the majority of NCATE's Standard 1 (*Candidate Knowledge, Skills, and Professional Dispositions*) is addressed through the Specialized Professional Association (SPA) reporting process, professional dispositions, while a part of the SPA reports' key assessments, are addressed largely as a separate process. And while professional dispositions are assessed in conjunction with student teaching experiences, the Master's programs in our Education unit do not "measure" candidates' dispositions upon entering our programs. Candidate's professional dispositions can be measured using a "pretest/posttest" method that seems to be more in line with what NCATE reviewers expect, as implied in the highest, or "Target," level of NCATE Standard 1.g.:

> Candidates work with students, families, colleagues, and communities in ways that reflect the professional dispositions expected of professional educators as delineated in professional, state, and institutional standards. Candidates demonstrate classroom behaviors that create caring and supportive learning environments and encourage self-directed learning by all students. Candidates recognize when their own professional dispositions may need to be adjusted and are able to develop plans to do so. (NCATE, 2008, p. 20)

In terms of determining initial professional dispositions, analyzing examples of "expected" professional dispositions in motion, and "develop[ing] plans" to modify them, it is clear that NCATE would like to see "evidence" (e.g., as reported through rubrics) of teacher candidates explicitly learning about, and reflecting on, professional dispositions before they begin student teaching. In light of this accreditation-based expectation, we began exploring sample tools and developing our own tool to measure the professional dispositions of all teacher candidates upon entry into our master's degree programs.

Unfortunately, the process of developing and implementing a new assessment tool occurred within the context of addressing the NCATE standards—most notably, the development of standards-based rubrics for each key assignment per course, all of which would be gathered using a new system (TaskStream) as a part of an e-portfolio capstone project and most of which would be used as "key assessments" during SPA reporting.[2] Rubrics are designed to provide information about which local and national standards are being addressed by linking standards to rubrics (typically, one standard per rubric row) and by infusing the rubrics themselves with standards-based language. If faculty members had previously used rubrics to evaluate the key assignments for their courses, then the language in them had to be modified to align with the standards. And if faculty members were not using rubrics, or if their rubrics had been more generic, then they needed to use these new rubrics to evaluate the key assignments for their courses. Faculty members can provide comments to candidates per rubric row or in an "Overall Comment" area. However, should faculty find themselves using these areas extensively due to the limits of the rubric, the effectiveness of rubrics as tools for evaluation are then called into question. In this way, rubrics have increasingly become a venue for reporting compliance with multiple bodies of standards rather than serving as one of multiple tools used to evaluate candidates' progress through our master's programs.

Faculty members were already overwhelmed, not only by determining which course assignments should be used as "key assignments," known as "key assessments" to SPA reviewers, but also by the task of aligning standards with their courses, key assignments, and key assignment rubrics drawn from the following bodies of standards:

- Association for Childhood Education International (ACEI) SPA standards
- Council for the Accreditation of Educator Preparation (CAEP) initial draft standards
- Council for Exceptional Children (CEC) SPA standards
- Initial Licensure/Post Baccalaureate (IL/PB) SPA standards

- Interstate Teacher Assessment and Support Consortium (InTASC) 2011 standards
- National Council for the Accreditation of Teacher Education (NCATE) standards
- New York State (NYS) Teaching standards
- Teaching English to Speakers of Other Languages (TESOL) SPA standards

When the complexity of the InTASC and NYS Teaching standards' sub-criteria *and* the pressure to align with SPA standards to gather data for reports due during the Fall 2013 semester are taken into account (not to mention the ongoing responsibilities associated with teaching, research, and committee and community service), it is understandable that faculty members perceived the task of measuring candidate dispositions as an additional burden. The collective intellectual, physical, and emotional energy required to take on this process can take a toll on the functioning of other aspects of our programs. This, then, is the context for the initial development of the Dispositions Assessment Form.

The Task: Development of a Dispositions Assessment Form

The Education Department's actions relative to the accreditation mandate for measurable dispositions could be classified as "survivalist." As noted earlier, the Department was engaged simultaneously with so many *different* accreditation mandates, that the three staff members on the committee formed to address the disposition issue were deeply involved in numerous subcommittees addressing *other* critical areas. Consequently, in order to "survive," the committee decided not to re-create the wheel, but simply to borrow one from another institution. Though the source of the model rubric cannot be shared, early in the fall semester (specifically, the document was retrieved on August 13, 2012), the committee members were able to gain access to a disposition measurement form used by another accredited institution. If that institution had gained accreditation using that form, it was reasoned, why can't it be adapted and then adopted as our own?

Entitled "Assessment of Dispositional Professional Qualities in Teacher Education Program Candidate," the 2-page form consisted of five major headings (Caring, Communicative, Creative, Critical, and Professional Requirements). Each heading also included a one-sentence explanation of the term followed by the phrase "The following list comprises many, but not all, of the qualities, tendencies, and/or behaviors which characterize a set of (e.g., caring, communicative, creative, etc.) dispositions." This phrase was followed by four to six subheadings to which candidates (rating themselves) and instructors (rating each candidate) were to provide a score: N.A. for *Not Applicable* or *Not Observable*, 0 for *Serious Concerns*, 1 for *Needs Improvement*, 2 for *Emerging*, and 3 for *Acceptable*. At the end of each of the five major headings, a small blank space was provided under the heading "Comments." The document was created as a rubric for evaluating dispositions. Delving into all the subheadings would not be possible in the space of this chapter, but focusing on one—Creative—will shed some light on the complexity (or perhaps foolishness) of the rating exercise. Under Creative, the subheadings included Flexibility, Inventiveness, Resourcefulness, and Resilience. Attaching a number to any of these subheadings is to assert, for example, that a candidate's Resilience might be "Emerging" or that his/her Inventiveness might "Need Improvement."

Modifying the Rubric

The committee was hopeful that minor changes could be made to make the form more consistent with other department rubrics. The first modification was to change the N.A/0/1/2/3 scoring scale to an N.A./1/2/3/4 scoring scale. That made the form consistent with all other department rubrics (apparently, giving a score of 0 was anathema to educators). Additional modifications were essentially deletions. As subheadings, Passion was deleted from the Caring category; Authenticity was deleted from the Communicative category; and under the Critical heading, the committee deleted a subheading listed as Open-mindedness and replaced it with Perspective.

The committee members revisited the form periodically throughout the fall semester, making minor changes to the language, essentially simplifying long descriptors of a subcategory. For example, under the subheading Presence, the cumbersome descriptor "has keen with-it-ness and engagement in human interactions and other's needs" was replaced with (what the committee felt was) a cleaner "is sensitive to, and aware of, human interactions and other's needs."

Finally, the committee decided to administer this evaluation in two phases: initially, during the third week of classes for the department's newest candidates as part of their Curriculum Planning in Education course; and about 18 months later as a part of a Reflective Paper submitted after completion of the practicum (student teaching).

During the middle of that academic year, the revised rubric, as well as the proposed implementation plan for the rubric, was presented to the Education Department. Meeting notes indicated that the rubric and pilot plan were approved with little discussion and no changes. It was agreed that the rubric would be piloted by the candidates who had completed the Curriculum Planning in Education class the previous fall, as well as those currently taking the course. This was done mainly because of the high degree of familiarity between the students and one of the committee members. That familiarity, the committee felt, would assure completion and possibly yield candid feedback.

Piloting the Rubric

In April of the spring semester, approximately 28 students piloted the rubric/disposition form, rating themselves on a scale of 1 to 4 on their dispositions relative to qualities such as Caring, Communicative, Creative, Critical, and Professional Requirements.

Candidates were told about the reason for the pilot. That is, for the purpose of program evaluation and improvement, a form was designed to quantify dispositions and that this activity would serve to refine that form. The term "disposition" was also defined for them as attitudes and beliefs exhibited, in this case, by a teacher. In response, one student said,

> So, if I want to make myself look good and make the Education Department look good for accreditation, then it would be in everyone's interest for me to give myself all 1's and 2's today, then give myself all 3's and 4's when I fill it out at the end of the program, right?

This approach to dispositions is what a colleague calls "strategizing dispositions"—in short, candidates giving the response they assume evaluators *want* to hear. Though the vast majority of individual scores were recorded in the 3 (Emerging) or 4 (Acceptable) categories, 19 of the 28 candidates listed a 2 (Needs Improvement) somewhere on the form. Three candidates scored themselves with a 1 (Serious Concern) for subcategories Voice, Resilience, and Collaborative.

As noted earlier, the Education Department retained the "Comments" box under each of the five main categories. Several students provided responses. One candidate indicated that she wanted to give herself a 2.5 for Resilience (splitting the difference!); under the subcategory of Humility, a candidate "objected" to the question. She maintained that there was no possible answer because of the contradiction of rating oneself highly (a 4) for a characteristic like "humility." Another candidate indicated that she could not respond to any of the subcategories under Professional Requirements "because she had 'not taught in a school yet.'" One candidate commented, "These are all qualities which I would like to strive for. However, I have not had many chances to experience them yet." She also wrote, "I am hoping when I enter the classroom I can uphold these (dispositions) as much as possible." Similar comments from another candidate included "I need to put more effort in these items."

One candidate simply wrote, "5.3 is not clear." When the committee members reviewed 5.3, they found that the statement was, in fact, not clear. It had read, "Work Ethic/Responsibility: attends to school policy for teacher attendance; completes teaching-related tasks in a thorough manner." There was no way a teacher candidate could respond to such a statement.

The most common theme from the "Comments" section was related to inexperience: that the candidates could not accurately complete a form about teacher dispositions because they simply had not taught yet, that they never had their own classroom, and that their experiences were limited to classroom observations.

Analyzing Results of the Pilot

The Education Department's NCATE Coordinator knew that reading and analyzing the results of the dispositions assessment would be viewed as a positive example of pursuing "continuous improvement" for the master's programs (which is NCATE's key goal). Disposition Committee members noted that the results of any assessment tool could be read in different ways. For instance, should the first tool's results between pre- and posttest reflect an *increase* in self-reported ratings (such as a level 2 during pretesting to a level 3 during posttesting)? If so, the Education Department could use these results to argue that candidates developed their professional dispositions after engaging in coursework and the practicum. Likewise, if the ratings *decreased*, the Education Department could argue that candidates became more self-aware throughout the course of their programs, discovering that they were not as ready as they thought they had been and feeling that they needed to continue working on developing their professional dispositions. The only trend that would be more difficult to explain is if the ratings remained the same, at which point the rubric likely would need to be modified; but even this outcome would qualify as a "continuous improvement" activity, thereby showing that our faculty members were using assessment outcomes to improve the program and increase candidate learning. In short, no matter what kind of data was secured through the use of a professional dispositions rubric, the Education Department could "spin" the results to reflect programs that are (a) running smoothly, involving the usual ongoing review/improvement processes, or (b) encountering some obstacles, indicating the need for more review, analysis, and revision of the rubric.

On the faculty side of this process, we must note the overwhelming exhaustion with which committee members approached this project. Within this context, the three faculty members who worked on revising the dispositions rubric did so in a way that attempted to balance the programs' focus on developing thoughtful, reflective practitioners with the need to integrate the new the InTASC standards (having worked with these standards to facilitate program improvement since 2009) into the assessment of candidates' professional dispositions.

Revising the Disposition Rubric

The disposition rubric, as well as a summary of the results of the pilot, was shared with the Education Department. Each of the issues that appeared in the previous section of this chapter (e.g., the strategizing of responses, responses made impossible by the lack of direct teaching experience, the contradiction of rating one's self on "humility," and the lack of clarity for certain statements) was presented and discussed. It is important to note that this same group—a group that accepted the original form without questions or comments—now readily saw the problems inherent in the disposition form following the pilot. Recommendations for improvement were both numerous and specific. Among the changes recommended was the addition of two blank lines below each statement in which respondents, after providing a self-rating of 1, 2, 3, or 4, were asked to "Provide an example." One might wonder why the flaws in the rubric (and the changes that seemed so obvious) were not seen as necessary when it was first presented months earlier. A possible response (revealing the fundamental flaw in the current reform initiatives at all levels, K–12 through higher education) is that "top-down" reforms, like the ones imposed by NCATE, disconnect the laborer from his/her labor. The initial lack of "buy-in" from the Education Department was a function of the "disconnect" between faculty and the accreditation process.

CONCLUDING THOUGHTS

In order to balance the contemporary obsession with accountability with the need for authenticity in education, we must attend to the development of critical reflection. A critically reflective approach will reveal the "continuous improvement" mandated by accrediting bodies like NCATE. The real issue here is *not* the measurement or assessment of dispositions. We see that task as a critically important component of the teacher education process. The problem, as described in this chapter, is the *mechanism* that the accreditation process mandates as the means to measure and assess dispositions—the rubric. Our concerns lie in three interrelated areas: First, the accreditation process forces teacher education programs to evaluate many qualitative concepts such as dispositions, as well as levels of student or employer satisfaction. Second, there is an expectation that these qualitative concepts, as well as an array of teacher education outcomes, can and should be *quantified*. And third, the go-to mechanism for measuring any of these dispositions, perceptions, and program outcomes is the rubric.

Despite the best efforts of all involved, we found that a rubric can never truly measure anything. It presents the *perception* of measurement but not the reality of it. A rubric can open a door that teacher educators and candidates can enter together to begin a dialogue; but the "data" collected through a rubric is not—and cannot—be an end in itself. The strength of the rubric is also its weakness: it is a surface-level tool. But, used intentionally, it can be a lever for continuous improvement. Teacher educators can use them to establish a dialogic relationship with preservice teachers by modeling rubric use as a critical, dynamic, *nonstandardized* endeavor.

Finally, our challenge as teacher educators is to avoid the temptation to use rubrics strategically; if we want our candidates to be critically reflective, we need to be critically reflective ourselves. If we allow rubrics to limit our imaginations, we abdicate our responsibility to shape the profession. Therefore, it is imperative for teacher educators to model the kinds of critically reflective practices that we hope to foster in teacher candidates. These include a commitment to assessment that is ongoing, multifaceted, and meaningful; an understanding of the need to develop and apply dispositions that support student learning without reverting to formulaic, restrictive pedagogies; and a dedication to the promotion of education as a means of transforming society in ways that are culturally sustaining, with explicit attention to equity and excellence.

NOTE

1. For example, in order to track whether or not a particular key assessment addresses NCATE Standard 4.a., both within and across program-based cohorts, rubrics become the go-to mechanism for "collecting data" from "candidate performances."

REFERENCES

Corcoran, P. B., Walker, K. E., & Wals, A. E. J. (2004, February). Case studies, make-your-case studies, and case stories: A critique of case-study methodology in sustainability in higher education. *Environmental Education Research, 10*(1), 7–21.
Drake, S., & Burns, R. (2004). *Meeting standards through integrated curriculum.* Alexandria, VA: Association for Supervision and Curriculum Development.

Helm, C. M. (2006). Teacher dispositions as predictors of good teaching. *The Clearing House, 76*, 117.

Hodkinson, P. (2005). Learning as cultural and relational: Moving past some troubling dualisms, *Cambridge Journal of Education, 35*(1), 107–119.

Huber-Warring, T., & Warring, D. F. (2006). Are you teaching for democracy? Developing dispositions, promoting democratic practice, and embracing social justice and diversity. *Action in Teacher Education, 28*(2), 38–52.

Jung, E., & Rhodes, D. (2008). Revisiting disposition assessment in teacher education: Broadening the focus. *Assessment and Evaluation in Higher Education,* 33(6), 647–660.

Katz, L. G., & Raths, J. D. (1985). Dispositions as goals for teacher education. *Teaching and Teacher Education, 1*(4), 301–307.

Katz, L. G., & Raths, J. D. (1986). *Dispositional goals for teacher education: Problems of identification and assessment.* Paper presented at the World Assembly of the International Council for Teaching. (ERIC Document Reproduction Service No. 272-470)

Lees, P. J. (2007). Beyond positivism: Embracing complexity for social and educational change. *English Teaching: Practice and Critique, 6*(3), 48–60.

National Council for Accreditation of Teacher Education (NCATE). (2008). *Professional standards for the accreditation of teacher education institutions.* Washington, DC: NCATE.

Petty, N. J., Thomson, O. P., & Stew, G. (2012). Ready for a paradigm shift? Part 2: Introducing qualitative research methodologies and methods. *Manual Therapy, 17*, 378–384. doi:10.1016/j.math.2012.03.004

Phelps, P. H. (2006). The dilemma of dispositions. *The Clearing House, 79*(4), 174–178.

Raths, J. (2001). Teachers' beliefs and teaching beliefs. *Early Childhood Research and Practice, 3*(1). Retrieved January 15, 2013, from http://ecrp.uiuc.edu/v3n1/raths.html

Ripski, M. B., LoCasale-Crouch, J., & Decker, L. (2011). Pre-service teachers: Dispositional traits, emotional states, and quality of teacher-student interactions. *Teacher Education Quarterly, 38*(2), 77–96.

Shulman, J. H. (2002). *Happy accidents: Cases as opportunities for teacher learning.* Paper presented at the annual meeting of the American Educational Research Association. New Orleans, LA.

Unluer, S. (2012). Being an insider researcher while conducting case study research. *The Qualitative Report, 17*(58), 1–14. Retrieved July 10, 2013, from http://www.nova.edu/ssss/QR/QR17/unluer.pdf

CHAPTER 10

COLLABORATION, RUBRICS, AND TEACHER EVALUATION

Susan Dreyer Leon and Laura Thomas

Does using a rubric-based teacher evaluation system like Charlotte Daniel-son's *Framework for Teaching* (2013) or Robert Marzano's Teacher Evaluation Model (2013) improve teaching or student learning? This straightforward question turns out to have a pretty complicated answer, rooted in the lack of quality data linking teacher evaluation systems to either teacher improvement or student success (Murphy, Hallinger, & Heck, 2013). In this chapter, we will illustrate that rubric-based systems do show promise if they are well implemented as part of a broader professional development and collaboration initiative with sufficient funding, training, and time. Unfortunately, our analysis also reveals that the factors that increase the potential for successful implementation of these rubric-based systems are frequently absent in U.S. schools and even less likely to be present in schools that serve poor, African American, or Latino students. We are also concerned that data derived from substandard implementation of these evaluation systems can and are being inappropriately used as a high-stakes public assessment for teachers and are being linked to teacher ratings, compensation, and dismissal.

Rubric Nation, pages 149–166
Copyright © 2015 by Information Age Publishing
All rights of reproduction in any form reserved.

The Teacher Quality Movement

Before we look at these evaluation systems in more detail, we need to explore something about the recent history of what has come to be known as the "Teacher Quality" movement. With the passage in 2001 of the No Child Left Behind Act (NCLB, 2002), policymakers focused on the basic foundations of teacher preparation by requiring schools to document the extent to which their teachers were "highly qualified," which has meant documenting that they have appropriate training and credentials for the subjects they teach (NCLB, 2002). This was an important first step in trying to guarantee all students access to good teachers, especially in chronically underperforming and underfunded schools serving poor students and students of color. In her book, *The Flat World and Education* (2010), Stanford University professor and teacher education expert Linda Darling-Hammond reports, "By every measure of qualification—certification, subject-matter background, pedagogical training, selectivity of college attended, test scores, or experience—less qualified teachers are found in schools serving greater numbers of low-income and minority students" (p. 43). Lest anyone doubt the significance of these preparation factors, Darling-Hammond goes on to illustrate the magnitude of the impact, saying,

> While each of these traits made teachers more effective, the combined influence of having a teacher with most of these qualifications as compared to having few of them was larger than the effects of race and parent education combined ... the achievement gap would be much reduced if low-income minority students were routinely assigned such highly qualified teachers rather than those they most often encounter. (pp. 43–44)

If the quality of the teacher in the classroom is among the most important variables in student success (Darling-Hammond, Bransford, LePage, Hammerness, & Duffy, 2007), then being able to describe and measure effective teaching suddenly takes center stage in educational reform. President Barack Obama defines the current policy direction:

> If a teacher is given a chance or two chances or three chances but still does not improve, there is no excuse for that person to continue teaching. I reject a system that rewards failure and protects a person from its consequences. The stakes are too high. We can afford nothing but the best when it comes to our children's teachers and the schools where they teach (as cited in Weisberg, Sexton, Mulhern, & Keeling, 2009, p. 3).

In this case, effective teaching is defined by measurable growth in student learning. This might seem obvious, but it has not historically been the benchmark for teacher evaluation. It has long been argued that the tasks of teaching are too complex to measure well and that so many factors influence a student's ability to learn that we cannot isolate and measure the impact of an individual teacher (Coggshall, Ott, & Lasagna, 2010, p. 19). This perspective is radically and rapidly changing, and student learning has moved to the center of teacher evaluation (Bill & Melinda Gates Foundation, 2013). With the advent of *Race to the Top*, the signature piece of educational policy to come from the Obama White House, high-stakes teacher evaluation has been catapulted to the top of the education agenda in every participating state and the fast-moving, highly publicized changes to teacher hiring, evaluation, and dismissal systems have the attention of everyone in the field.

The *Race to the Top Executive Summary* (U.S. Department of Education, 2009) includes explicit criteria related to placing effective teachers and leaders in "high poverty and/or high minority schools" (p. 9), which begins to address the equity issues raised by Darling-Hammond, but it also goes much further in requiring participating states to find new ways to evaluate and reward teacher effectiveness, which include

- Design and implement rigorous, transparent, and fair evaluation systems for teachers and principals that differentiate effectiveness using multiple rating categories that take into account data on student growth as a significant factor, and are designed and developed with teacher and principal involvement;
- Conduct annual evaluations of teachers and principals that include timely and constructive feedback; as part of such evaluations, provide teachers and principals with data on student growth for their students, classes, and schools;
- Use these evaluations at a minimum, to inform decisions regarding developing teachers and principals, including by providing relevant coaching, induction support, and/or professional development;
- Compensating, promoting, and retaining teachers and principals, including by providing opportunities for highly effective teachers and principals to obtain additional compensation and be given additional responsibilities;
- Whether to grant tenure and/or full certification to teachers and principals using rigorous standards and streamlined, transparent, and fair procedures; and removing ineffective tenured and untenured teachers and principals after they have had ample opportunities to improve, and ensuring that such decisions are made using rigorous standards and streamlined, transparent, and fair procedures. (U.S. Department of Education, 2009, p. 9)

Although fewer than half of states have been awarded *Race to the Top* funds, the use of student testing data as part of teacher evaluation has also been made a requirement for the 45 states seeking "flexibility" in the implementation of the *Elementary and Secondary Education Act* (U.S. Department of Education, 2014). This flexibility is highly desirable for states because the ESEA, popularly known as *No Child Left Behind*, says that as of 2014 all students in all schools must be proficient in reading and math as measured by the states' standardized testing systems. All parties recognize that this goal is functionally unattainable in the vast majority of schools, hence the flexibility program. Without the so-called "waivers," all states would have to designate virtually all of their schools as failing and then begin implementing of a set of onerous and expensive interventions. Since states do not want to do that, they are accepting the teacher evaluation conditions attached to the waiver, at least in theory. In practice, the requirements have sent states scrambling to find valid and reliable measures of teacher effectiveness they can implement quickly, despite push back from local leaders, districts, teachers unions, and state legislatures. We will discuss the politics of this in more detail further below, but first let us look at the elements of the evaluation systems that are being implemented by many states.

The Changing Nature of Teacher Evaluation

The high-stakes nature of new teacher assessments has raised a host of extremely important questions in teacher evaluation. Can effective teaching be validly and reliably measured? How do we do that? What does it mean to provide "timely and constructive feedback?" What data sources do we use to show impact on student learning? Are there any existing teacher evaluation systems that can be universally applied to satisfy the requirements of *Race to the Top*, and what resources do states need to implement those systems as quickly as possible?

Teacher evaluation has long been identified as a systemic weakness in U.S. schools. In a 2009 report entitled "The Widget Effect: Our National Failure to Acknowledge and Act on Differences in Teacher Effectiveness" (Weisburg et al., 2009), the authors present research to support their fundamental indictment of the state of teacher evaluation in the United States. They summarize the problem this way,

> The failure of evaluation systems to provide accurate and credible information about individual teacher's instructional performance sustains and reinforces a phenomenon that we have come to call the Widget Effect. The Widget Effect describes the tendency of school districts to assume classroom effectiveness is the same from teacher to teacher. This decades-old fallacy fosters an environment in which teachers cease to be understood as individual

professionals, but rather as interchangeable parts. In its denial of individual strengths and weaknesses, it is deeply disrespectful to teachers; in its indifference to instructional effectiveness, it gambles with the lives of students. (p. 4)

They go on to summarize what the data show about the elements that need to be included in a high quality teacher evaluation system. They say that teachers' ratings need to be

based on their ability to fulfill their core responsibility as professionals—delivering instruction that helps students learn and succeed. This demands clear performance standards, multiple rating options, regular monitoring of administrator judgments, and frequent feedback to teachers. Furthermore, it requires professional development that is tightly linked to performance standards and differentiated based on individual teacher needs. The core purpose of evaluation must be maximizing teacher growth and effectiveness, not just documenting poor performance as a prelude to dismissal. (p. 5)

The idea of "multiple rating options" is a key reason for the rise of rubrics in teacher evaluation. In many traditional systems, teachers were simply rated as satisfactory or unsatisfactory. This pass/fail approach tends to make administrators less likely to assign a high-stakes "U" rating, especially to teachers who are not great, but certainly not the worst. This gives rise to the phenomenon where 98% of teachers in the United States are rated as satisfactory. In addition, the ratings give teachers almost no information on their own performance, how to improve, or in what areas. This is information that 85% of teachers surveyed say they would like to have (Gates & Gates, 2011).

In a 2012 *Phi Delta Kappan* opinion piece entitled "Evaluating Teacher Evaluation," Darling-Hammond, Amrein-Beardsley, Haertel, and Rothstein also call for standards-based evaluation practices, and in particular recognize that

standards-based evaluation processes have also been found to be predictive of student learning gains and productive for teacher learning.... Effective systems have developed an integrated set of measures that show what teachers do and what happens as a result. These measures may include evidence of student work and learning, as well as evidence of teacher practices derived from observations, videotapes, artifacts, and even student surveys.

These tools are most effective when embedded in systems that support evaluation expertise and well-grounded decisions, by ensuring that evaluators are trained, evaluation and feedback are frequent, mentoring and professional development are available, and processes are in place to support due process and timely decision making by an appropriate body.

We can see from the above that the field has begun to coalesce around some key elements of high quality teacher evaluation, including that it be standards based, performance based, and embedded in a high quality, collaborative, professional learning environment. Good evaluation requires trained evaluators, a culture of ongoing, frequent feedback, and a connection to professional development and teacher career ladders.

In *The Flat World and Education* (2010), Darling-Hammond notes that support for quality teaching in the United States looks like "swiss cheese" (p. 194) She admits that in some states the holes are smaller, but "in no case is there a fully developed system of instructional support even remotely comparable to that in high-achieving nations...and of course...the system is weakest in the communities where students' needs are greatest" (p. 194). Darling-Hammond goes on to point out that "no other country in the world goes about training, supporting and evaluating its teaching force in such an individualistic and haphazard manner" (p. 194). We are making some progress in terms of defining teaching standards, but adoption and implementation of both teaching standards and teacher evaluation systems still varies by state and often by district.

In 1987, as a partial response to *A Nation at Risk* (1983), the Council of Chief State School Officers (CCSSO) launched the Interstate Teacher Assessment and Support Consortium (InTASC). The CCSSO worked with the Carnegie Foundation's newly formed National Board for Professional Teaching Standards, the American Association for Colleges of Teacher Education, and both the National Education Association and the American Federation of Teachers, among many others, to develop a set of standards that could inform states in their work to improve teacher performance and evaluation. The group issued its first set of teaching standards for teacher practice in 1992 and has been updating and revising these ever since (Hunt & Lasley, 2010). The latest InTASC Model Core Teacher Standards were released in 2011. The 10 standards prioritize the new emphasis on teacher effectiveness and include both personalized learning for students and teacher collaboration (CCSSO, 2011). Each standard includes performance indicators, essential knowledge, and critical dispositions that help to define the standard in detail.

Many states have based their evaluation systems at least in part on the InTASC standards, and most commercial teacher evaluation models, like Danielson or Marzano, make a point to present some documentation that "cross-walks" their standards with InTASC standards to demonstrate how well the systems align. Some states offer their school districts a choice of accepted models, and the decision about which to use is made at the district level. Other states require specific systems or system elements that all districts must use in common. The data on the effectiveness of these new systems is perforce uneven as all players wrestle simultaneously with new standards, new tools, and new levels of oversight and accountability (Saw-chuk, 2013). A great deal of time and money, both public and private, is being poured into finding out which systems work best and what we need to support those systems; meanwhile, states have to take action immediately. Some states, like New York, have started by quickly tracking and publicizing teacher evaluation data for individual teachers and mandating the use of evaluation models like the Danielson *Framework for Teaching* (2013), which are already developed, have some evidence of being effective, and can be implemented now, off the shelf.

Value-Added Modeling

Because *Race to the Top* requires multiple measures of teacher effective-ness, including observations and evidence of student learning, many states and school districts are requiring a mixture of evaluation systems, since no one existing system includes all the required elements. One of the first systems out of the gate—"value-added modeling" or VAM—has garnered a lot of attention from the press, teachers, policymakers, and researchers. VAM uses statistical methods to try to capture the impact that an individual teacher has on the standardized test scores of their students in a given year. So far, the data do not support VAM as either a valid or reliable method for teacher evaluation (Amrein-Beardsley, 2008; Koedel & Betts, 2007; RAND, 2004). Standardized tests of student learning have not been designed to capture teacher effectiveness, so when they are used that way, the data that they produce has to be massaged to account for things like prior academic level, socioeconomic factors, and so on (Santos & Gebeloff, 2012). The sta-tistical means for doing this work have not yet been rigorously tested, and the results have not been correlated against other, better-known methods for teacher evaluation (Hill, Kapitula, & Umland, 2011). In effect, we do not actually know if the VAM data are accurate on any level. A 2010 study from the National Center for Analysis of Longitudinal Data in Educational Research concludes,

> Given the problems with the assumptions underlying commonly estimated value-added models, caution in using value-added measures of teacher pro-ductivity for high-stakes decisions would be advised, but it is still conceivable (and indeed the Rockoff et al. study already suggests) that there may be ways to use the information in conjunction with other measures to increase teach-er productivity. (Harris, Sass, & Semykina, 2010, p. 36)

As value-added modeling gets better and more sophisticated, it may be-come a more reliable way to gauge teacher effectiveness, but right now, it remains problematic. However, this academic skepticism is not stopping states from currently using VAM in high-stakes teacher evaluation because if they are part of *Race to the Top* or if they have received a *No Child Left Behind* waiver from the federal government, they are required to use at least some testing data in teacher evaluation. This has come to a head most recently in the state of Washington, where the legislature has refused to approve using student standardized test performance data in teacher evaluation. As a result, the U.S. Department of Education has revoked the state's *No Child Left Behind* waiver (Klein, 2014). Similar battles are looming in other states as they begin to challenge the validity and reliability of VAM methods and the right of the federal government to impose teacher evaluation systems on the states.

Performance-Based Teacher Evaluation

Evaluation systems that assess the long list of attributes of effective teaching described by the InTASC standards (2011) and other models like Danielson (2013) and Marzano (2013), are called "standards-based" and "performance-based" evaluation models. All of these systems use rubrics, because, as Robert Marzano argues, rubrics are the most effective way to describe a teacher's progress along the continuum of performance described by a given standard (Marzano, 2012). The rubric is the tool used to measure the degree to which a given teacher behavior accords with what we know about best practices in the field. The more specific the rubric is, the more precise feedback can be for teachers (Marzano, 2012). Rubric-based systems like Danielson (2013) or Marzano's (2013) are often embedded as the tool or instrument inside other evaluation practices. This means their implementation can look quite different across settings depending on how they are used. Rubrics can be used by teachers for self-evaluation, by peers, by administrators, and by outside evaluators. Rubrics can be used for observations only or along with portfolios, teacher artifacts, student surveys, and other measures of student learning to create a robust portrait of teacher activity. Other features of teacher evaluation systems specify how often evaluation occurs, how the evaluation is used, and who gets the data. Most school districts put together their own evaluation systems, which include required elements from their state departments of education, negotiated elements with their teachers' associations, and the preferences of their principals and superintendents.

In a review of state education department websites, we found that viewers are often given Internet links to the Danielson Group website, Marzano's website, and the InTASC standards. Many states also have their own teaching standards, which are likewise almost always aligned to InTASC. One intention here may be to provide district-level decision makers with as much information as possible about the available approved systems for evaluation in their state. Generally the documents on these websites that give standards, domains, and the rubrics to evaluate them are many pages long and provide significant detail about the contents of the evaluation systems and the rubrics being used to assess them. It is impossible in a chapter of this size to capture all of this information succinctly, but we strongly suggest that readers spend a little time browsing some state websites. In particular, it is helpful to view their recommended links to Web information on approved teacher evaluations systems, where readers can gain a more thorough understanding of exactly what these evaluation systems are attempting to measure and how they propose to do it.

Both the Danielson *Framework for Teaching* (2013) and Marzano's *Teacher Evaluation Model* (2013) "systematically describe various components of research-based effective classroom practices" (Mielke & Frontier, 2012). Marzano (2013) uses a set of 10 rubrics, with exemplars of practice, and Danielson (2013) has four domains (with 22 components and 76 subdomains). Both systems have the goal of capturing, as fully as possible, all the complexity of a teacher's work and giving teachers and administrators a common language to talk together about teacher effectiveness. The rubrics used in these two systems are somewhat different, but they have common elements. Danielson uses the categories *Unsatisfactory, Basic, Proficient,* and *Distinguished*; and Marzano employs *Not Using, Beginning, Developing, Applying,*and *Innovating.* Both systems include detailed descriptions of the domain of practice and specific exemplars of what practice looks like at each level of performance.

Because our space here is limited and because the *Framework for Teaching* (2013) is more widely used than Marzano's (2013) system and has a "small but consistently positive" correlation between its ratings and student learning (Bill & Melinda Gates Foundation, 2010), we are going to dig into the data and controversy surrounding Danielson's model as it is being implemented in some states in the *Race to the Top* era. We believe that what follows is a fair description of the potential benefits and pitfalls of most similar rubric-based teacher evaluation systems. As a starting point, it is worthwhile to get a good look at one of the specific "elements" within one of the domains of the *Framework for Teaching* to illustrate the degree of specificity that the system entails. We strongly recommend that our readers access *The Framework for Teaching* online and review at least one domain all the way down to the "element" level in order to see the degree of specificity involved in the design of this evaluation system. Marzano (2013) argues that this level of specificity is a key characteristic of a system that encourages improved teacher effectiveness rather than just evaluating teacher performance.

It is fair to ask the question, what are educators supposed to do with a teacher development tool of this size and scope? What is the most effective way to introduce and approach the task? In a 2013 interview (Griffin, 2013), Danielson talks about her vision,

> Ideally, districts could take a year and talk about the framework as a tool to improve instruction before using it as an evaluation tool. Districts and state efforts that are successful include pilot projects to allow people sufficient time to gain a deep understanding of the framework and what good teaching looks like. (p. 29)

During this introductory period, the Danielson Group (2010) identified four key processes that need to happen at the school site. Teachers and administrators need to *get familiar with the four domains* and their 22 component parts. This includes *learning how to identify and collect evidence for the domains.* Two of these domains, Classroom Environment and Instruction, are primarily based on classroom observation, and the other two, planning and preparation and professional responsibilities, require the collection and assessment of a variety of teacher artifacts like lesson plans, letters to families, student work, and so on. Classroom *observers need training* in both what to look for and how to have effective conversations with teachers about what they see. Next, everyone has to learn how to *compare the evidence to the rubric accurately* and "calibrate their judgments against those of their colleagues" (Danielson, 2010, p. 39) so that at the end of this exploration year, there is broad agreement about what unsatisfactory, basic, proficient, and distinguished work looks like in and out of the classroom (Danielson, 2010).

We believe that the greatest benefit of all rubric-based evaluation systems is in the quality and depth of school-level, standards-based community conversations about effective teaching and learning. To make these conversations and the evaluation systems effective, we argue that schools need strong leadership, time for collaboration, and money to support high quality training. Our concern is that schools are not—and will not be—getting this support, and furthermore, that the schools that serve the most at-risk students will get even less of this support than their neighbors in more affluent areas.

The Critical Importance of Leadership

School leaders play an incredibly pivotal roll in the potential effectiveness of a rubric-based evaluation system. Danielson herself feels so strongly about this that in 2009, she published the book *Talk About Teaching: Leading Professional Conversations* (Danielson, 2009). The book is a guide for school leaders on how to facilitate these key conversations in their schools. Making sure leaders have the level of training and capacity necessary to properly manage a rubric-based system is a critical factor in implementation success.

Quality leadership is also a major implementation concern. Danielson says, "My experience is many principals still don't understand what instructional leadership means or how to do it" (as cited in Griffin, 2013, p. 30). The best-researched definition of instructional leadership (Leithwood, Seashore-Louis, Anderson, & Wahlstrom, 2004) includes a leader's ability to define the school's mission, manage the instructional program, and promote a positive learning climate (Leithwood et al., 2004, p. 66). In 2011, a large-scale Chicago study (Sartain, Stoelinga, & Brown, 2011) of the implementation of the *Framework for Teaching* included two areas where leadership issues came to the fore. The first was whether teachers found principals to be credible instructional leaders, and the second was the principals' personal capacity to lead the conversations around teaching and learning that the rubrics require (Sartain et al., 2011). The study also captured principals' own perspectives on implementing the *Framework for Teaching*. In general, principals thought it was a significant improvement over the checklist system they had been using, but they also reported emerging professional development needs of their own, including wanting more training in the following areas:

- How to have honest, reflective conversations with teachers about their practice
- How to use the Framework data to guide professional development decisions
- How to have difficult conversations with teachers who are underperforming
- How to talk to teachers about the new system and the impetus for replacing the checklist
- How to schedule observations, as well as pre-and postconferences (Sartain et al., 2011, p. 37)

Leadership for teacher evaluation is also a major equity issue because failing schools, which we have seen disproportionately serve poor and non-White students, also tend to have the weakest leadership (Loeb, Kalogrides, & Horng, 2010), so in the very environment in which teachers have the greatest need for instructional improvement, they are least likely to have access to one of the key factors for successful implementation of a rubric-based evaluation system.

Rush to Implement Without Time and Training

School budgets have been hard hit by the economic downturn of 2008 and the federal budget sequester (Leachman & Mai, 2014), and time for teacher collaboration is shrinking (Darling-Hammond, 2013). With these two factors as a backdrop, we worry that the *Framework for Teaching* is being improperly implemented in many settings and that the quality of the data gathered will be compromised. Even more importantly, in our view, the real support for effective teaching will be severely reduced. Our perspective is bolstered by a 2013 General Accounting Office report that found

> officials in most RTT states cited challenges related to developing and using evaluation measures, addressing teacher concerns, and building capacity and sustainability. State and district officials also discussed capacity challenges, such as too few staff or limited staff expertise and prioritizing evaluation reform amid multiple educational initiatives. (GAO, 2013)

Anecdotal reports found in local media, teacher blogs, and union papers are equally disturbing. In New York State, where the *Framework for Teaching* is being required as the primary teacher evaluation tool, the time frame from adoption to high-stakes implementation was a scant 2 months (and in the summer at that). Teachers were provided a total of 6 hours of professional development on the use of the model (Singer, 2013). During a recent listening tour, a member of New York's governing Board of Regents, Harry Phillips, described Danielson's framework as "impossible" (Gibney, 2013). On the blog *The Assailed Teacher* (2013), the anonymous author gives her perspective on what implementation of the *Framework for Teaching* looks like in her school.

> Our administrators will come in, observe us and literally check off which parts of Danielson they saw in our lesson. For those areas that are either unobservable in a classroom . . . or that the administrator has yet to check off, we can submit up to 8 "artifacts" a year to our administrators. . . . Based upon those artifacts, our administrator might check off more Danielson boxes on our evaluation, or they might not check off any. (para. 11)

> It is not a journey of professional self-discovery for teachers and administrators. It is a highly pressurized atmosphere which is causing teachers to do things they would not otherwise do mostly for the purpose of getting a few tick marks checked off so they do not end up getting fired. (para. 18)

Although this may be a worst-case scenario or a case of reporter bias, the conversion of the *Framework for Teaching* to a checklist is one of the great risks of rubric-based evaluation systems. What makes this so frustrating is that the choice of Danielson in the first place validates the idea that teacher evaluation should be a tool for teacher improvement, which the *Framework for Teaching* has shown it can do (Bill and Melinda Gates Foundation, 2010). But in rushing the implementation and reducing the *Framework* to a checklist, most of its capacity to improve teacher effectiveness is being lost. We also worry that poor implementation, like what is described above, is more likely to occur in schools that are already the least functional because they lack organizational integrity, strong professional community, and high quality teachers and leaders who can help guide and shape the implementation process.

Professional Learning Communities and Teacher Evaluation

The rough start for the *Framework for Teaching* in New York does not leave us completely depressed about the possibility of success for rubric-based teacher evaluation systems. However, we must be explicit about what will be required to make implementation of these systems actually function to improve instruction, increase student learning, and help administrators make good decisions about promotion and dismissal. Milbrey McLaughlin and her colleague R. Scott Pfiefer identified key elements of successful teacher evaluation systems back in 1986. They said that

> A meaningful evaluation effort requires at a minimum a hospitable institutional setting. Our research joins that of organization theorists (e.g., March and Olsen, 1976; Kerr and Solcum, 1981; Etzioni, 1975; Argyris, 1982) to suggest that the responses of teachers and administrators to a teacher evaluation plan depend firstly not on the teacher evaluation instrument, but on the extent to which a district's organizational environment exhibits:
>
> * mutual trust between teachers and administrators
> * open channels of communication
> * commitment to individual and institutional learning
> * viability of evaluation activities and associated learning efforts
>
> These four factors comprise the organizational enabling conditions that play a significant role in determining the extent to which choices about design or instrumentation can make a difference to the success of a teacher evaluation effort. (p. 3)

Although these words were written nearly 30 years ago, the finding still represents the most significant challenge that schools and districts face when implementing any teacher evaluation system. The success or failure of that system is based first and foremost not on the evaluation technique but on the quality of the professional climate into which it is introduced.

We've already talked about the leadership issue above. Another big problem with many school cultures is the degree to which teachers and administrators still work in isolation. This too is a historic failing of the American educational system. The Change Leadership group at Harvard (Wagner & Kegan, 2006.) describes the problem this way:

> Isolation of adults at all levels in the education system actively discourages
> their learning and capacity to improve their practice. Indeed, virtually every
> other profession in modern life has transitioned to various forms of team-
> work, yet most educators still work alone so that when teachers work in isola-
> tion good teaching exists as random acts of excellence in the system and there
> is little dissemination of best practice. (p. 72)

The implementation of a rubric-based system like the *Framework for Teaching* could be an outstanding catalyst for a reimagining of the nature of
teacher's work and professional collaboration across all levels of the school
or even within a district. In fact, this process has been going on for some
time in many school reform submovements around the country. Hundreds
of school districts have participated in professional development around
the creation of professional learning communities through the trainings
offered by Richard and Rebecca Dufour (Solution Tree, 2014) or the Critical Friends Group training, which is provided by universities, colleges,
nonprofit professional development service providers, School Reform Initiative, the National School Reform Faculty, and numerous independent
education consultants (SRI, 2014). Teachers and administrators in the most
successful schools have been quietly engaged in a collaboration revolution
for several decades, and not all of these schools are in wealthy communities.
Data on high performing, high poverty schools show that the level of collaboration and communication among adults in the schools is a key common element in their success (Shannon & Bylsma, 2007).

The data about the connection between professional learning communities, teacher effectiveness, and improved student learning are very convincing (Bryk, Sebring, Allensworth, Luppescu, & Easton, 2010; Vescio, Ross, &
Adams, 2008). The results of a recent large-scale school effectiveness study
in Chicago are illustrative of the point:

> When examining professional capacity in the school, we found that the indi-
> vidual qualifications of teachers were not nearly as important as the ways in
> which teachers worked together. When tied to strong instructional practices,
> the extent to which teachers took collective responsibility for the school and
> formed a professional community were the most important elements for in-
> creasing learning gains.
>
> Schools with strong collaboration were more effective as a whole than schools
> with strong individuals but little collaboration. (Allensworth, 2012, pp. 30–31)

We also have rigorous research to help identify which key features of professional community are linked to improved student and teacher performance. These include shared norms and values, a focus on student learning, deprivatized practice, reflective dialogue, and collaboration (Kruse,
Louis, & Bryk, 1995).

In our view, too much of the current dialogue and research agenda about teacher quality and evaluation in the *Race to the Top* era are ignoring the data on professional learning communities and instead choosing to focus on the improvement of individual teachers. We are concerned that the implementation of any rubric-based teacher development and evaluation system cannot reach its full potential without a corresponding commitment to a reasonable time frame for implementation, highly qualified and specifically trained instructional leadership to guide the process, and the development of a high quality professional learning community in which to embed, support, and sustain the work of teacher improvement.

REFERENCES

Allensworth, E. (2012, Fall) Want to improve teaching? Create collaborative, supportive schools. *American Educator, 36*(3), 30–31

Amrein-Beardsley, A. (2008) Methodological concerns about the education value-added assessment system, *Educational Researcher, 37*(2), 65–75.

Assailed Teacher. (2013, September 13). *How the Race to the Top evaluations look so far in NYC.* [Blog post]. Retrieved from http://theassailedteacher.com/tag/danielson

Bill & Melinda Gates Foundation. (2010, October). Danielson's framework for teaching for classroom observations. *MET project.* Retrieved from http://met-project.org/resources/Danielson%20FFT_10_29_10.pdf

Bill & Melinda Gates Foundation. (2013). Ensuring fair and reliable measures of effective teaching. *MET project.* Retrieved from http://metproject.org/downloads/MET_Ensuring_Fair_and_Reliable_Measures_Practitioner_Brief.pdf

Bryk, A. S., Sebring, P. B., Allensworth, E., Luppescu, S., & Easton, J. Q. (2013). *Organizing schools for improvement: Lessons from Chicago.* Chicago, IL: University Of Chicago Press.

Coggshall, J. G., Ott, A., & Lasagna, M. (2010). Retraining teacher talent: Convergence and contradictions in teachers' perceptions of policy reform ideas. *Learning Point Association.* Retrieved from http://www.learningpt.org/expertise/educatorquality/genY/Convergence_Contradiction.pdf

Council of Chief State School Officers (CCSSO). (2011, April). *InTASC model core teaching standards: A resource for state dialogue.* Washington, DC: Council of Chief State School Officers.

Danielson, C. (2009). *Talk about teaching! Leading professional conversations.* Thousand Oaks, CA: Corwin/National Staff Development Council.

Danielson, C. (2010). Evaluations that help teachers learn. *Educational Leadership, 68*(4), 35–39.

Danielson, C. (2013). The framework for teaching: Evaluation instrument (2013). Princeton, NJ: *Danielson Group.* Retrieved from http://danielsongroup.org/framework

Darling-Hammond, L. (2010). *The flat world and education: How America's commitment to equity will determine our future.* New York, NY: Teachers College Press.

Darling-Hammond, L. (2013, April 11). What teachers need and reformers ignore: Time to collaborate. *The Answer Sheet.* Retrieved from http://www.washingtonpost.com/blogs/answer-sheet/wp/2013/04/11/what-teachers-need-and-reformers-ignore-time-to-collaborate/

Darling-Hammond, L., Bransford, J., LePage, P., Hammerness, K., & Duffy, H. (2007). *Preparing teachers for a changing world: What teachers should learn and be able to do.* San Francisco, CA: Jossey-Bass.

Darling-Hammond, L., Amrein-Beardsley, A., Haertel, E., & Rothstein, J. (2012, February 29). Evaluating teacher evaluation. *Education Week.* Retrieved from http://www.edweek.org/ew/articles/2012/03/01/kappan_hammond.html

Gates, B., & Gates, M. (2011) Grading the teachers. *The Wall Street Journal.* Retrieved from http://online.wsj.com/news/articles/SB10001424052970204485304576641123767006518

General Accounting Office (GAO). (2013, September 18). *Race to the Top: States implementing teacher and principal evaluation systems despite challenges.* Retrieved from http://www.gao.gov/products/gao-13-777

Gibney, J. (2013, December 3). Regents Phillips calls for civil disobedience! *Hudson Valley United.* Retrieved from http://hudsonvalleyunited.org/regents-phillips-calls-for-civil-disobedience/

Griffin, L. (2013, January). Charlotte Danielson on teacher evaluation and quality. *School Administrator, 70*(1), 27–31. Retrieved from http://aasa.org/content.aspx?id=26268

Harris, D., Sass, T., & Semykina, A. (2010). *Value-added models and the measurement of teacher productivity.* Washington, DC: Urban Institute.

Hill, H. C., Kapitula, L., & Umland, K. (2011). A validity argument approach to evaluating teacher value-added scores. *American Educational Research Journal, 48*, 794–831.

Hunt, T. C., & Lasley T. J., II (2010). *Encyclopedia of educational reform and dissent.* Thousand Oaks, CA: Sage.

Klein, A. (2014, April 30). NCLB waiver loss puts Washington State on uncertain ground. *Education Week.* Retrieved from http://www.edweek.org/ew/articles/2014/04/30/30washington.h33.html

Koedel, C., & Betts, J. R. (2011). Does student sorting invalidate value-added models of teacher effectiveness? An extended analysis of the Rothstein critique. *Education Finance and Policy, 6*(1), 18–42.

Kruse, S. D., Louis, K. S., & Bryk, A. S. (1995). An emerging framework for analyzing school-based professional community. In K. S. Louis & S. D. Kruse (Eds.), *Professionalism and community: Perspectives from urban schools.* Thousand Oaks, CA: Corwin.

Leachman, M, & Mai, C. (2014, May 20). Most states funding schools less than before the recession. *Center on Budget and Policy Priorities.* Retrieved from http://www.cbpp.org/cms/?fa=view&id=4011

Liethwood, K., Seashore-Louis, K. S., Anderson, S., & Wahlstrom, K. (2004). Review of research: How leadership influences student learning. *Wallace Foundation.* Retrieved from http://www.wallacefoundation.org/knowledge-center/school-leadership/key-research/Documents/How-Leadership-influences-Student-Learning.pdf

Loeb, S., Kalogrides, D., & Horng, E. L. (2010). Principal preferences and the uneven distribution of principals across schools. *Educational Evaluation and Policy Analysis, 32*(2), 205–229.

Marzano, R. (2012, November). The two purposes of teacher evaluation. *Educational Leadership, 70*(3), 14–19. Retrieved from http://www.ascd.org/publications/educational-leadership/nov12/vol70/num03/The-Two-Purposes-of-Teacher-Evaluation.aspx

McLaughlin, M. W., & Pfeifer, R. S. (1986). Teacher evaluation: Learning for improvement and accountability. *National Institute of Education*, SEPI-86-5, 253.

Mielke, P., & Frontier, T. (2012, November). Keeping improvement in mind. *Educational Leadership, 70*, 10–13.

Murphy, J., Hallinger, P., & Heck, R. H. (2013). Leading via teacher evaluation: The case of the missing clothes? *Educational Researcher, 42*(6), 349–354. doi:10.3102/0013189X13499625

National Commission on Excellence in Education. (1983). *A nation at risk: The imperative for educational reform: A report to the Nation and the Secretary of Education, United States Department of Education.* Washington, D.C.: The Commission.

No Child Left Behind Act of 2001, Pub. L. No. 107-110, § 115

RAND Education Research Brief. (2004) *The promise and peril of using value-added modeling to measure teacher effectiveness.* Retrieved from http://www.rand.org/pubs/research_briefs/RB9050/RAND_RB9050.pdf

Santos, F., & Gebeloff, R. (2012, February 24). Teacher quality widely diffused, ratings indicate. *The New York Times.*

Sartain, L., Stoelinga, S. R., & Brown, E. R. (2011). *Rethinking teacher evaluation in Chicago: Lessons learned from classroom observations, principal-teacher conferences, and district implementation.* Research Report, Consortium on Chicago School Research, University of Chicago Urban Education Institute.

Sawchuk, S. (2013, February 5). Teachers' ratings still high despite new measures. *Education Week, 32*(10), 1, 18–19.

School Reform Initiative (SRI). (2014). Retrieved from http://www.schoolreforminitiative.org

Singer, A. (2013, June 10). Who is Charlotte Danielson and why does she decide how teachers are evaluated? *Huffington Post.* Retrieved from http://www.huffingtonpost.com/alan-singer/who-is-charlotte-danielso_b_3415034.html

Shannon, G. S., & Bylsma, P. (2007). *Nine characteristics of high-performing schools: A research-based resource for schools and districts to assist with improving student learning.* Olympia: Washington Office of Superintendent of Public Instruction.

Solution Tree. (2014). PLC Locator [Map]. *All Things PLC.* Retrieved from http://www.allthingsplc.info/plc-locator/us

U.S. Department of Education. (2009). *Race to the Top program executive summary.* Retrieved from http://www2.ed.gov/programs/racetothetop/executive-summary.pdf

U.S. Department of Education (2014). *ESEA flexibility.* Retrieved from http://www2.ed.gov/policy/elsec/guid/esea-flexibility/index.html

Vescio, V., Ross, D., & Adams, A. (2008). A review of research on the impact of professional learning communities on teaching practice and student learning. *Teaching and Teacher Education, 24*(1), 80–91.

Wagner, T., & Kegan, R. (2006). *Change leadership: A practical guide to transforming our schools.* San Francisco, CA: Jossey-Bass.

Weisberg, D., Sexton, S., Mulhern, J., & Keeling, D. (2009, June 8). The Widget Effect: Our national failure to acknowledge and act on differences in teacher effectiveness. *TNTP.* Retrieved from http://widgeteffect.org/downloads/TheWidgetEffect.pdf

CHAPTER 11

GETTING TEACHER-EVALUATION RUBRICS RIGHT

Kim Marshall

When I was first introduced to the idea of rubrics in a summer workshop with Grant Wiggins in the mid-1990s, the idea was immediately appealing: what a good way to get a handle on the perennially difficult task of evaluating students' written work. I was a principal of a large elementary school in Boston, and that fall we created grade-by-grade rubrics with three domains: Mechanics and Usage, Content and Organization, and Style and Voice. This was an extraordinarily helpful exercise, forcing us to make clear what writing looked like at four different levels of proficiency. For several years, we used the rubrics to evaluate students on a quarterly basis and inform and improve instruction.

I didn't become aware of teacher-evaluation rubrics until several years later. Charlotte Danielson published her *Framework for Teaching* in 1996, but a committee to revamp Boston's teacher-evaluation process, on which I served, did not adopt her work; we were still wedded to the narrative evaluation model with a two-point evaluation scale—Satisfactory and Unsatisfactory. We did create a list of desirable teacher attributes in each

Rubric Nation, pages 167–184
Copyright © 2015 by Information Age Publishing
All rights of reproduction in any form reserved.

domain, which, in retrospect, was a baby step toward the development and use of rubrics for teacher evaluation.

Writing a Teacher-Evaluation Rubric

In 2002, I left the Boston schools and started coaching principals. I also began writing *The Marshall Memo*, a newsletter summarizing educational research and best practices. Reading a wide range of publications, I saw more and more mentions of rubrics for teacher evaluation and was drawn to the idea. I had been trained in the traditional approach to teacher evaluation and had written hundreds of lengthy narratives, and rubrics struck me as having the potential to be more time-efficient for supervisors and more informative for teachers.

In 2006, one of the principals I was coaching asked me to write a rubric for his charter school in Newark, New Jersey. I inquired why he did not just use Danielson's or one of the other rubrics that were available. He said he wanted to use something a little different and I accepted the job. Creating a teacher-evaluation rubric from scratch was an interesting challenge. I gathered several rubrics and saw a number of common flaws that I was determined to avoid:

- Most rubrics were long and wordy—very cumbersome for supervisors to fill out and teachers to digest in the busy world of schools.
- Some rubrics divided teaching into domains that were illogically conceptualized or too academic.
- Most used "fixed mindset" language for the levels (e.g., *Distinguished, Proficient, Basic,* and *Unsatisfactory*), which could convey the idea that good teachers are born, not made.
- Some rubrics did not describe observable classroom behaviors in clear, vivid language.
- Some put two or more teaching behaviors into individual boxes, making it difficult for supervisors to give a single score for that portion of the rubric.
- Some underemphasized or completely left out important aspects of teaching (e.g., homework, teacher attendance, and parent involvement).
- In most rubrics, each domain sprawled over two or more pages, making it difficult to see the overall picture of a teacher's performance in that area.
- Some rubrics used shortcuts that failed to capture important variations in teaching quality (e.g., starting each of the four levels with

words like *Always, Mostly, Sometimes, Never,* and not providing detail on the gradations of classroom actions).

With these potential pitfalls in mind, I set about trying to create a better mousetrap.

The first decision any rubric writer needs to make is how teachers' work should be divided up. After examining the available rubrics, research on effective teaching, especially *The Skillful Teacher* by Jon Saphier and Robert Gower (1997), *What Works in Schools* by Robert Marzano (2003), and *Linking Teacher Evaluation and Student Learning* by Pamela Tucker and James Stronge (2005), and insights from my years as a teacher, central office administrator, and principal, I decided on six domains:

1. Planning and preparation for learning
2. Classroom management
3. Delivery of instruction
4. Monitoring, assessment, and follow-up
5. Family and community outreach
6. Professional responsibilities

I thought these covered all of teachers' day-to-day responsibilities, were logically sequenced, and had about the right proportions—two thirds focused on classroom instruction, one third on aspects of the job outside the classroom.

The rubric writer's second decision is how many scoring levels there should be and how they should be labeled. Currently, virtually all teacher rubrics use a 4-3-2-1 scale, and I agreed with the logic of that approach. A 4-point scale makes it possible to identify truly outstanding teaching (Level 4), solid professional performance (Level 3), mediocre practices (Level 2), and unacceptable teaching (Level 1). Tennessee educators are using a statewide 5-point scale, but interestingly, this rubric has written descriptions only at Levels 5, 3, and 1, leaving it to supervisors to "eyeball" Levels 2 and 4 (Team Tennessee, n.d.).

The labels used for each level are also important; they embody the rubric's philosophy about performance and convey important messages to teachers and administrators. Over the last few years, there has been a shift from "fixed mindset" language for Levels 4 and 3 (*Distinguished, Exemplary, Excellent,* and *Proficient*) to "growth mindset" language (*Highly Effective* and *Effective*). Finding the right label for Level 2 is particularly tricky—how to describe mediocre performance without labeling and discouraging the teacher. Here are some attempts: *Needs Improvement, Partially Effective, Minimally Effective, Basic,* and *Developing.* My thinking on labels has evolved, and I believe these are best:

4. *Highly effective*
3. *Effective*
2. *Improvement necessary*
1. *Does not meet standards*

Each is designed to convey general feedback about the teacher's performance, focus on standards and results, and encourage improvement.

Having made these decisions, I zeroed in on Level 3 (Effective), gathered descriptions of good teaching practices from multiple sources, sorted them into the six domains, arranged them in a logical sequence, eliminated duplication, and worked hard to make each one as clear, descriptive, and brief as possible (I kept each description to one line). Without question, this was the most intellectually demanding part of the entire process.

When my Level 3 descriptions were finished, I took each one up a notch to create Level 4, pegging them to the kind of outstanding teaching practices exemplified in Doug Lemov's (2010) book, *Teach Like a Champion*. I then took each Level 3 description down a notch to create Level 2 (decidedly mediocre practices that no teacher should be proud of), then took each one down another notch to create Level 1 (clearly unsatisfactory and ineffective practices). The final step was giving each row a one-word "headline" on the left side. Figure 11.1 is a sample page from the rubric.

The Newark charter school was pleased with the rubrics I created and proceeded to use them for teacher evaluation. With the principal's permission, I began to share the rubrics with other schools and wrote an article about them for Phi Delta Kappan *EDge Magazine* (2006). I decided to offer the rubrics as free and open source documents, and they are used widely around the country and have been included on the New York and New Jersey lists of approved rubrics.

Over the last 10 years, I have conducted hundreds of professional development workshops on how to make rubrics (not just mine) part of an effective teacher-evaluation process and made thousands of classroom visits with school leaders with debriefings afterward. What follows are my insights on introducing rubrics to teachers and administrators and implementing them in ways that will maximize positive impact on teaching and learning. I will also address a number of commonly asked questions.

Introducing Rubrics

When teachers and administrators are first handed a copy of an evaluation rubric, the most common reaction is, "Holy cow!" (or words to that effect). Many educators are overwhelmed as they leaf through page upon page of densely packed matrices and hardly know where to begin. I have found that the most effective way for a superintendent, principal, or consultant to get teachers

C. Delivery of Instruction

The teacher:	4 **Highly Effective**	3 **Effective**	2 **Improvement Necessary**	1 **Does Not Meet Standards**
a. **Expectations**	Exudes high expectations, urgency, and determination that all students will master the material.	Conveys to students: This is important, you can do it, and I'm not going to give up on you.	Tells students that the subject matter is important and they need to work hard.	Gives up on some students as hopeless.
b. **Mindset**	Actively inculcates a "growth" mindset: take risks, learn from mistakes, through effective effort you can and will achieve at high levels.	Tells students that effective effort, not innate ability, is the key.	Doesn't counteract students' misconceptions about innate ability.	Communicates a "fixed" mindset about ability: some students have it, some don't.
c. **Goals**	Shows students exactly what's expected by posting essential questions, goals, rubrics, and exemplars; virtually all students can articulate them.	Gives students a clear sense of purpose by posting the unit's essential questions and the lesson's goals.	Tells students the main learning objectives of each lesson.	Begins lessons without giving students a sense of where instruction is headed.
d. **Connections**	Hooks virtually all students in units and lessons by activating knowledge, experience, reading, and vocabulary.	Activates students' prior knowledge and hooks their interest in each lesson and new vocabulary.	Is only sometimes successful in making the subject interesting and relating it to things students already know.	Rarely hooks students' interest or makes connections to their lives.
e. **Clarity**	Presents material clearly and explicitly, with well-chosen examples and vivid, appropriate language.	Uses clear explanations, appropriate language, and examples to present material.	Sometimes uses language and explanations that are fuzzy, confusing, or inappropriate.	Often presents material in a confusing way, using language that is inappropriate.
f. **Repertoire**	Uses a wide range of well-chosen, effective strategies, questions, materials, technology, and groupings to accelerate student learning.	Orchestrates effective strategies, questions, materials, technology, and groupings to foster student learning.	Uses a limited range of classroom strategies, questions, materials, and groupings with mixed success.	Uses only one or two teaching strategies and types of materials and fails to reach most students.
g. **Engagement**	Gets virtually all students involved in focused activities, actively learning and problem-solving, losing themselves in the work.	Has students actively think about, discuss, and use the ideas and skills being taught.	Attempts to get students actively involved but some students are disengaged.	Mostly lectures to passive students or has them plod through textbooks and worksheets.
h. **Differentiation**	Successfully reaches virtually all students by skillfully differentiating and scaffolding and using peer and adult helpers.	Differentiates and scaffolds instruction and uses peer and adult helpers to accommodate most students' learning needs.	Attempts to accommodate students with learning deficits, but with mixed success.	Fails to differentiate instruction for students with learning deficits.
i. **Nimbleness**	Deftly adapts lessons and units to exploit teachable moments and correct misunderstandings.	Is flexible about modifying lessons to take advantage of teachable moments.	Sometimes doesn't take advantage of teachable moments.	Is rigid and inflexible with lesson plans and rarely takes advantage of teachable moments.
j. **Closure**	Consistently has students summarize and internalize what they learn and apply it to real-life situations and future opportunities.	Has students sum up what they have learned and apply it in a different context.	Sometimes brings closure to lessons and asks students to think about applications.	Moves on at the end of each lesson without closure or application to other contexts.

Overall rating:_____ Comments:

Figure 11.1 A sample Marshall Teacher Evaluation Rubric.

to move past this initial negative reaction and see the benefits of a rubric is to proceed in a step-by-step fashion, alternating between a broad overview (general) and granular specifics (particular). Here is a sample rubric introduction using this approach:

- *Step 1* (General)—Briefly review the rubric's domains and rating scale. This gives people a sense of how the document is structured.
- *Step 2* (Particular)—Have everyone turn to one page (I suggest domain D, Monitoring, Assessment, and Follow-up) and silently read the vertical column at Level 3. When people have finished, pick one cell at Level 3 and read it aloud (for example, "Has [teacher] students set goals, self-assess, and know where they stand academically at all times"). This demonstrates that Level 3 is a solid, expected professional performance—nothing that any teacher should be ashamed of—which preempts one of the most common pushbacks: teachers' resistance at getting a rating that feels like a B.
- *Step 3* (Particular)—Read aloud the horizontal row from which the Level 3 example was taken, moving from right to left. For example:
  - Level 1: Allows students to move on without assessing and improving problems with their work.
  - Level 2: Urges students to look over their work, see where they had trouble, and aim to improve those areas.
  - Level 3: Has students set goals, self-assess, and know where they stand academically at all times.
  - Level 4: Has students set ambitious goals, continuously self-assess, and take responsibility for improving performance.

This gives people a sense of how the language of the rubric moves from unsatisfactory to excellent.

- *Step 4* (General)—Display that page of the rubric on a screen and read the headings of each horizontal row to give an overview of the areas covered in that domain—for example, Criteria, Diagnosis, On-the-spot, Self-assessment, Recognition, Interims, Tenacity, Support, Analysis, and Reflection.
- *Step 5* (Particular)—Display that page of the rubric with the ratings of a sample teacher circled or highlighted. A winning strategy is to show how you would rate *yourself* as a teacher (the more mixed your self-assessment, the better). This shows the audience what a realistic evaluation looks like—and models humility.
- *Step 6* (General)—Display the final summary page of the rubric, again with a sample teacher's ratings in all the domains circled or highlighted. Again, it's helpful if this is your own self-assessment.
- *Step 7* (Particular)—Now have people think of a teacher they know well and silently rate the teacher on all the lines on that page. Emphasize that it's important to read Level 3 of each row first, and if that doesn't describe the teacher's performance, look left or right

for the best description. A room full of educators usually gets very quiet as people fill out the page.

- S*tep 8* (General)—When everyone is finished (this usually takes about 3–4 minutes), ask if any teacher got all Level 4 ratings. It's very rare for there to be a single hand in the air. Ask if there was at least *one* Level 4 rating. Several hands usually go up, which makes the point that in any school, there will be a few top ratings, but not a lot.

After Step 8 is a good time to invite people to discuss in small groups the possible advantages and disadvantages of using rubrics to evaluate teachers. After 5 or so minutes of group discussion, reconvene the audience and have participants share their thoughts. Begin with advantages—this is an important tactical move to prevent skeptics from setting a negative tone up front. These are some of the positive points that are usually mentioned by workshop participants:

- Rubrics provide a shared conceptual framework and a common language about good and not-so-good teaching.
- Rubrics tell teachers exactly where their performance in each area stands on a 4-3-2-1 scale.
- Since most teachers naturally aspire to the highest level, a 4-level rubric has a built-in push toward excellence.
- For teachers with scores at Levels 3, 2, and 1, the language of the cell just above where they scored provides a specific description of what they need to do to improve.
- The comprehensive scope of a rubric makes it easier for a teacher to accept criticism (Level 2 or 1 ratings), since there are many other areas in which they are (hopefully) scoring at Level 3 and 4.
- The rubrics can easily be used by teachers to self-assess and set goals for a school year, and then track their progress over time.
- Rubrics are much quicker for supervisors to fill out than traditional narratives, since the writing is done for them.

Turning to the disadvantages of rubrics (and it is important to air critical feedback and apprehensions), these are some of the concerns that are often voiced:

- If supervisors have not visited classrooms frequently, they will not be able to fill out the rubrics knowledgeably.
- If supervisors have observed only "glamorized" lessons put on for their benefit, their rubric scoring will not reflect the kind of teaching students are experiencing on a daily basis, which is what really matters for long-term learning.

- The rubric might limit supervisors' perceptions and prevent them from seeing and commenting on important aspects of instruction.
- Some supervisors might not be considered credible evaluators in certain subject areas or grade levels.
- Some administrators might be uncomfortable judging teachers on a 4-3-2-1 scale or uncertain of their ability to make fair judgments in so many areas.
- Supervisors might not be fully candid and refrain from giving Level 2 or 1 scores to teachers who deserve them, undermining the potential for useful feedback.
- Conversely, some administrators might decide to give very few Level 4 scores, "grading on a curve" irrespective of the amount of excellent classroom performance in their school.
- Supervisors might complete the rubrics and present them to teachers without providing the teacher the opportunity to voice disagreements.
- Some educators do not like this type of precise, prepackaged evaluation tool. As one private-school administrator in Washington DC said to me, "I don't like being put in a box."
- Teachers might count up and compare points with colleagues (4 for each top-level rating, 3 for each next-to-top, etc.), turning the evaluation process into a numbers-driven competition to gain an advantage over their colleagues.
- Supervisors might require teachers to provide evidence for each rating, which makes filling out the rubric extremely time-consuming and can distract teachers from their work with students (a Connecticut teacher who was asked to do this in late 2013 said, "I've never worked so hard and taught so little.")
- Making rubric scores high-stakes—for example, giving merit pay bonuses for Level 4 performance or moving to dismiss teachers scoring at Level 1—might make it less likely that teachers would be candid about their shortcomings and work effectively with their supervisor.

In my experience, this kind of pro-and-con discussion almost always leaves an audience of teachers and school administrators with a positive feeling about using rubrics—along with some legitimate concerns. And indeed, the devil is in the details. Even with all their potential benefits, rubrics can be implemented in ways that damage staff morale and do little or nothing to improve teaching and learning. As I have learned over the years, thoughtful implementation is as important as the quality of the rubric itself.

Hurdles to Successful Implementation

The most important question is when and how teacher-evaluation rubrics should be used. Back in 2006, my assumption was that rubrics were summary evaluation tools and that supervisors would wait until the end of the school year to fill them out. But teachers naturally want to know where they stand month by month, and many superintendents want to keep track of how principals are handling the evaluation process as the year unfolds. This hunger for real-time evaluation data has led many supervisors to fill out rubrics throughout the year—either during classroom visits or in postobservation conferences with teachers.

Using rubrics in this manner appeals to busy school leaders since it makes the teacher-evaluation process seem quicker and more efficient. However, I believe real-time rubric scoring undermines effective coaching, supervision, and evaluation. For starters, it is next to impossible to fill out a comprehensive, multipage rubric while observing the fluid and complex dynamics of a classroom. To be good observers, supervisors need to have their heads up, walk around the room, listen carefully to the teacher, look over students' shoulders at the work they're being asked to do, ask one or two students "What are you working on?" and look at some of the material on the walls. The challenge—and it is challenging—is to decide on the most important thing to address with the teacher afterward and jot down a few quick notes. What affirmation, question, or concern is most likely to move the teacher's practice forward? Trying to rubric-score a teacher during an observation distracts the supervisor from focusing on those key insights and makes his or her feedback to the teacher seem bureaucratic and inauthentic.

Regardless, a number of software companies (among them Rally, Teachscape, and iObservation) have created electronic applications that allow supervisors to fill out checklists, and/or make comments on iPads or laptops during observations and even send them electronically to teachers before leaving the classroom. While these products are highly seductive to school leaders, I believe there are several practical problems: (a) the supervisor is making snap judgments about what is happening in the classroom without giving the teacher a chance to explain the bigger picture, (b) the teacher's anxiety level is likely to spike knowing that the supervisor is making evaluative comments in electronic form in real time, and (c) it's less likely that there will be a follow-up conversation because it appears that the supervisor has already made up his or her mind. This is a perfect example of one of Charlotte Danielson's (2007) most telling critiques of conventional evaluation: It is done *to* teachers, not *with* them.

Some proponents of in-class rubric scoring (whether it be through using an app or traditional paper and pencil) acknowledge the problem of supervisors being overwhelmed by how much happens during a classroom visit and suggest that only one segment of the rubric be filled out (perhaps the school has decided to focus on teacher's questioning strategies or classroom management). But this seriously limits the supervisor and might lead him or her to miss important interpersonal or pedagogical events. And even with only one page of the rubric to evaluate, there is still the problem of finding the right line in the rubric and making immediate evaluative judgments while so much is occurring simultaneously.

Filling out the rubric during postobservation conferences with teachers creates a different set of problems. First, rubrics are inherently evaluative, and most principals I work with find that scoring teachers on a 4-3-2-1 scale after each observation undermines productive coaching since the teacher tends to remember only the ratings. Second, receiving evaluative feedback on 20 or 30 areas is overwhelming, and the result is likely to be a stressed-out teacher with no clear focus for improvement. Third, being required to use rubric language after a classroom visit may prevent supervisors from articulating in their own words the one or two most important commendations or suggestions that the teacher needs to hear.

What Is to Be Done?

I have argued that using rubrics during classroom visits or immediately afterward is problematic. But waiting until the end of the year to fill out the rubric runs the risk of teachers not receiving timely feedback on their performance and possibly getting blindsided by negative feedback in the final evaluation meeting. The solution, I have come to believe, is using rubrics formally at three points in the year:

- As school opens, teachers score themselves on the entire rubric, meet with their supervisor, and set 2–3 improvement goals based on areas of the rubric with relatively low scores;
- At midyear, teacher and supervisor meet and compare the teacher's updated self-assessment with the supervisor's tentative scoring page by page, discuss any differences, assess progress on the teacher's goals, and identify areas for growth and support;
- At the end of the year, teacher and supervisor repeat this process and reach closure on the year's ratings.

I have found that the midyear and year-end evaluation meetings work best if the teacher and supervisor fill out the rubrics beforehand (in pencil), discuss only the areas where they disagree (and perhaps one or two other areas that are particularly important to the teacher or supervisor), and base the conversation on the teacher's actual performance (versus secondhand information or philosophical viewpoints). This approach makes rubric meetings quick, focused, and efficient—usually not more than 30 minutes.

As the year-end meeting proceeds, the supervisor provides an overall rating for each domain (with a brief comment if needed). When all the domains have been scored, the supervisor fills out the final summary page, gives an overall rating, they both write brief summative comments, and they sign off.

The only exception to this three-times-a-year process is with teachers whose performance shows clear signs of being unsatisfactory (Level 1). As soon as serious performance problems become apparent, these teachers should receive scores on the relevant areas of the rubric, an improvement plan, and intensive support.

Frequently Asked Questions

When schools and districts implement teacher-evaluation rubrics, a number of questions come up. Here are my thoughts on a selection of these.

How Many Classroom Visits Are Needed to Fill Out the Rubric?
I have long believed that the traditional model (announced full-lesson observation with preconference, lengthy write-up, and postconference) has built-in design flaws that make it inaccurate (the supervisor is not getting a sense of what students are experiencing on a day-to-day basis), ineffective (not seeing typical daily practice, the supervisor can't provide appropriate coaching suggestions), and dishonest (if lay people knew that teachers were being evaluated on an annual "dog-and-pony show," they would be scandalized). In addition, the traditional process consumes hundreds of hours of supervisors' time. Instead, I believe that short, frequent, unannounced classroom visits followed by brief face-to-face postobservation conversations (with very brief write-ups afterward) allow supervisors to sample day-to-day instruction, have regular coaching conversations, and gradually gather most of the information they need to complete the rubric at year's end (Marshall, 2006).

How many short observations there should be is open to debate; my experience, as a Boston principal and as a coach of principals, is that 10 visits per teacher per year is about the right frequency (Marshall, 2013). In most schools, this means two or three classroom visits a day. Some districts are asking supervisors to make fewer visits (sometimes combined with one or two full-lesson observations). Other educators advocate more-frequent visits; for example, Newark, New Jersey, charter school leader Paul

Bambrick-Santoyo (2012), in his book, *Leverage Leadership*, makes the case for *weekly* classroom visits for each teacher.

It is difficult for school leaders to squeeze more than two or three observations into their incredibly busy days, and we need empirical research on how many visits provide a reasonably accurate picture of a teacher's performance and understand whether there is a point of diminishing returns on classroom observations. Equally important, in my experience, is supervisors having a good "eye" for instruction, genuinely listening to teachers' insights when they talk to them after each visit and when necessary, reaching out to content-area instructional coaches and subject-area specialists for guidance.

How Can Teachers' Professional Work Outside the Classroom Be Evaluated?

This includes extra duties, paperwork, attendance and punctuality, working with colleagues on curriculum planning and data analysis, professional development workshops and courses, book study groups, and so on. To assess these important areas, supervisors must rely on other points of contact with teachers: dropping in on team meetings, observing staff meeting interactions, attending student performances and athletic events, watching teacher interactions with parents, and monitoring data on attendance, paperwork, and other areas. Supervisors who are visible around their schools can form a fairly accurate picture of teachers' nonclassroom performance, but there will inevitably be gaps in their knowledge. This is where teachers' input in midyear and end-of-year rubric conversations is so helpful. It's also a good idea to have more than one administrator monitoring teachers' performance so the leadership team can compare notes and fill in gaps.

In Evaluation Conferences, Who Has The Burden of Proof?

When a supervisor and teacher disagree on a particular line of the rubric, here is a possible rule of thumb: if the teacher is advocating for a Level 4 score and the supervisor believes Level 3 or 2 is more accurate, the teacher needs to convince the supervisor. If the supervisor is arguing for a Level 1 score but the teacher believes a higher score is more accurate, the supervisor needs to have evidence. If there are disagreements between Level 2 and 3 scores, there should be a free-flowing debate on the evidence. At the end of the day, however, the supervisor has the final say.

How Much Are Teachers and Supervisors Likely to Differ When They Compare Ratings?

In one New York City elementary school that used this approach during the 2012–2013 school year, the principal reported to me that 60% of teachers' self-assessments were virtually identical to her ratings, 30% of teachers rated themselves lower, and 10% scored themselves significantly higher than the principal believed they deserved (personal communication, June 2013). She was glad she had done midyear check-ins, because it offered her time to address these discrepancies in her classroom visits and coaching conversations.

Should Novice Teachers be Evaluated With a Modified Rubric?

The rationale for creating a less-demanding rubric is that new teachers will not receive many ratings at Level 3 and 4 on the standard rubric and might become discouraged. However, new teachers are working with students every day, and I believe they should be held to the same expectations as everyone else. Administrators should explain that it is not the end of the world for new teachers to have some Level 2 ratings (even a few at Level 1) in the first year; the school will provide lots of support to put them on a steep learning curve so they reach the effective level in virtually all areas in their second and third year of teaching.

Should Fractional Scores Be Permitted?

If a teacher's performance in one area straddles Level 2 and 3, is it appropriate to give a 2.5? Since secondary teachers work with four or five different groups of students and elementary teachers cover several different subjects, this seems like a logical approach. On the other hand, there is an argument for keeping things simple and asking supervisors to use only whole numbers based on the preponderance of the evidence. A compromise might be to allow supervisors to straddle ratings in the midyear conference (which would give the teacher a clear signal to step up performance in a particular area) but require whole-number ratings in final evaluations.

How Should Teachers' Absences Be Counted?

Not all rubrics have a line for attendance, but for those that do (in my rubric, Level 4 is 98%–100% present, Level 3 is 95%–97% present, Level 2 is 6%–10% absence, and Level 1 is 11% or higher absence), should teachers be considered absent for taking personal days, attending a professional conference, or visiting another school? My recommendation is that only sick days be counted as absences, and there should be a place to note if there are exceptional circumstances that explain unusually low attendance—for example, a serious illness or a death in the immediate family. Some teachers disagree with a percentage approach to attendance, but I think it is important that the rubric sends a clear signal that a teacher's presence in the classroom is critical—substitutes almost never deliver instruction that is as rigorous and effective as the regular teacher (Clotfelter, Ladd, & Vigdor, 2007; Miller, Murnane, & Willet, 2007).

How Should Nonclassroom School Staff Be Evaluated?

These include librarians, nurses, guidance counselors, instructional coaches, and other nonteaching roles. Charlotte Danielson (2007) has published a series of rubrics for nonteaching staff, and the Westwood, Massachusetts, schools have done similar work branching off from my teacher rubrics. For educators who work with students in confidential settings (e.g., psychologists and guidance counselors), direct observation is not possible, and supervisors need to schedule regular check-in meetings and perhaps use anonymous student surveys to assess the quality of the work.

Should Teachers' Ratings Be Made Public?

In my view, absolutely not. I believe rubric scores are confidential personnel records and should not be released, even in aggregated form at the building level. Public disclosure of rubric scores not only violates the trusting relationship that must be nurtured between supervisors and teachers, but also runs the risk of putting pressure on supervisors to inflate scores (Who wants their school to look bad in the community?). However, principals and superintendents should create a confidential spreadsheet of teachers' ratings for their leadership teams, highlighting the areas where there is solid performance and where additional work and professional development are needed.

Should Top-Rated Teachers Receive Merit Pay?

My interpretation of the research on performance pay is that even in the business world, it's not an effective practice, and a few experiments in K–12 education have not produced positive results and have been discontinued, sometimes for financial reasons (Frey & Osterloh, 2012; Johnson & Papay, 2010; Springer & Gardner, 2010; Yuan et al., 2013). However, there are several ways that rubric evaluations might be used to tweak the traditional salary scale:

- Top-rated teachers might be offered opportunities to perform extra work for extra pay; for example, mentoring colleagues, designing curriculum, and running professional development.
- Districts might consider eliminating or scaling back salary increments for advanced degrees, since the research shows very little correlation between master's and doctoral degrees and classroom effectiveness (Goldhaber, 2002; Hattie, 2008). For example, Hattie's (2007) meta-analyses rank teacher credentials 124th out of 138 in overall impact on student achievement. The money saved could go to compensating highly effective teachers for additional duties.
- Teachers scoring at Level 2 might be denied a step increase the following year and receive an improvement plan and intensive sup-

port; if they have not progressed to Level 3 by the end of that year, they might be dismissed. The Hillsborough, Florida, school district used this approach with union approval; the union president has stated that she would not want her own children in a mediocre classroom and didn't think anyone else would either (Wingert, 2010).

- Teachers evaluated at Level 1 should get an immediate improvement plan and intensive support, and if they do not improve in a reasonable period of time (preferably within that year), should be counseled out or dismissed.

This approach allows rubric ratings to play a part in teachers' income without using the ineffective strategy of merit pay.

Should Teachers' Rubric Scores Be Recorded in Numerical Form?

One built-in feature of rubrics is that it's easy to tabulate teachers' performance in a very precise manner; for example, Valerie Williams scored 29 out of a possible 40 in classroom management. But there are several problems with this approach. First, adding up ratings assumes that each line in the rubric has equal value, which is not true. The research is clear that some teacher actions have more impact on student learning than others. For example, Hattie's (2008) comprehensive compilation of meta-analysis data ranks effective use of formative assessment data third (out of 138) in its impact on student achievement, while homework is ranked 88th. Using numerical rubric scores conveys a false sense of precision to teachers and school leaders.

Second, certain parts of the rubric are more important for some teachers than others. Perhaps Valerie set a personal goal of working with her grade-level team on interim assessment follow-up, developing a class website, and communicating with hard-to-reach parents by text messages; for her, those rubric areas have more weight than areas in which she is doing fine.

Third, numerical scores do not capture a teacher's growth in specific areas. Perhaps Valerie and her team have made great strides in the quality of their unit plans and use of Essential Questions, meriting a special commendation from the principal, but only a one-point rise in her rubric score.

Fourth, a teacher might perform quite differently depending on the challenge level of students and the working conditions within a school; for example, teaching an AP history class versus a group of ninth-grade repeaters. The context in which a teacher teaches has tremendous impact on rubric scores, and supervisors need to take that into account, not by grading on a curve, but by making sure that nobody overemphasizes the importance of numerical scores.

Finally, reducing rubric ratings to numbers might very well lead teachers to compare their evaluations and cause morale problems, especially since, as was argued above, the numerical scores do not reflect precisely how a teacher is performing in a particular year. For these reasons, I think summative rubric evaluations should be reported using only the labels for each domain. For example, a given teacher's work was *Effective* in Planning and Preparation, *Highly Effective* level in Classroom Management, and so on, with an overall rating (e.g., *Effective*) summing up all the domains, accompanied by brief written comments where appropriate.

Will Rubrics Improve Teaching and Learning?

This, of course, is the most important question of all. It could be argued that rubrics are old wine in new bottles—merely a streamlined way of delivering top-down evaluative judgments that will not improve much of anything. That's possible, but I believe well-constructed rubrics, if used appropriately by competent supervisors, can add significant value. The key factors are a skillful introduction of the rubrics to teachers, teachers self-assessing and setting goals, well-trained supervisors making frequent classroom visits with feedback conversations and coaching throughout the year, and teacher input in midyear and year-end evaluation meetings. In schools with these factors in place, rubrics bring much greater clarity to teacher supervision and evaluation, push educators to higher levels of performance, and provide a powerful boost to students' achievement and life chances.

DEVELOPING A RESEARCH AGENDA FOR RUBRICS

Since rubrics are a relatively new development in K–12 schools, there are a number of unanswered questions that would be helpful for researchers to address in the years ahead. While this is not an exhaustive list, the following represents unanswered questions about teacher evaluation rubrics:

- Under what circumstances will the use of rubrics improve teacher evaluation and teacher learning?
- What is the ideal length and level of detail for a teacher-evaluation rubric (i.e., number of domains, number of lines per domain, total number of pages)? Similarly, what is the ideal number of rating levels?
- What kinds of professional development best prepare principals and teacher leaders to use rubrics effectively?
- What is the optimal supervisor/teacher ratio for effective supervision and evaluation?
- How and to what extent do electronic devices (e.g., iPads, laptops, smartphones) enhance the supervision and evaluation of teachers and when do they impede it?

- When, during the school year, do teacher-evaluation rubrics best promote improvements in teaching and learning?
- Should teachers self-assess on rubrics? If so, at what point or points in the school year? And what is the most effective role of supervisors in this process?
- What is the value of releasing teachers' rubric scores to the public and does the practice have an impact on teaching and learning?

Teaching is an exceptionally complex enterprise, and evaluating teachers fairly and accurately has always been a challenge. Considering that the average instructor teaches 5 lessons a day, which adds up to 900 lessons a year, and the teachers in a medium-size school collectively teach about 27,000 lessons a year, the job of supervision and evaluation seems impossible, especially with the traditional evaluation process. Teacher-evaluation rubrics have great potential in terms of building a shared understanding of good teaching and streamlining the process of evalution—*if* they are well-constructed, *if* they are introduced to teachers in a way that builds ownership and trust, and *if* they are used wisely by thoughtful and well-trained administrators who regularly visit classrooms and follow up with teachers.

REFERENCES

Bambrick-Santoyo, P. (2013). *Leverage leadership.* San Francisco, CA: Jossey-Bass.

Clotfelter, C., Ladd, H., & Vigdor, J. (2007, November). Are teacher absences worth worrying about in the U.S.? *The National Bureau of Economic Research.* Retrieved from http://www.nber.org/papers/w13648

Danielson, C. (1996). *Enhancing professional practice: A framework for teaching.* Alexandria, VA: ASCD.

Danielson, C. (2009). *Talk about teaching: Leading professional conversations.* New York, NY: Corwin Press.

Frey B., & Osterloh, M. (2012, January/February). Stop tying pay to performance. *Harvard Business Review, 90*(1/2), 51–52.

Goldhaber, D. (2002, Spring). The mystery of good teaching. *Education Next, 2*(1), 50–55. Retrieved from http://educationnext.org/the-mystery-of-good-teaching/

Hattie, J. (2008). *Visible learning. A synthesis of over 800 meta-analyses relating to student achievement.* New York, NY: Taylor & Francis.

Johnson, S. M., & Papay, J. (2010). Merit pay for a new generation. *Educational Leadership, 67*(8), 48–52.

Lemov, D. (2010). *Teach like a champion.* San Francisco, CA: Jossey-Bass.

Marshall, K. (2006, September/October). The why's and how's of teacher evaluation rubrics. *EDge Magazine, 2*(1), 1–19

Marshall, K. (2013). *Rethinking teacher supervision and evaluation* (2nd ed.).San Francisco, CA: Jossey-Bass.

Marzano, R. (2003). *What works in schools.* Alexandria, VA: ASCD

Miller, R., Murnane, R., & Willett, J. (2007, August). Do teacher absences impact student achievement? Longitudinal evidence from one urban school district. *National Bureau of Economic Research.* Retrieved from http://www.nber.org/papers/w13356

Saphier, J., & Gower, R. (1997). *The skillful teacher.* Acton, MA: Research for Better Teaching.

Springer, M., & Gardner, C. (2010). Teacher pay for performance: Context, status, and direction. *Phi Delta Kappan, 91*(8), 8–15.

Team Tennessee. (n.d.). *General educator rubric.* Retrieved from http://team-tn.cloudapp.net/wp-content/uploads/2013/12/General-Educator-Rubric.pdf

Tucker, P., & Stronge, J. (2005). *Linking teacher evaluation and student learning.* Alexandria, VA: ASCD.

Wingert, P. (2010, December 6). When school reformers and union leaders unite. *Newsweek.* Retrieved from http://www.newsweek.com/when-school-reformers-and-union-leaders-unite-68989

Yuan, K., Vi-Nhuan L., McCaffrey, D., Hamilton, L., Stecher, B., Marsh, J., & Springer, M. (2013). Incentive pay programs do not affect teacher motivation or reported practices: Results from three randomized studies. *Educational Evaluation and Policy Analysis, 35*(1), 3–22.

CHAPTER 12

THE DANIELSON FRAMEWORK FOR TEACHING AS AN EVALUATION RUBRIC

One Size Fits None

Leslie David Burns

Throughout this text, the editors and authors grapple with the paradox that well-designed rubrics *can* increase the quality of a subject's performance despite the fact that little evidence exists to document this claim. The editors cite one reviewer of this volume who states rubrics have become so ubiquitous and unhealthy that they constitute an "evil" in the implementation of educational evaluations (Personal communication, February 14, 2014). But rubrics are not evil. Rubrics are tools. As tools, they may be used well or poorly. They may be soundly designed or not. They may be chosen wisely or unwisely and implemented in principled or slavish ways.

The problem is that even when soundly designed, wisely chosen, and used well, rubrics have unintended consequences because they are *always* products of the subjective values and assumed or unarticulated presumptions of their authors (Fairclough, 1995). This is true for any public policy

Rubric Nation, pages 185–200
Copyright © 2015 by Information Age Publishing
All rights of reproduction in any form reserved.

instrument (Stone, 2002). Any such instrument's utility depends on people working in diverse contexts that are deeply complex and unpredictable, especially in education (Spiro, Coulson, Feltovich, & Anderson, 1988). Because rubrics are texts that position users to act and think in certain ways rather than others (Fairclough, 1995), they often lead to paradoxically un-intended/negative results even if their uses are well-intended.

In this chapter, I explore how the Framework for Teaching rubric designed by Danielson (2013) presents cautionary tales about rubric design and the use of rubrics to evaluate teacher quality during classroom instruction. Teaching is performed in what Spiro et al. (1988) have described as an ill-structured domain requiring flexible thinking for successful performance, multiple methods and approaches, and the constant need to adapt those methods and approaches depending on the demands of the context in which they are used. I begin by discussing standards-based accountability reform, the style of reform for which the Danielson Framework was explicitly designed. I highlight its limitations as a policy instrument and its intimate relationship with corporate education reformers and as a product of those reformers' goals. I analyze the Danielson Framework for Teaching's (FFT) claims to scientific validity and its claims to a foundation in constructivist learning theory. I describe its inherent incapacity for evaluating teacher quality based on its limitations, and offer explanations of why this is the case.

The FFT is rife with potential unintended consequences, has deep ties to corporate/state reform efforts (CCSSI, 2010; Danielson, 2014), and is designed in a way that *prevents* quality teaching in favor of documenting needs for continuous improvement that favor a politicized model of standardized teaching despite what is scientifically known about teaching and learning. The FFT's implementation via state/corporate alliances has less to do with instituting good teaching for classroom success and more to do with corporate discourses of efficiency and effectiveness that require the de-skilling and deprofessionalization of teachers. To begin, I explore how standards and standardization have become oversimplified due to their imposition on the U.S. public education system by a corporate movement that regards quality teaching in ways that often have negative consequences on the system they are supposed to improve.

The Problems of "Common" Education, Standards, and Standardization

According to Delandshere and Petrosky (2004), research about accountability reform in the United States focuses on *how* to develop standards, not why or how to implement them. The bulk of this literature treats the process as unproblematic. Apple (1990) calls such a fabrication based on manufactured consensus a consistent part of most rational policymaking decisions (Bardach, 2005; Stone, 2002). Apple (1990) goes on to underscore the fact that complexity is usually the first challenge to be ignored in such decisions, which favor simplistic solutions that enable large bureaucracies to offer the *appearance* of consensus when they often simply overlook potential problems to appear legitimate. These fabrications frequently result in negative yet unintended consequences that make projects like determining the qualities required to be a successful teacher difficult if not impossible. In discussing the impulse toward oversimplification, Delandshere and Petrosky write that from reformers' perspectives, "Ensuring a common vision for teacher education is perceived as necessary in order for all teachers to develop the knowledge, skills, and dispositions that are *assumed* to have a positive effect on the achievement of all students" (2004, pp. 4–5; emphasis added). The current accountability reform movement represented by the Common Core State Standards Initiative (CCSSI, 2010) and concurrent efforts to attach reform to certain evaluation frameworks such as ACT's College and Career Readiness and the Danielson FFT follow from historically traditional assumptions that "knowledge is a commodity that can be objectified and measured in terms of immediately visible outcomes," that what teachers know and do is "the most important" influence on student learning, and that it is possible to reach consensus about these matters (Delandshere & Petrosky, 2004, pp. 5–6, 8).

Similar to Delandshere and Petrosky (2004), a collective of curriculum experts and critical literacy theorists known as the New London Group (2000) finds that although many reformers represent accountability goals as opportunities for professionalization and worker empowerment, they actually *increase* workers' responsibilities while *reducing* their abilities to perform at high levels. Such reforms decrease or eliminate workers' status as autonomous professional experts, a finding echoed by Smagorinsky in his study of language arts teachers (1999). Existing research has already highlighted that reform-based focus on teachers as *the* most important factor determining student achievement represents a simplistic attempt to resolve a complex problem. Delandshere and Petrosky conclude that *any* reform that "prescribes alignment, consensus, and consistency through bureaucratic and authoritarian control is antithetical to learning, inquiry, and true democratic participation" (2004, p. 6).

Prescriptive rubrics for teachers' continuous improvement, of which the FFT is the most prominent, circumscribe the complexity of teaching and impose "a fixed political will that shapes [teachers'] capacities, who they become as teachers, and positions them primarily as implementers of content and pedagogy as defined by the standards" (Delandshere & Petrosky, 2004, p. 7). In the current reform regime, teacher accountability as it is presently represented constitutes a monopoly on thought that requires professionals to submit to and help maintain a status quo that makes erroneous use of progressive educational language and concepts. These are all problems identified by the New London Group (2000) as predictable consequences of accepting a reform ideology that applies corporate ideals to educational institutions in ways that fail to account for the many ways in which corporate and educational contexts differ, sometimes to the point of being antithetical. The FFT's design and widespread use are both reflective of that corporate approach that has been historically harmful in U.S. public schools.

The Problem of the FFT As a Corporatist Instrument in Education

Some readers might wonder how something as seemingly harmless as a rubric could be capable of wreaking havoc on an entire profession, let alone preventing the kinds of improvement and growth the rubric was created to support. It is important to emphasize that I make no assertion that Charlotte Danielson, the Danielson Group, representatives of the CCSSI, or any others advocating the FFT are engaged in a plan to destroy public education. It is likely such individuals and groups perceive themselves as well-intentioned people trying to fix a system they believe is broken. From the corporate/state perspective, it is predictable they would design policies and instruments to fulfill public interests as *they* perceive them (Stone, 2002). If public schooling's purpose is framed as a project of preparing children for college and career, as is the case with the CCSSI and thus the FFT, it makes sense that corporate/bureaucratic actions will utilize discourses of efficiency, standardization, effectiveness, and instrumentalism. Each of these impulses is unhealthy because each ignores the inherent complexity of contemporary public schools. Instead, they standardize practice in a misguided attempt to reduce that complexity.

Standardization is an efficiency practice with roots in U.S. public education that go back to Taylorism and Fordism—efficiency models for engineering used in the early 20th century and applied to education as a form of *social* engineering (Null, 2011). Taylorism entails assumptions that it is possible to observe a worker, identify the tasks and decisions that a worker makes, and thus identify essential ways to increase productivity and eliminate redundancies or seemingly purposeless activities. Taylorism is pathologically rational in assuming tasks and decision-making remain constant across time and context, and as a result entails assuming it possible to design systems that will improve *anyone's* performance of a given job in the same ways at the same times to achieve the same results at all times. Similarly, Fordism projected corporate concepts of effectiveness onto education and is also based on assumptions that standardizing tasks and processes increases productivity and requires less knowledge and fewer skills. Fordism is definitively a project of deprofessionalizing workers and training them to follow procedures rather than make decisions to complete tasks on their own (Ash, 2008).

Taylorism and Fordism were used for education reform in the early 20th century in ways that unfortunately standardized educational processes and deprofessionalized the fields of teaching and education. Today, these same approaches underlie discourses of college and career readiness that use the same assumptions with the same (potentially unintended) consequences. In fact, the discourse of effectiveness in teacher education has proven to be a startlingly complex problem for policymakers. Denotatively, the term *effective* is defined as *having a predictable result,* and the Danielson Framework utilizes that term on a consistent basis along with its antonym, *ineffective.* Such discourse is consistent with its Taylorist/Fordist roots. However, it is widely understood amongst professional educators that teaching, learning, human development, and the nature of schools are almost never predictable. Regardless of teacher quality, constructivist theories and their resulting scientific findings document that both teaching and learning processes are all extremely variable and unpredictable. *Effectiveness* is not the actual goal of a constructivist education system. Rather, it has become a proxy term for *successful*—a term that denotes accomplishing a purpose or attaining a goal regardless of method, and a term that means something very different than *predictability* (Burns, 2014). When reformers talk now about becoming *effective,* they miss their intended goal of being more *successful* because predictability is impossible in ill-structured domains like education.

Beginning in fall, 2014, the state of Kentucky will implement the FFT as its sole instrument for evaluating teacher quality in concert with the Common Core State Standards Initiative. Several districts in Kentucky have been piloting the FFT, and it has been revised as early as February, 2014 (Danielson, 2014). Its expressed purpose is to comprise the state's "Teacher Professional Growth and *Effectiveness* System" (Danielson, 2014, p. 2, emphasis added). As such, it is explicitly an instrument for standardization. Using the language of constructivist theories, it represents itself as a tool for professional growth. However, it is much more likely to *stifle* growth and deprofessionalize the system so that teachers function as technicians following procedures rather than experts making professional decisions. If we accept even the most arguable findings that teachers are *the* most significant variables in increasing student success, use of the FFT seems likely to render their influence on student growth completely immaterial.

In Kentucky, the FFT is asserted as a research-based document aligned with standards from the Interstate New Teacher Assessment and Support Consortium, the Kentucky Teacher Standards, the Kentucky Board of Education's Program of Studies, the Common Core Academic Standards

(CCS), and the state's own Characteristics of Highly Effective Teaching and Learning, developed in 2010 via collaboration with WestEd and Harvard University (Danielson, 2014). According to the Danielson Group (Danielson , 2013), the FFT is designed so that the "complex activity of teaching" is divided into 4 domains, 22 components, and 76 discrete indicators to support the evaluation of teachers via a rating system across domains of Planning and Preparation, Classroom Environment, Instruction, and Professional Responsibilities" (Danielson , 2013, para. 1). This is reflective of Taylorist efforts to conduct task-analysis of a given job, reduce it to a finite and predictable set of skills and steps, and establish procedures that must be followed by all workers at all times under all circumstances. As the editors of this volume note, the FFT seeks to define what teachers should know and be able to do, and its designers assert that the rubric delivers a comprehensive, research-based instrument for evaluating teacher quality. These are not legitimate claims.

The 2013 version of the FFT, though it has since been slightly revised, was a direct response to calls for teacher accountability aligned with the Common Core State Standards (CCSS). Kentucky became the first state to officially adopt the Common Core in 2010. Evidence that the Danielson FFT has been scientifically validated with the CCSSI is claimed by both the state and the Danielson Group, but the evidence is questionable. While the original FFT was published in 1996, the Danielson Group claimed it was scientifically validated in a 2007 study (2014). This is a problematic claim. While the FFT was tested for validity and reliability in 2007, there is *no* evidence offered that it was tested again for alignment with the CCSS in 2013. At best, this means that the Danielson Group disingenuously claimed that its 2007 validation via the Measures of Effective Teaching Project (MET) was sufficient to claim alignment with a set of standards that were not published until 3 years later. It is unlikely the current FFT is aligned in any scientific way with the CCSS, let alone with Kentucky's own internally developed research bases for "effective teaching" (Kentucky Department of Education, 2010) and other initiatives. It cannot be, because those policy instruments literally did not exist at the time the FFT was validated.

The fact that the Measures of Effective Teaching Project was sponsored by the corporate reform group the Bill and Melinda Gates Foundation should not be overlooked or underestimated in this case (Bill and Melinda Gates Foundation, 2013). The Gates Foundation has become one of the foremost leaders of Common Core reform efforts designed by government and corporate interests to reform schools and prepare students for college and career, effectively making public schools feeder systems for the U.S. workforce (an intensely Taylorist and Fordist approach). While the Gates Foundation is ostensibly nonprofit, its monetary grants to various states like Kentucky have regularly entailed agreements that the funded state adopt and/or pilot educational reform instruments and resources. This fact makes the Gates Foundation's grants seem very much like trading money for goods and services—an act that would otherwise be treated as a capitalistic transaction. Such grants and their ties to Taylorist/Fordist discourses lend credence to Delandshere and Petrosky's (2004) warning that such standardization constitutes a monopoly on thought. If schooling is standardized in these ways, our historic experiences with such reforms predict that the results will not be successful (Stone, 2002; Tyack & Cuban, 1995). They will be inequitable, limiting, unsuccessful, and even unjust in that they penalize professionals and their students for any perceived lack of conformity, regardless of what may be strong evidence that would otherwise justify their variances and demonstrate better results.

The lack of nonpartisan tests of validity automatically calls use of the FFT into question. Similar to the Danielson Group's claims that the FFT is scientifically valid for use with the CCSS, there is no evidence of research issued by the state of Kentucky, for example, that the FFT was independently validated for use with that state's internal policies and resources. Kentucky claims it validated the FFT through the Educational Testing Service (ETS) in 2013. However, the link provided by the Kentucky Department of Education leads to an Educational Testing Service (ETS) promotional web page offering no information regarding validation studies of the FFT in Kentucky. The ETS does make the following claim regarding such work on the page: "Due to ETS's experience, our clients typically accept more than 90 percent of our items on the first review" (ETS, 2014, para. 4). In other words, for a fee, the ETS offers states customized evaluation instruments that those states typically accept as valid simply because ETS claims to be "experienced" and therefore trustworthy. This is equivalent to accepting the claim that a customer should trust a salesman simply because the salesman has been selling things for a long time. It is not a sufficient claim, and certainly not for supporting assertions that the ETS validated Kentucky's materials and found no problems with alignment across the several policy texts, resources, and other instruments specified as part of Kentucky's project in relation to the FFT.

The additional fact that both the ETS and other ostensibly nonprofit groups like the Gates Foundation are somehow nonpartisan and devoid of corporatist interests is also misleading, in that their status as "nonprofit" groups lends them an air of being unbiased or disinterested parties. This is not the case. Both the ETS and the Gates Foundation are effectively corporate entities designed to accomplish the monopoly on thought that Delandshere and Petrosky (2004) warn about. It is notable that ETS' annual *revenue* was reported to be $411,000,000 as early as the mid-1990s, even though ETS is technically a *nonprofit* entity (Nordheimer & Frantz, 1997). The Gates Foundation reports having a total of $40.2 *billion* in its endowment fund as of April 2014. Such revenues and corporate endowments (profits) raise questions about how such nonprofit groups interact with for-profit corporations and state governments in the creation and trade of public education goods and services. Given the FFT's scant evidence for scientific validity, it is troubling that such a rubric would be advocated for use to evaluate all teachers in all contexts based on deeply flawed claims from nonprofit subsidiaries and special-interest groups with corporate ties and methods that have long been found to do harm in education.

Giroux (2012) points out corporate measures of teacher quality constrain teachers' choices of method, design, and resources, and they undermine innovation for students' future success—both explicit goals of the CCSSI, the Danielson Group, and Kentucky's Department of Education. Under an accountability regime like this, teachers are forced to set aside any innovative ideas or alternatives they would otherwise use as professional experts and conform to the requirements of policy even if that means ignoring knowledge and evidence. Using the FFT in false alignment with the CCSSI makes Giroux's claims likely, if paradoxical. Educators working with the FFT will be positioned to work within the constraints of an accountability system that, intentionally or not, is designed in ways that systematically de-skill and deprofessionalize their work. Following Giroux's logic, even professionals who would seek to resist such things, the FFT as it is currently being used decreases the likelihood that they will have the opportunity to consider resistance or even reform viable options. They will not merely fail to prepare their students for college and careers due to incompetence. They will be *positioned to fail* to meet criteria for success by that policy regime's evaluation instrument (the FFT) to become persistently ineffective (Fairclough, 1995). The FFT as a proposed solution could easily become antithetical to reformers' goals.

The above conclusion raises an additional question: Is the FFT actually an efficient instrument that addresses the complex and comprehensive nature of teaching? No. It is not and it does not. In the next section, I explore ways in which the FFT represents a practically impossible approach to teacher evaluation.

The FFT As a Tool for Systematic Failure

The Problem of Time

While there are numerous problems that might be identified when considering how users of the FFT may use it, it is useful to simply consider the scope of the rubric. With 4 domains, 22 components, and 76 indicators for rating teacher quality, the evaluation is not even possible on a purely practical level in public schools. Immediately, *time* becomes a central concern for any individual, group, or institution seeking to use the FFT. It is possible to offer the following scenarios and identify serious flaws in FFT implementation based on simple math.

For the purposes of this thought experiment, I take the example of a large suburban high school in Kentucky that plans to hire a single, full-time employee who will be responsible for *all* FFT evaluations across all grade levels and all content areas. Based on state policy, all nontenured teachers must be evaluated three times per year, and one third of all tenured teachers will be evaluated twice each year in a 3-year rotating cycle. The high school currently employs 120 teachers. To be realistic, I assume the evaluator will *not* spend time rating the FFT domain of Professional Responsibilities during classroom observation time because that domain's indicators are generally unrelated to classroom teaching. Approximately 36 teachers at the school are untenured, requiring a total of 108 evaluation observations. The remaining 84 tenured personnel mean the school's evaluator will need to conduct evaluations of an additional 28 employees twice each. The result is 164 total evaluations per year. Several considerations of time within the FFT process become highly relevant: preparation, observation, data collection, data analysis, and feedback.

For each evaluation the school's FFT evaluator conducts, we must assume that the evaluator will do at least the following: conduct a thorough review of standards- and research-based instructional plans used/designed by the teacher being evaluated, spend a full instructional period conducting each observation according to the domains of the FFT, analyze evidence based on data collected during classroom observation, and oversee conferences with the evaluated teachers to communicate results and set goals for future continuous improvement.

Let us presume the evaluator spends just one hour analyzing instructional materials a teacher has designed for an evaluation. With 164 evaluations to complete each year, the evaluator would require, at minimum, 164 hours for review and preparation. After reviewing plans and conducting evaluations, the evaluator is further required to meet with each teacher in order to analyze results, set goals, and plan for improvement. Again, I will allot one hour per teacher per performance for data analysis by the evaluator, and one hour for conferencing with the teacher—activities that require the FFT evaluator spend an additional 328 hours.

Through simple addition, the total amount of time spent completing basic FFT implementation is 492 hours of work. Now, recall that the FFT evaluator is required to observe each teacher for a full instructional period. In a 90-minute block-style schedule, this evaluator would require an additional 162 hours. The total time for the FFT evaluator to review teachers' designs, observe and evaluate implementation, and confer with the teacher to set goals for improvement in this school will be 654 hours, minimum, based on an assumption that there are no significant problems at any point and the teachers perform at an adequate level at all times. Given that Kentucky requires 185 days of school, and each daily schedule lasts approximately 7 hours (1,295 hours), the time for FFT implementation alone constitutes over 50% of the school year. It is important to note that these hours include built-in, mandatory time for instructional planning, noninstructional meetings, professional development, lunch, standardized testing, and more—all of which render an estimate of 1,295 hours extremely generous. This makes implementation of the FFT in Kentucky seem more or less reasonable, if the evaluator's tasks ended there and we ignored the fact that the allotted time entails the implementation of many noninstructional activities. However, this approach to the problem of time remains deceiving. It is not the larger context of the school year that should be used to realize the futility of the FFT. It is the time allotted for classroom teaching and learning that reveals the FFT's flaws.

At a finer-grained level, we can calculate the time an FFT evaluator has to observe each teacher for the 56 indicators on the rubric focused explicitly on teaching. With 56 indicators to observe, document, and explain using concrete evidence in a 90-minute block period, the evaluator would have to rate a teacher for one indicator once every 1.6 minutes. In a traditional 55-minute class period, the evaluator would have to complete one indicator per minute. In either case, completion of an indicator evaluation would require observing a discrete behavior in one of the FFT domains, identifying it as relevant, noting its instance and quality, identifying and citing evidence of outcomes, and rating the teacher. Given the scope of the rubric and the tasks it requires, completing a full FFT rubric in a single 90-minute teaching episode is simply impossible unless the evaluator is allowed to focus on just one domain at a time per episode. However, if that were allowed, we could easily calculate how much additional time a thorough evaluation would require to the extent that no evaluator could conceivably maintain such a pace of evaluation, data analysis, and conferencing. If the evaluator focused on rating teachers for just one domain per teaching episode, it would triple the number of required observations, the time spent reviewing instructional designs, and the time conferencing with teachers to set improvement goals. That total would amount to 1,962 hours, which is 150% of the time officially scheduled for a full academic year in the state of Kentucky. As such, division of the FFT is definitively unworkable in a single-evaluator system, and that only accounts for the evaluator's direct implementation of the FFT in absurd conditions. No evaluator could reasonably complete a fair, thorough evaluation of all the FFT's indicators in the time allotted. It would be both physically, mentally, and logistically impossible.

Again, the FFT (and the corporatist regime in which it is being implemented) are easily and simply found to be too unwieldy. In this case, we have not even attempted to account for evaluation of teachers' nonclassroom-based Professional Responsibilities, the fourth domain of the FFT. Simply put, the Danielson FFT rubric is designed in a way that makes authentic assessment (let alone evaluation) impossible without doing serious harm and rendering extremely questionable findings. That conclusion does not account for the rubric's additional limitations with regard to how it defines quality teaching, ineffective practices, and accomplished performances such as those the editors of this volume enumerate in their introduction.

The Problems of Constructivism

As the editors rightly point out (this volume), the FFT presents evaluation options that are at best ignorant of cultural differences in particular and sociocultural interactions in general (e.g., the FFT does nothing to define students' "civil" behavior, even though the concept of civility differs across cultures and contexts). The FFT also has a tendency toward incoherence in its claims of alignment with constructivist principles of teaching and learning. For example, Domain 1B: Planning and Preparation, "Demonstrating Knowledge of Students" would appear to align with constructivist teaching principles on a superficial level. However, one guiding example of data that would result in an "accomplished" rating for the teacher according to the Kentucky/Danielson FFT is described as follows: "The teacher realizes that not all of his students are Christian and so he plans to read a Hanukkah story in December" (2014, p. 8). Another offers, "The teacher plans to ask her Spanish-speaking students to discuss their ancestry as part of their social studies unit on South America" (p. 8). These are appallingly ignorant examples of teachers who do not simply fail to demonstrate knowledge of their students but in fact indicate that the teacher *lacks* significant knowledge about his/her students' diverse identities or how to utilize them for enhanced teaching. Still, in the FFT, these are offered as examples of "accomplished" practice and sufficient professional quality.

In the first example, the Judeo-Christian focus requires any user to ask whether the teacher is aware that many students adhere to neither of those religions and will thus be less likely to engage. It also raises questions about why such texts would be used to teach at all, simply because the time of year coincides with Judeo-Christian holidays. Many professionals would evaluate such a basis for instructional planning as far short of "accomplished" as specified in the FFT. Many would find such examples unprofessional and "ineffective" because they violate prominent constructivist precepts of designing curriculum based on learners' identities, prior experiences, purposes, impulses, and interests. In this case, and many more, the FFT fails its own claim to alignment with constructivist pedagogies and may even position teachers to fail if they use constructivist precepts well.

Similarly, under the same indicator, an "accomplished" teacher would notice that several students spoke Spanish and therefore design lessons requiring them to explore their heritage during a unit of study about "South America." This example of "accomplished" practice is at best ignorant and practically racist in its stereotypical representation of Latino cultures and students. Spanish is spoken in many countries *not located in South America*, and not all South American countries utilize Spanish as their official language. Many professionals would rate such a plan as highly *ineffective* in constructivist terms. It could easily cause students' performance and engagement to decrease due to stereotype threats that impair their abilities to think, concentrate, and perform at optimal levels (Steele, 2011).

The Problem of Teachers As "the" Most Significant Variable

Even if a teacher is considered the single most important factor in improving student achievement in any classroom (RAND Corporation, 2014), it is generally understood by education experts that most external factors cannot be controlled by those teachers (e.g., the learner's educational history, social class, access, opportunity, etc.). It is further accepted that these uncontrollable variables have far greater collective impacts on student success than any individual teacher. Still, many student behaviors that are definitively outside of a teacher's control are used to inform the use of the FFT. However, because these uncontrollable variables are integral to using the FFT, that rubric positions evaluators to make teachers accountable for controlling them in all anyway despite the fact that they have been found to be invalid criteria (Sawchuck, 2011).

In short, classroom teaching entails the evaluation of too many unquantifiable or unknown variables that make anything more than subjective assessment of teacher quality a lie (Berliner, 2005). Add to that the fact that any user of the FFT rubric *must* possess the full range of both content knowledge and pedagogical content knowledge of the discipline in which the teacher is working (English, mathematics, biology, physics, history, economics, music, drama, and many more), and the project of evaluating teacher quality becomes even more untenable.

The Problems of Disciplinary and Pedagogical Expertise

As Moje et al. (2004) have found, each discipline entails a set of unique literacy practices, specialized terminology, ways of thinking and communicating, and ways of determining success and even truth in ways that are different than those used in other disciplines. As a result of these differences, Ippolito, Lawrence, and Zaller (2013) note that each content area must use unique or adapted methods in ways that are not the same as those in other subjects. Any FFT evaluator would have to be a fully trained disciplinary expert in *all* of the content areas s/he is assigned to for teacher evaluation. In the case presented here, that would require a single employee to master *every* discipline and subdiscipline taught in a school's curriculum and also recognize the peculiar teaching practices of each discipline in order to observe successfully.

CONCLUSION

In short, the FFT is a standardized one-size-fits-all rubric. It is framed using a corporate, Taylorist/Fordist discourse of continuous improvement that actually ensures no teacher can ever be rated as entirely successful on a consistent basis, and makes it even less likely for a teacher to be deemed as "exemplary" for more than a few indicators regardless of actual performance and ability. In fact, the FFT is designed so that even the most successful teacher will receive at least some "ineffective" ratings each time s/he is evaluated simply because the rubric is designed to result in the need for continuous improvement.

As Fairclough (1995) would argue, the FFT utilizes that discourse of continuous improvement to mask its actual purpose as a tool for ensuring a fabricated state of *in*effectiveness for most teachers most of the time. It makes teacher quality evaluation a project specifically designed to identify goals for continuous improvement because the accountability regime requires the institutionalization of continuous improvement—a circular argument that makes evaluating actual teacher quality meaningless.

As Labaree (2012) finds, this is all very unfortunate but entirely predictable, and it actually fulfills the many contradictory purposes imposed on public education. As Labaree details, the U.S. education system has been designed by states to serve both public and private interests, serve politics and markets as well as liberal democratic values, and promote both equality and inequality, all at the same time. He notes that "These educational goals represent the contradictions embedded in any liberal democracy, contradictions that cannot be resolved without removing either the society's liberalism or its democracy (p. 17). Few professional educators, regardless of ideology or politics, are likely to advocate the abandonment of democratic values. Education is both a public *and* private good wherein people reasonably expect to find consistent quality and measures to hold those who operate the system accountable when it does not work. However, as Labaree (2000) has also found, teaching is hard work that seems easy to many people, including professionals who may work in the education system despite their ignorance of its complexities. None of this is to say that rubrics for teacher evaluation constitute an evil. Rather, it is to say rubrics like the FFT are inadequate for the tasks at hand. We must do better.

Designing good rubrics requires deep knowledge of content, pedagogies, and social contexts related to education. It requires consideration of school logistics. It requires the ability to equitably structure assessments that, frankly, *assess* rather than *rate* teacher quality. It also highlights the fact that educators might have greater success developing assessments that are adaptable and flexible rather than standardized. Rubrics should be capable of translation across disciplines and classrooms, or specialized to respond to particulars in those myriad contexts.

Policymakers and professional educators must be suspicious of "claims based on appeals to precision, certainty, clarity, and rigor," and proceed with the realization that accountability is always "temporal, fallible, limited, compromised, negotiated, incomplete, and contradictory" (Cherryhomles, 1988, pp. 142–143). By standardizing what "good" teaching looks like, the FFT is a rubric that does not promote success. It fabricates needs, and in doing so, it standardizes curriculum in ways that are utterly counter to the positions of the CCSSI policies and constructivist principles it purports to uphold. Given that the Kentucky Department of Education, as one example, adopted the CCSSI's standards, its use of them explicitly asserts that it is implementing those policies and principles in their totality, when that is not the actual case. Reflecting Delandshere and Petrosky's (2004) finding that advocates of standards-based reform tend to treat such a project as simple, Kentucky's use of the CCSSI in conjunction with the FFT treats deeply complex concepts, challenges, and variables as if they were a simple, easily accounted for, and uniform set of problems that can be addressed in a standardized rubric.

As a matter of policy, the CCSSI cautions that teachers must be "free to provide students with whatever tools and knowledge their professional judgment and experience identify as most helpful" (National Governors Association Center for Best Practices, 2010, para. 4). They also state the standards "do not—indeed, cannot—enumerate all or even most of the content that students should learn" (National Governors Association Center for Best Practices, 2010, para. 15). Finally, for the purposes of this critique, the CCSSI states explicitly that no standards "can fully reflect the great variety in abilities, needs, learning rates, and achievement levels of students in any given classroom" (2010, para. 18). Given that these are the policies of the Common Core that the Danielson Group claims to align with, we must conclude that there is a tremendous amount of work to be done if the FFT, or *any* rubric, can be made valid and sustainable for use in teacher assessment or evaluation. For now, the FFT is a product of corporate standardization. It is a one-size-fits-all rubric that actually fits none.

REFERENCES

Apple, M. (1990). *Ideology and curriculum.* New York, NY: Routledge.

Ash, A. (2008). *Post-Fordism: A reader.* New York, NY: Wiley.

Bardach, E. (2005). *A practical guide to policy analysis: The eightfold path to more effective problem solving* (2nd ed.). Washington, DC: CQ.

Berliner, D. (2005). The near impossibility of testing for teacher quality. *Journal of Teacher Education, 56*(3), 205–213.

Bill and Melinda Gates Foundation. (2013). Ensuring fair and reliable measures of effective teaching: Culminating findings from the MET's three-year study. *MET Project.* Retrieved from http://metproject.org/downloads/MET_Ensuring_Fair_and_Reliable_Measures_Practitioner_Brief.pdf

Burns, L. D. (2014). *Moving targets: A critical discourse analysis of standards and teacher preparation in English language arts.* Saarbrücken, Germany: Scholars.

Cherryholmes, C. (1988). *Power and criticism: Poststructural investigations in education.* New York, NY: Teachers College Press.

Common Core State Standards Initiative (CCSSI). (2010). *Common Core State Standards Initiative: Preparing America's students for college and career.* Retrieved from http://www.corestandards.org/

Danielson, C. (2013). The framework for teaching evaluation instrument. Princeton, NJ: *Danielson Group.* Retrieved from http://danielsongroup.org/framework

Danielson, C. (2014, August 1). Kentucky framework for teaching. *Kentucky Department of Education.* Retrieved from http://education.ky.gov/teachers/pges/tpges/pages/kentucky-framework-for-teaching.aspx

Delandshere, G., & Petrosky, A. (2004). Political rationales and ideological stances of the standards-based reform of teacher education in the U.S. *Teaching and Teacher Education, 20*(1), 1–15.

Educational Testing Service (ETS). (2014). *Educator licensure: Custom state solutions.* Retrieved from https://www.ets.org/educator_licensure/custom/

Fairclough, N. (1995). *Critical discourse analysis: The critical study of language.* London, UK: Longman.

Giroux, H. A. (2012). Education and the crisis of public values: Challenging the assault on teachers, students, & public education. New York, NY: Peter Lang.

Ippolito, J., Lawrence, J. F., & Zaller, C. (Eds.). (2013). *Adolescent literacy in the era of the Common Core: From research to practice.* Cambridge, MA: Harvard University Press.

Kentucky Department of Education. (2013, July 31). Characteristics of highly effective teaching and learning (CHETL). *Kentucky Department of Education.* Retrieved from http://education.ky.gov/curriculum/docs/pages/characteristics-of-highly-effective-teaching-and-learning-(chetl).aspx

Labaree, D. L. (2000). On the nature of teaching and teacher education: Difficult practices that seem easy. *Journal of Teacher Education, 51*(3), 228–233.

Labaree, D. L. (2012). *Someone has to fail: The zero-sum game of public schooling.* Cambridge, MA: Harvard University Press.

Moje, E., Ciechanowski, K. M., Kramer, L., Ellis, L., Carrillo, R., & Collazo, T. (2004). Working toward third space in content area literacy: An examination of everyday funds of knowledge and Discourse. *Reading Research Quarterly, 39*(1), 38–70.

National Governors Association Center for Best Practices, Council of Chief State School Officers. (2010). *English language arts standards.* Washington, DC: Author. Retrieved from http://www.corestandards.org/ELA-Literacy/ introduction/key-design-consideration/

New London Group. (2000). *Multiliteracies: Literacy learning and the design of social futures.* New York, NY: Routledge.

Nordheimer, J., & Frantz, D. (1997, September 30). Testing giant exceeds roots, drawing business rivals' ire. *The New York Times.* Retrieved from http://www. nytimes.com/1997/09/30/us/testing-giant-exceeds-roots-drawing-business-rivals-ire.html

Null, W. (2011). *Curriculum: From theory to practice.* Lanham, MD: Rowman & Littlefield.

RAND Corporation. (2014). *Teaching matters: Understanding teachers' impact on student achievement.* Retrieved from http://www.rand.org/education/projects/ measuring-teacher-effectiveness/teachers-matter.html

Sawchuk, S. (2011). *EWA research brief: What studies say about teacher effectiveness.* Washington, DC: Education Writer's Association.

Smagorinsky, P. (1999). Time to teach. *English Education, 32,* 50–73.

Spiro, R., Coulson, R., Feltovich, P., & Anderson, D. (1988). Cognitive flexibility theory: Advanced knowledge acquisition in ill-structured domains. In V. Patel (Ed.), *Tenth annual conference of the cognitive science society* (pp. 375–383). Hillsdale, NJ: Erlbaum.

Steele, C. (2011). *Whistling Vivaldi: How stereotypes affect us and what we can do.* New York, NY: Norton.

Stone, D. (2002). Policy paradox: The art of political decision making (Rev. ed.). New York, NY: Norton.

Tyack, D., & Cuban, L. (1995). *Tinkering toward utopia: A century of public school reform.* Cambridge, MA: Harvard University Press.

CHAPTER 13

RACING THE UNCONSIDERED

Considering Whiteness, Rubrics, and the Function of Oppression

Joseph E. Flynn, Jr.

Little boxes on the hillside,
Little boxes made of ticky tacky,
Little boxes on the hillside,
Little boxes all the same . . .
And the children go to school . . .
And then to the university,
Where they are put in boxes
And they come out all the same.

—*Little Boxes,* Malvina Reynolds (1962)

A central question that drove the creation of this edited volume is what are the ways in which the ever-growing use of rubrics for teacher and student evaluation have had an impact on education and society? This is a challenging question that is rarely entertained when the issue of rubrics arises. Typically, when we talk about rubrics, the focus is on how to design or use them more effectively. Extending the discussion to consider the tacit implications of rubrics is imperative in the spirit of furthering keen examinations of the ways in which hidden curricula (Apple, 2004; Giroux, 1981; Jackson, 1990;

Rubric Nation, pages 201–221
Copyright © 2015 by Information Age Publishing
All rights of reproduction in any form reserved.

Lewis, 2001) are perpetuated. One can argue that rubrics are not tools of instruction and therefore do not necessarily contribute to the hidden curriculum, but that is dependent upon how one defines curriculum, which is a contested issue itself (Lunenberg, 2011; Null, 2011; Pinar, 2011). Simultaneously, teachers (and administrators for that matter) are not inoculated from these hidden curricula either. Teachers at all levels of education are often locked into a strange position with rubrics. Not only do teachers design and employ rubrics to evaluate the learning of their students, but also teachers are subjected to the use of rubrics for the oftentimes high-stakes evaluations of their own performance. In short, the ubiquity of rubrics has a direct impact on all stakeholders in the classroom, despite the lack of critical dialogue about the implications of rubrics. One such implication is how rubrics further epistemologies of Whiteness and inadvertently contribute to the creation of structures of racial oppression in the United States.

One of the greatest challenges to understanding racial oppression (i.e., racism) is seeing past discrete instances of prejudice and discrimination toward an understanding of systemic and institutional racism. As defined by social scientists and antiracist educators, racism as a system of advantage based on race (Hitchcock, 2011; Tatum, 2002; Wellman, 1993), which conflicts with popular conceptions of racism. To be exact, Sensoy and DiAngelo (2011) define racism as follows:

> In the United States and Canada, racism refers to White racial and cultural prejudice and discrimination, supported by institutional power and authority, used to the advantage of Whites and the disadvantage of people of color. Racism encompasses economic, political, social, and institutional actions and beliefs that perpetuate an unequal distribution of privilege, resources, and power between Whites and people of color. (p. 187)

Although personal proclivities, actions, and opinions (acts of individual racism) are important to consider in the reproduction of racism in our society, what is far more crucial is an interrogation of how our institutions further racism through discursive practices and the ways in which a particular set of epistemologies frames our contexts, decisions, and actions. Focusing on the discrete actions of individuals is essential, as those discreet actions encapsulate examples of how individuals can live (or not live) an antiracist life. However, that does not eclipse the ways in which epistemologies and discursive practices further the institutional nature of racism.

If racism is sustained and furthered through institutional discursive practices and epistemologies, then the question is how does this happen, especially given a social context that roundly chastises individuals for perceived racist acts? After all, the United States has a bevy of laws and policies that regulate workplaces, schools, and other institutions against racism. Individuals are charged with discouraging discriminating or racist behaviors, and the hope is that through the imposition and adjudication of laws and policies prohibiting racist practices in institutions, the collective actions and attitudes of individuals will result in the dismantling of racism. Unfortunately, the hope does not match reality; for after 50 years of the Civil Rights Act, Affirmative Action, and other policies and legal decisions, racism remains an intractable problem in the United States. There are numerous explanations of how racism is furthered through educational practices (Gillborn, 2008; Howard, 2006; Leonardo, 2013; Leonardo & Grubb, 2013; Nougera & Wing, 2006; Pollock, 2005; Vaught, 2011), but an aspect that has been missing from the analysis of racist institutional practices is the ways in which seemingly innocuous tools and strategies can also further racism. In this case, the objects of scrutiny are rubrics.

How do rubrics promote racism? Simply, the assumptions that underlie the use of rubrics promote particular epistemologies of Whiteness, and those assumptions are recirculated without question. This chapter will explore the notions of Whiteness and White epistemologies and their relationship to rubrics (inadvertently and/or deliberately). Although there are competing constructions of Whiteness, the work of Judith Katz (2003) and AnaLouise Keating (2007) yield valuable frameworks for thinking about how Whiteness is embedded in social and educational contexts through institutional policies and practices.

By understanding rubrics as a manifestation of Whiteness, we can further our understanding the subtleties of how institutional racism functions and sustains a position of privilege for Whiteness. As Turley and Gallagher (2008) point out, "Instead of declaring all rubrics 'good' or 'bad,' we need to examine what they do, why, and in whose interests" (p. 92). This is essential because as rubrics have become institutional mainstays in education, they invariably have an effect on how students—of all racial and ethnic groups—conform to the subtle and overt habits of mind furthered through rubrics (Maslow, 1948). Students, teachers, and administrators are constantly exposed to rubrics and therefore are exposed to the assumptions that are embedded in rubrics as a phenomenon. The repercussions of the use of rubrics over time hard wire students, teachers, and administrators into particular discursive practice that further promotes and privileges Whiteness, even though that assimilative process is not clearly recognized. Rubrics promote habits of mind that reflect White epistemologies and aid in the shaping of worldviews—an essential step in the internalization of oppression. To begin this discussion, I will first consider Whiteness Studies as a field of inquiry and further provide characteristics of White epistemologies. Then I will offer examples of White epistemologies embedded in rubrics, primarily the ideas of objectivity/neutrality, single-voiced perspectives, and nonrelationality.

Whiteness Studies and the Construction of White Epistemologies

Whiteness Studies emerged as a formal field of study in the late 1980s into the 1990s (Kennedy, Middleton, & Ratcliffe, 2005). It is defined as an area of study that uses a number of different disciplines (anthropology, economics, history, law, political science, psychology, philosophy, sociology, etc.) and critical frameworks (Critical Pedagogy, Critical Race Theory, Critical Multiculturalism, etc.) to move the phenomenon of Whiteness and White people to the "center of analysis in an unprecedented and unforeseen way . . . *Whiteness becomes the center of critique and transformation*" (Leonardo, 2013, pp. 6–7; emphasis in original). Leonardo (2013) goes on to comment that Whiteness Studies "poses critical questions about the history and status of Whiteness (a process not to be equated with Blackness or Otherness)" (p. 7). In effect, Whiteness Studies asks long-ignored questions regarding why and how Whiteness, and by extension those defined as White, became privileged in the U.S. social context, how that privileging is lived, and its implications for all citizens. In short, Whiteness Studies scholars ask a simple question: How and why is Whiteness privileged and what is the impact of that privileging?

Although Whiteness Studies did not necessarily emerge as a field of academic study until the latter 1980s, David Roediger (1999), a leading Whiteness Studies scholar, opined that Whiteness has been studied and critiqued since the first African stood on an auction block. Through narratives of captured, kidnapped, and enslaved Africans and African Americans (Douglass, 1845/2004; Equiano, 1789/1999; Jacobs, 1861/2011; Northup, 1853/2014), a great deal of text has been presented that explores the actions of White people, but theorizing the creation, impact, and privileging of Whiteness and White people is something different, requiring the use of a broad range of scholarly tools and frameworks.

W. E. B. DuBois was one of the first scholars to mount a discussion about how White superiority and privilege function. In his classic essay, "The Souls of White Folk," DuBois (1920) directly challenges the rise of White privilege:

> The discovery of personal whiteness among the world's peoples is a very modern thing,—a nineteenth and twentieth century matter, indeed. The ancient world would have laughed at such a distinction. The Middle Age regarded skin color with mild curiosity; and even up into the eighteenth century we were hammering our national manikins into one, great, Universal Man, with fine frenzy which ignored color and race even more than birth. Today we have changed all that, and the

world in a sudden, emotional conversion has discovered that it is white and by that token, wonderful! ("The Souls of White Folk," para 3).

In effect, DuBois was mounting a serious critique and historic contextualization of Whiteness as early as 1920. Rabaka (2007) summarizes the power of DuBois' ideas as follows:

> Long before the recent discourse on racism and critical white studies, DuBois called into question white superiority and white privilege, and the possibility of white racelessness and/or white racial neutrality and universality. He was one of the first theorists to chart the changes in race relations from de jure to de facto forms of white supremecy, referring to it, as early as 1910, as "the new religion of whiteness." (p. 2)

Similarly, Carter G. Woodson's (1933/1992) classic analysis, *The Miseducation of the Negro*, directly challenged the privilege of Whiteness by calling into question the ability of White folks to shape the understanding and marginalization of Blackness and Black folks through educational and curricular misrepresentations.

Critiques of Whiteness and the ways of White folk are by no means limited to African American scholars. Sanchez (1995) offered a stunning exploration of the history of the Americanization of Mexicans in California in the early 1900s. Key to his analysis is not only the narrative history but also the inclusion of expectations of assimilation for Mexicans that reflected White ways of being. In a more contemporary analysis, Lee (2005) explored the expectations of assimilation for Asian immigrants at a predominantly White school in the Midwest. In effect, non-Whites have critiqued and analyzed White people and Whiteness for quite some time, but it was not until fairly recently that the field of inquiry, Whiteness Studies, found a solid foothold in academia.

Peggy McIntosh's (1988) essay "White Privilege and Male Privilege: A Personal Account of Coming to See Correspondences through Work in Women's Studies," popularly known as "Unpacking the Invisible Knapsack" brilliantly and courageously defined White privilege and further offered a substantial number of examples of White privilege she observed in her own life. The essay served as a watershed moment in the examination of racial oppression and the privilege of Whiteness and White people. The essay has inspired a legion of White (and non-White) people to further critique the role of Whiteness in society. Through the detailed discussion of the epistemologies, actions, motivations, fears, traits, and characteristics of White folks, Whiteness Studies moved Whiteness and White people from the periphery to the center of critique. But that begs the question of what is Whiteness?

Whiteness Versus White People or Epistemology Versus Socially Constructed Identity

When talking about Whiteness, it is easy to conflate Whiteness with White people. However, there is a difference. White people are a socially constructed identity group, typically defined by skin color (Guess, 2006; Harris, 1993; Higginbotham, 1980). Those deemed White were able to access a range of rights and privileges at the expense of those not deemed White. In fact, the definition of a White person has shifted many times throughout the history of the United States. This idea can be seen in the struggles and marginalization of European ethnic groups like the Irish, Italians, and eastern Europeans during 1800s and 1900s (Ignatiev, 2008; Jacobson, 1999).Also, a key fact to consider in the political construction of race is states in the U.S. South had discrete sets of laws that defined who was and who was not White, typically assessed by maternal lineage and legal decisions (Higginbotham, 1980, 1998). In addition to the history of variances of racial definitions in Southern states, U.S. Supreme Court cases, particularly *Ozawa v. the United States* (1922) and the *United States v. Thind* (1923), denied Asians the opportunity for full citizenship because they could not be defined as free White persons. In the Ozawa case, the Court argued that White was synonymous with Caucasian, which Ozawa was not since he was of Asiatic descent. However, the Court, in less than a year, reversed its logic for Thind, who was scientifically classified as Caucasian but was a darker-skinned Indian. In short, what constitutes a White person is wholly dependent upon political and social forces.

Whiteness, on the other hand, is a racially framed set of epistemologies generally constructed as a system of thoughts, values, and beliefs that shape the ways in which an individual interacts with and interprets her/his environment (Feagin, 2014; Harris, 1993; Keating, 2007; Sensoy & DiAngelo, 2011). In effect, Whiteness is not necessarily a possession of those deemed White. To the contrary, anyone of any race or ethnicity can adopt Whiteness as an epistemological framework, although assimilating the epistemologies of Whiteness does not guarantee that one will be deemed White or receive all the privileges of being White. Whiteness is such a powerful force to reckon with because it encompasses ideas and values (not merely actions) that aid in shaping everything from social behaviors and mores to educational practices. Sayles-Hannon (2009) further defines Whiteness as "a way of thinking and understanding that influences how we (human beings of all 'races,' classes, genders, and sexualities) construct, perceive, and regulate our identities" (p. 711).

Whiteness, as a privileged institutionalized condition, positions everyone engaged with the project of education (virtually all institutions for that matter) to further approaches, constructs, and discourses informed by Whiteness. It is essential to consider the fact that our primary institutions were historically created and developed by White American and historically privileged those who embraced White epistemological frames, and the institution of education is not exempt from that history. This includes decisions like whether or not to use rubrics and the reasons generated to legitimate their use. The problem is that as a benefit of its privilege, the impact of Whiteness typically goes unacknowledged (Delpit, 1988; McIntosh, 1988; Yancy, 2004). Yancy (2004) forthrightly challenges the invisibility of Whiteness:

> Whiteness fails to see itself as alien, as seen, as recognized. To see itself as seen, Whiteness would have to deny the imperial epistemological and ontological base from which it sees what it wants (or has been shaped historically) to see . . . It refuses the difficult process of alienation and return, that is return to a different, antiwhiteness place of knowing and being. To refuse this process, Whiteness denies its own potential to be Other (to be "the not-same"), to see through the web of White meaning that it has spun. Whiteness refuses to transcend an economy of White discourse and action that creates the illusion of a social world of natural, immutable arrangements, arrangements that get axiological assignments (black = bad; white = good) from within a rigid system of White totalization. (p. 13)

Further commenting on the challenge and need for critically exploring Whiteness, Keating (2007) points out that "We are all, in various ways, inscripted into this 'white'/supremacist framework. Because this framework functions to benefit 'white'-raced people, they can be more invested in it" (p. 131). Her comment is especially important because when we consider something seemingly innocuous like rubrics, they are often talked about with the assumption that they are merely helpful tools for evaluation; the conversation about their use tends to stop there. Discussions of whose interests are served through rubrics or how rubrics reinscribe various assumptions that promote a particular worldview (in this case, White epistemologies) tend not to be entertained. Kincheloe and Steinberg (1998) also speak to the necessity of critiquing and challenging Whiteness. They say that "White ways of being can no longer be universalized, white communication practices can no longer be viewed unproblematically as the standard, and issues of race can no longer be relegated to the domain of those who are not White" (p. 18). Naturally, this begs the question of what exactly are White epistemologies?

By reviewing the research about Whiteness and White privilege, Katz (2003) created a typology of Whiteness that detailed its general aspects and assumptions. Included in her typology are aspects and assumptions like rugged individualism (i.e., self-reliance, centering of the individual, and control of the environment); the Protestant work ethic; respect for authority; the equivocation of wealth and worth; a winner/loser binary; time as a commodity; a future orientation (i.e., planning for the future, delayed gratification, progress is always a good thing); hierarchical decision making; emphasis on English and the written tradition; avoidance of conflict and minimization of emotions; avoidance of personal life in public dialogue; history and holidays based on Judeo-Christian, Western European, ancient Greek and Roman, and White experiences; and an action orientation. Katz also highlights the emphasis of the scientific method as central to Whiteness. The scientific method promotes ideas like objectivity, rationality, linear thought, cause/effect relationships, and the emphasis of quantitative data. These ideas have become central organizing concepts that have shaped educational practices and policies in the current era, particularly in reference to the *No Child Left Behind* requirement of scientifically based research and subsequent data-driven decision making (Learning Point Associates, 2007; Ravitch, 2011; Taubman, 2009; U.S. Department of Education, 2001).

Along with Katz (2003), Keating also delineated a number of primary characteristics of Whiteness. In her text, *Teaching Transformation: Transcultural Classroom Dialogues* (2007), she includes characteristics like nonrelational, discrete boundaries, unspoken norms, and separates and divides; overreliance on reason; dualisims, binary-oppositional thinking, and hierarchies; monolithic, single-voiced, and authoritative; neutral, distanced objectivity, examinablity/detachment, ahistorical; and finally, self-enclosed hyper-individualism (pp. 133–137).

It is crucial to point out that these aspects and assumptions are not solely the providence of Whiteness. In other words, the idea that if you work hard you will succeed (the Protestant work ethic) is singularly unique to Whiteness is not necessarily accurate. (To say that *only* White folks embrace hard work is also a racist statement because it further denigrates non-Whites). Rather, these general aspects, assumptions, and characteristics are privileged through Whiteness and all are expected to acquiesce to them. Epistemological frameworks, like Afrocentricity, feminism, or indigenous perspectives, for example, are constructed as *other* (or deviant at the extreme). The challenge is to see how one epistemological framework is privileged institutionally, for the privileging of one epistemology—in this case Whiteness—is a key element of oppression because the privileged epistemology establishes cultural norms and expectations at the expense of other groups.

There is a long history of the racial oppression of non-White racial groups and epistemologies (Higginbotham, 1980; Sanchez, 1995; Spring, 2012; Zinn, 2003). Central to these relationships is the idea that the epistemologies and cultural norms of the privileged or agent group are forced onto marginalized or target groups. Speaking specifically about the dichotomy of White America and Black America, Hacker (1992) wrote, "America is inherently a 'White' country: in character, in structure, in culture. Needless to say, Black Americans create lives of their own. Yet as a people, they face boundaries and constrictions set by the white majority (p. 4).

An example of the clashing and imposition of epistemologies also can be found in the story of indigenous Americans and Western Europeans (who ultimately created the idea and became known as White).[1] As the presence of many Western Europeans expanded westward, they felt that the cultural norms of the indigenous groups they encountered were primitive and unenlightened. Indigenous groups' cultural norms related to gender roles, relationship to land, notions of play and work, language, spirituality, and other social practices contrasted with those of the Western Europeans, resulting in the idea that indigenous Americans needed to be assimilated into what became White epistemologies and cultural norms and the subsequent establishment of boarding schools where indigenous American children were separated from their families and forced to adopt White ways of being (Spring, 2012).

These decisions and actions marginalized indigenous cultures and cemented the connection between Whiteness and oppression. Sensoy and DiAngelo (2011) say that oppression is

> the prejudice and discrimination of one social group against another, *backed by institutional power*. Oppression occurs when one group is able to enforce its prejudice and discrimination throughout society because it controls the institutions. Oppression occurs at the group and macro level, and goes well beyond individuals (p. 40).

What is of particular importance is the idea that oppression is *backed by institutional power*. By shaping policies, practices, and discourse, institutions privilege particular epistemologies that often go unquestioned (Cherryholmes, 1988), and in the United States, privileged epistemologies are largely rooted in Whiteness. Rubrics are not exempt from these forces.

It is essential to consider the Whiteness of rubrics as an effort to uncover how institutional practices inadvertently further oppressive practices. As stated above, the United States has expressed intolerance toward oppressive practices; all the while racism continues to have an indelible impact on the educational achievement and social opportunities for non-Whites (Gillborn, 2008; Leonardo & Grubb, 2013; Nougera, 2008; Pollock, 2004; Vaught, 2011). The lion's share of research on rubrics constructs them as a benefit for students, teachers, and administrators when designed well. Unfortunately, the research on rubrics has thus far steered clear of the epistemological influences that undergird them and the far-reaching effects they entail.

As Cherryholmes (1988) declares, we "are more concerned with performing expected actions than with analyzing them" (p. 6). In the spirit of a full analysis of rubrics, considering the racial implications is crucial to expanding our understanding of the subtle ways in which institutional racism functions. Furthermore, a racial analysis of White epistemologies that ground rubrics can help us understand how Whiteness sustains its privileged status and establishes social practices and expectations that all are expected to embrace, in effect making us all think and engage the same.

Rubrics: A Racial Framing

It may seem strange to mount an examination of the racial epistemologies and assumptions that are embedded in rubrics. But, as explicated above, the United States has a long and storied history with race, initially based on the assumption that the ways of being and epistemologies of non-White groups were somehow inferior or unenlightened and needed to be corrected. The seeds of racism sewn 400 years ago did in fact produce some troublesome crops, and we have been eating those crops ever since the first notions of Whiteness were inculcated into laws, policies, and social practices. To assume that rubrics are exempt from that history minimizes the power and reach of institutional racism and the privilege of Whiteness across the history of the U.S. social and institutional context. The issue that manifests in relation to Whiteness and rubrics is that the critically unquestioned nature of rubrics sustains and institutionally reinforces Whiteness because the assumptions that undergird rubrics that are directly related to epistemologies of Whiteness are left unexamined. Since students, teachers, and administrators are routinely exposed to rubrics, they are also exposed to the assumptions and epistemologies that serve as the foundation of rubrics. Especially in the case of students and teachers, rubrics encourage particular habits of mind and experience that, in this analysis, promote long-standing institutionalized epistemologies of Whiteness. In effect, rubrics become more than simple tools for evaluation and assessment; they become a tacit tool in the sustaining of institutional and systemic racism.

In an earlier chapter in this volume, Tenam-Zemach discussed Maslow's (1948) notion of *rubricization* and the sustaining of the status quo. She stated,

> Basically, Maslow [1948] posits that our nature is to attend to the world in a way so that it already conforms to how we perceive it. It is a human's way of maintaining the "status quo, rather than a true recognition of change, novelty and flux" (p. 23). We tend to force what is new to align as much as possible with what is familiar and comfortable. (Tenem-Zemach, this volume, p. 3).

The perception of the world in the U.S. social and institutional context is racially framed through Whiteness (Feagin, 2014), and it is the consistent reinscription and privileging of the White racial frame that serves as the foundation of institutionally racist practices. In effect, the assumptions, aspects, and characteristics that are privileged through Whiteness serve as the metaphorical air we all are expected to breathe. And much like the air we breathe, we have the tendency to not question its quality. In a context wherein a particular epistemology—Whiteness—is privileged, the status quo is to continue the privileging of Whiteness in all areas of existence. Regardless of whether or not we are talking about the trivial (e.g., popular culture) or the foundational (like the sacrosanctity of the Protestant work ethic or the scientific method and their assumptions), Whiteness is privileged. Rubrics are not outside that framing.

This chapter does not offer the space to mount a full consideration of the relationship between rubrics and Whiteness, but a few examples can be considered. As introduced above, Katz (2003) and Keating (2007) offered a number of assumptions, aspects, and characteristics of Whiteness, many of which are directly reflected in and sustained through rubrics. Let us consider for a moment the characteristics of objectivity and neutrality, single-voiced perspectives, and nonrelationality.

Objectivity and Neutrality

The ideas of objectivity and neutrality are key to the epistemologies of Whiteness and its social and institutional privileging. Sayles-Hannon (2009) discusses the notion of neutrality and points out "In academic multiculturalism, neutrality can often be one of the trickiest characteristics of 'whiteness' to identify. Recognizing neutrality requires that we look at what is not-stated, assumed, or understood to be the most objective approach for research or assessments" (p. 715). This idea is especially important in the case of rubrics and encapsulates the heart of not only this chapter but also this book. Rubrics operate without much critical thought about their impact. But there is another side of the notions of objectivity and neutrality in the critical consideration of rubrics and White epistemologies.

Research has shown that a key assumption about the use of rubrics is that their use ensures a level of objectivity for the evaluator (Campbell 2005; Crank, 1999; Reitmeier, Svendsen, & Vrchota, 2004; Spandel, 2006). This objectivity, or neutrality, is evidenced by clearly delineated expectations, acceptable performance markers, and scoring strategies. Reitmeirer et al. (2004) declare that the use of rubrics moves evaluations from "subjective observations to specific performances" (p. 18). In other words, rubrics are used with the intent of minimizing subjective and personal influences in evaluation, as though somehow further framing the evaluation moment for an individual through a rubric ensures a neutral or objective stance for the evaluator. However, rubrics are social constructions and therefore are never objective since they are created by people from an often unexamined set of values, beliefs, and dispositions. Especially in the case of rubrics like Danielson's (2013) and Marzzano's (2007), rubrics are often created with guiding principles and strategies culled from decades of research about effective teaching. But as Kuhn (1996) discusses, research studies are neither objective nor are research paradigms and their attendant assumptions.

Research and commentary about rubrics popularly constructs them as tools to aid evaluators (Turley & Gallagher, 2008). The rubrics-as-merely-tools metaphor endorses the notion of objectivity and neutrality in that a tool, by its very nature, is only useful until someone picks it up and uses it for the purposes it was designed. Unfortunately, this proposition obscures the idea that the very creation of a tool happens in a context with a certain set of assumptions, intentions, and reprecussions (both intended and unintended assumptions). For example, language (in this example, Standard English[2] specifically) is also a socially constructed tool individuals learn in order to successfully navigate a social context. Language in and of itself is defined as an objective set of rules, but in practice it is used as a gatekeeping mechanism that marginalizes those who have not acquired or mastered the language. In context, an African American or Latino student who comes to school with a different primary language is marginalized or excluded as a result of not using the language of wider communication, Standard English. Because the student has not mastered the language, she is marginalized. In effect, so-called Standard English, although constructed as an objective or neutral phenomenon, is ultimately laden with a range of subjectivities and further employed in multiple ways that shape social conditions and possibilities. Objectivity is ultimately a myth that gives way to social conditions dependent upon space and power.

Despite the declaration of objectivity, rubrics are only as objective as the person(s) who created them. They are laden with imposed assumptions of quality, imposed assumptions of order, imposed assumptions of worth, and imposed assumptions of fairness. Rubrics are invariably created with a certain set of expectations in mind that an evaluator either declares herself or willfully accepts from others (states and districts adopting and requiring the use of the Danielson rubric (2013) for teacher evaluation, for example). However, Stellmack, Konheim-Kalkstein, Manor, Massey, and Schmitz (2009) showed that despite the extolled virtue of objectivity and neutrality through rubrics, they are not panaceas against subjectivity. One could argue that the promise of objectivity is in fact a false promise, a bamboozling of sorts. Regardless, objectivity is a key argument for the use of rubrics in assessment and evaluation, one that is almost blindly embraced in the United States while other regions around the globe are not as quick (Reddy & Andrade, 2009) to make large-scale adoptions of them.

Single-Voiced Perspectives

The primary contradiction inherent in the promotion of Whiteness through rubrics is that while rubrics sell the promise of objectivity, they also promote single-voiced perspectives about what is effective practice or performance. In the process of creating a rubric, it is essential to codify a set of standards or expectations the person being evaluated (student, teacher, or otherwise) must be held accountable to. Once those standards or expectations have been encoded into a rubric, they become a "fixed" idea and the representation of a singular perspective about what is and what is not an effective or proficient performance.

Consider the Charlotte Danielson *Framework for Teaching* rubric (2013), which is being adopted wholly or in adapted versions in many states and districts for the evaluation of teachers. Danielson posits that her rubric for teacher evaluation is culled from decades of best-practice research on effective teaching. Specifically she states,

> The Framework for Teaching identifies those aspects of a teacher's responsibilities that have been documented through empirical studies and theoretical research as promoting improved student learning. While the Framework is not the only possible description of practice, these responsibilities seek to define what teachers should know and be able to do in the exercise of their profession. (p. 1)

Although many researchers using a wide range of methodologies, research paradigms, philosophical orientations, and political beliefs offered a number of research studies and theories on best practices in education, once Danielson (2013) reviewed, summarized, and encoded those findings into a rubric, she created a document that provided a singular vision of what "good teaching" looks like, a document that is ultimately filtered and constructed through her own values, ideals, interpretations, and dispositions. This is not a challenge to the legitimacy of Danielson's values, ideals, or dispositions (or, by the same token, any other person or team who creates a rubric). Rather, it is a statement that points to the idea that a rubric, regardless of whom creates it, fixes a single perspective or voice and further expresses a singular set of values, beliefs, perspectives, and dispositions that become the singular guiding perspective of an evaluation.

Nonrelationality

The nonrelationality nature of Whiteness is key to sustaining White privilege in that it forces us to not see the fact that the matrix of our identities has an impact on all aspects of our individual lives, experiences, and interpretations. Sayles-Hannon (2009) discusses this characteristic in relation to the development of multicultural curriculum. She states,

> The non-relational characteristic of "whiteness" functions to maintain its
> authority by minimizing, erasing, or omitting the multiple and interlocking
> facets of identities. When one has to pick a single aspect of one's identity
> (i.e., "race," class, gender, or sexuality) to encompass and represent one's en-
> tire self, intersections are ignored. (p. 716)

In effect, Sayles-Hannon is pointing out the importance of understanding
the idea of intersectionality (Crenshaw, 1991, 1995; Flynn, Hunt, Wickman,
Cohen, & Fox, 2014), the idea that each of us, again, is a matrix of identities. This is a complicated notion, for embracing the notion of intersectionality disallows the simple stereotyping of individuals. When considering this
in terms of rubrics, it is essential to first consider the idea that experience
and identity are inextricably tied together. My experience as an African
American, middle-class, heterosexual, male from the Midwest is invariably
different than that of a Mexican, female, migrant worker. Moreover, the
ways in which the two of us are seen are invariably different as well.

Maslow's notion of rubricization (1948) points to the idea that the process of rubricization invariably creates categories for people, and those categories can slip into stereotypes of those who can and those who cannot.
Once a rubric is created, expectations are bracketed and other factors are
no longer of merit, worthy of consideration according to the rubric. If the
categories are created by actors outside classrooms on a macrolevel (for
instance, state-mandated rubrcis for teacher assessment), they will not be
responsive to the people in front of them unless the teacher is responsive
to them and mindful of discourses of Whiteness. Not that this needs to be
extinguished, but we need to be mindful of the phenomenon in order to
create practices that are responsive to students who have not been assimilated into Whiteness or those who are resistant to Whiteness.

The use of rubrics, in the least and as discussed above, is a way of feign-
ing objectivity; it is also a step in the standardization of an experience for
both the individual doing the evaluation or assessment and the individual
who is the object of evaluation or assessment. The objectives, descriptions,
and scoring contained in rubrics serve as a tools for standardization by
showing a group of individuals the expectations of performance. However,
that standardization will consistently dismiss what is not represented in the
standardization of expected performance. In other words, if only A, B, and
C are contained in the rubric, other factors like M, N, and O are not part of
the evaluation. Consider for a moment the following two examples, one on
the microlevel and one on the macrolevel.

A teacher designs a rubric for an assignment, any assignment. The teach-
er may be focusing on standards and expectations that are culled from the
Common Core State Standards for Langauge Arts, which are important.
However, the rubric more likely than not will not consider other aspects of

identity/experience that are equally essential to understanding the qual-ity of an individual student's performance on the task. Factors like the quality of previous instruction, the quality of the student's growth, the student's ability to perform the task in relation to home factors, the student's learning challenges or language acquisition, the student's comfort in the school's social context are all significant factors of experience that can have an empowering or devastating impact on performance. To assume that those outside-the-rubric factors are not worth consideration in the evaluation or assessment can further marginalize an individual student.

By the same token, consider the adoption of state-level required rubrics for teacher evaluation. The question to pose to those rubrics are do they include an assessment of the quality of a teacher's preparation program, personal challenges a teacher may be confronting like taking care of a sick parent or child, or the quality of the mentoring and induction offered the teacher? Some may argue that those issues are beyond the scope of an evaluation, which is precisely the point. Once the rubric has been implemented for evaluation, all subjected to the rubric are expected to perform to the standards and expectations represented in the rubric, despite any personal or institutional struggles the evaluee must confront. In other words, aspects of identity and experiences are left by the wayside and deemed irrelevant, even though they in fact are.

The nonrelationality of rubrics is a key step in the standardization of performance encouraged through rubrics. Furthermore, this is a privileging of a characteristic of White epistemologies because, as Sayles-Hannon (2009) explained, not recognizing the complexity of the intersections within individuals privileges one manifestation of performance and identity at the expense of others. The more rubrics are used in classrooms, the more that edict is reinforced.

CONCLUSION

To close this chapter, I want to reiterate an essential point. This chapter is in no way intended to chastise White people or those assimilated into Whiteness. Actually, my purpose for writing this chapter is to display two fundamental issues to be aware of in understanding and working through forms of oppression in general and racial oppression specifically. First, understanding racial oppression can be complicated. I suggest that understanding and correcting the behaviors of individuals is in fact the "easier" part of ameliorating racism. The challenge lies in encouraging and sustaining courageous conversations (Singleton & Linton, 2005) that clarify terminology, challenge assumptions, respect all involved, and shed light on understanding the lived experiences of oppression or racism. However, that is only part of the work. The more difficult task is the critical examination of our institutional practices in order to ascertain how the agent group is privileged through institutional and systemic practices at the expense of target groups. This requires critical lenses that take nothing for granted, especially the seemingly innocuous actions, procedures, and codes of behaviors perpetrated daily.

It is essential to examine not only overt acts of discrimination but also the tacit acts that discretely racially frame contexts by imposing epistemologies and shaping social interactions in ways that privilege some (in this case, White folks and those assimilated into Whiteness) and marginalize others (non-White folks and those not assimilated into Whiteness). The assumed rationality, objectivity, and linear thinking that undergirds rubrics promote a technology of racism that privileges ways of Whiteness and further requires stakeholders in education (students, teachers, administrators, etc.) to conform to a particular process of evaluation.

Because all claims to neutrality and objectivity, single-voiced perspectives, and nonrelationality (among other characterisitics) emerge from the institutionalized dominant discourse of Whiteness, White people are almost always allotted a privileged position and set of advantages that render educational work inequitable in terms of effort required to be recognized as "educated." That does not mean that all White people are overt racists with ill intentions to non-Whites. It means that, due to simple historical progressions of institutionalization (this nation was predominantly White for a very, very long time and its education systems have always been generated using White cultural ideologies, discourses, and epistemologies), it is only sensible that public schooling, from a historical perspective that includes now, is largely a set of projects designed through utilization of inherent institutional discourses of Whiteness. It is not an evil plot, though there are truly racist bad actors that do harm. Rather, it is a state of being that occurred systemically over time and without critique.

That leads to the second point. Institutions are built to be self-sustaining. I assume that proponents and users of rubrics have the best of intentions, and if rubrics are designed and used well, they can be helpful tools for teachers and students alike. This is a point many of the chapters in this edited volume and outsider research point out. However, a primary characteristic of privilege is that those who are privileged are least aware of it (Delpit, 1988; McIntosh, 1988). Racism is just as much a matter of how one group characterizes members of other groups as it is about the privileged epistemologies carried out across history that shape the ways we think and act.

In her keynote address at the 2013 National Association for Multicultural Education, Angela Davis introduced her speech by saying, "We cohabit this world with the ghosts of our histories" (personal communication, November 10, 2013). When discussing the institutional nature of oppression and racism, there are tendencies to dismiss ideas as misplaced or as conspiracy theories. But as considered above, if we live in a country of well-intentioned citizens (especially, in this case teachers, administrators, and policymakers), then why and how does racism persist? What is explicated in the previous section is the idea that institutionally racist practices persist because they are practices informed by certain epistemologies that privilege a particular worldview that has undergirded the creation of institutions and institutional practices. The peril that exists in not offering critical examinations of *all* institutional practices, including the nature and use of rubrics, rests in the idea that institutional practices are what further racism (a system of advantage based on race) and not solely the actions of individuals.

This chapter did not seek to denigrate rubrics or those who champion rubrics. Rather, my intention is for this chapter for it to be a provocation and invitation to approach the consideration of rubrics beyond whether or not they are good or bad, designed well or poorly. A discussion about how to "fix" this is beyond the scope of this chapter; but I challenge and encourage others to continue further thinking and research about this. Schools are institutionalized spaces of Whiteness by way of policies and practices. This chapter encourages us all to apply the full range of critical perspectives to rubrics in order to create a fuller understanding of more complicated questions like whose interests are served through the imposition of rubrics. What are the assumptions that undergird rubrics as a phenomenon and their use? Why are rubrics not used in other countries to the extent they are used in the United States? Are there more communal and/or egalitarian strategies for effective evaluation and assessment? And what are the ways in which individuals and groups are privileged or marginalized through the use of rubrics? Encouraging the critical examination of all aspects of educational practices and policies is the first step in ensuring that our actions are mindful of the fact that we are all different and will never come out just the same.

NOTES

1. Although the historic development of Whiteness and the social construction of White people is an important discussion, it is beyond the scope of this chapter to fully explore this. For a full discussion, see Cheryl Harris' "Whiteness as Property" (1993) or Jacqueline Battalora's Birth of a White Nation (2013).
2. The idea of Standard English is a greatly contested idea among linguists, but the discussion is beyond the scope of this chapter. For more, see the Conference on College Composition and Communication document "Students' Right to Their Own Language".

REFERENCES

Apple, M. (2004). *Ideology and curriculum* (3rd ed.). New York, NY: Routledge.

Battalora, J. (2013). *Birth of a White nation: The invention of White people and its relevance today.* Houston, TX: Strategic Book Publishing and Rights Co.

Campbell, A. (2005). Application of ICT and rubrics to the assessment process where professional judgment is involved: The features of an e-marking tool. *Assessment & Evaluation in Higher Education, 5*(30), 529–537.

Cherryholmes, C. (1988). *Power and criticism: Poststructural investigations in education.* New York, NY: Teachers College Press.

Crank, V. (1999). Chasing objectivity: How grading rubrics can provide consistency and context. *Journal of Teaching Writing, 17*(1/2), 56–73.

Crenshaw, K. (1991). Mapping the margins: Intersectionality, identity politics, and violence against women of color. *Stanford Law Review, 43*(6), 1241–1299.

Crenshaw, K. (1995). Mapping the margins: Intersectionality, identity politics, and violence against women of color. In K. Crenshaw, N. Gotanda, G. Peller, & K. Thomas (Eds.), *Critical race theory: The key writings that formed the movement* (pp. 357–383). New York, NY: New Press.

Danielson, C. (2013). *The framework for teaching: Evaluation instrument.* Princeton, NJ: Danielson Group.

Delpit, L. (1988). The silenced dialogue: Power and pedagogy in educating other people's children. *Harvard Educational Review, 58*(3), 280–298.

Douglass, F. (2004). *Narrative of the life of Frederick Douglass.* Cheswold, DE: Prestwick House. (Original work published 1845)

DuBois, W. E. B. (1920). Darkwater: Voices from within the veil. *Project Gutenberg.* Retrieved from http://www.gutenberg.org/files/15210/15210-h/15210-h.htm

Equiano, O. (1999). *The interesting narrative of the life of Olaudah Equiano, or Gustavus Vassa, the African. Written by Himself.* Mineola, NY: Dover. (Original work published 1789)

Feagin, J. (2014). *Racist America: Roots, current realities, and future reparations* (3rd ed.). New York, NY: Routledge.

Flynn, J. E., Hunt, R. D., Wickman, S. A., Cohen, J., & Fox, C. (2014). Architecting the change we want: Applied Critical Race Theory and the foundations of a diversity strategic plan in a college of education. In C. E. Sleeter, L. I. Neal, & K. K Kumishiro (Eds.), *Diversifying the teacher workforce: Preparing and retaining highly effective teachers,* (pp. 153–167). New York, NY: Routledge.

Gillborn, D. (2008). *Racism and education: Coincidence or conspiracy?* New York, NY: Routledge.

Giroux, H. (1981). Schooling and the myth of objectivity: Stalking the politics of the hidden curriculum. *Journal of Education, 16*(3), 282–304.

Guess, T. J. (2006). The social construction of Whiteness: Racism by intent, racism by consequence. *Critical Sociology, 32*(4), 649–673.

Hacker, A. (1992). *Two nations: Black and White, separate, hostile, and unequal.* New York, NY: Macmillan.

Harris, C. (1993). Whiteness as property. *Harvard Law Review, 106*(8), 1707–1791.

Higginbotham, A. L. (1980). *In the matter of color: Race and the American legal process: The Colonial period.* New York, NY: Oxford University Press.

Higginbotham, A. (1998). *Shades of freedom: Racial politics and presumptions of the American legal process.* New York, NY: Oxford University Press.

Hitchcock, J. (2011). *Lifting the White veil: A look at White American culture.* Roselle, NJ: Crandall, Dostie & Douglass.

Howard, G. R. (2006). *We can't teach what we don't know: White teachers, multiracial schools* (2nd ed.). New York, NY: Teachers College Press.

Ignatiev, N. (2008). *How the Irish became White* (Routledge Classics Ed.). New York, NY: Routledge.

Jackson, P. (1990). *Life in classrooms.* New York, NY: Teachers College Press.

Jacobs, H. (2011). *Incidents in the life of a slave girl* (Reprint ed.). Mineola, NY: Dover. (Original work published 1861).

Jacobson, M.F. (1999). *Whiteness of a different color: European Immigrants and the alchemy of race.* Cambridge, MA: Harvard University Press.

Katz, J. (2003). *White awareness: Handbook for anti-racist training* (2nd ed.). Oklahoma City: University of Oklahoma Press.

Keating, A. (2007). *Teaching transformation: Transcultrual classroom dialogues.* New York, NY: Palgrave Macmillan.

Kennedy, T. M., Middleton, J. I., & Ratcliffe, K. (2005). The matter of Whiteness: Or, why Whiteness studies is important to rhetoric and composition studies. *Rhetoric Review, 24*(4), 359–373.

Kincheloe, J. L., & Steinberg, S. R. (1998). Addressing the crisis of Whiteness: Reconfiguring White identity in a pedagogy of Whiteness. In J. L. Kincheloe, S. R. Steinberg, N. M. Rodriguiz, & R. E. Chennault (Eds.), *White reign: Deploying Whiteness in America* (pp. 3–30). New York, NY: Palgrave Macmillan.

Kuhn, T. (1996). *The structure of scientific revolutions* (3rd ed.). Chicago, IL: University of Chicago Press.

Learning Point Associates. (2007). *Understanding the No Child Left Behind Act: Scientifically based research.* Naperville, IL: Learning Point Associates.

Lee, S. J. (2005). *Up against Whiteness: Race, school, and immigrant youth.* New York, NY: Teachers College Press.

Leonardo, Z. (2013). *Race frameworks: A multidimensional theory of racism and education.* New York, NY: Teachers College Press.

Leonardo, Z., & Grubb, N. (2013). *Education and racism: A primer on issues and dilemmas.* New York, NY: Routledge.

Lewis, A. (2001). There is no "race" in the schoolyard: Color-blind ideology in an (almost) all White school. *American Educational Research Journal, 38*(4), 781–811.

Lunenburg, F. (2011). Theorizing about curriculum: Conceptions and definitions. *International Journal of Scholarly Academic Intellectual Diversity, 13*(1), 1–6.

Marzano, R. J. (2007). *The art and science of teaching: A comprehensive framework for effective instruction.* Alexandria, VA: Association for Supervision and Curriculum Development.

Maslow, A. (1948). Cognition of the particular and of the generic. *Psychological Review, 55*(1), 22–40.

McIntosh, P. (1988). *White privilege and male privilege: A personal account of coming to see correspondences through work in women's studies.* Working Paper No. 189. Wellesley, MA: Wellesley College, Center for Research on Women.

220 ▪ J. E. FLYNN, Jr.

Northup, S. (2014). *Twelve years a slave.* CreateSpace Independent Publishing Platform. (Original work published 1853)

Nougera, P. A., & Wing, J. Y. (2006). Introduction: Unfinished business: Closing the achievement gap at Berkeley High School. In P. A. Nougera & J. Y. Wing (Eds.), *Unfinished business: Closing the racial achievement gap in our schools* pp. 3–28). San Francisco, CA: Jossey-Bass.

Null, W. (2011). *Curriculum: From theory to practice.* Lanham, MD: Rowman & Littlefield.

Pinar, W. (2011). *What is curriculum theory?* (2nd ed.). New York, NY: Routledge.

Pollock, M. (2004). *Colormute: Race talk dilemmas in an American school.* Princeton, NJ: Princeton University Press.

Rabaka, R. (2007). The souls of White folk: W. E. B. DuBois's critique of White supremacy and contributions to critical White studies. *Journal of African American Studies, 11*(1), 1–15.

Ravitch, D. (2011). *The death and life of the great American school system: How testing and choice are undermining education* (Rev. & Exp. ed.). New York, NY: Basic.

Reddy, Y. M., & Andrade, H. (2009). A review of rubric use in higher education. *Assessment and Evaluation in Higher Education, 35*(4), 435–448.

Reitmeier, C. A., Svendsen, L. K., & Vrchota, D. A. (2004). Improving oral communication skills of students in food science courses. *Journal of Food Science Education, 3*(2), 15–20.

Reynolds, M. (1962). Little boxes. On *Malvina Reynolds sings the truth* [Record album]. New York, NY: Columbia Records (1967).

Roediger, D. R. (1999). *Black on White: Black writers on what it means to be White.* New York, NY: Schoken.

Sanchez, G. (1995). *Becoming Mexican American: Ethnicity, culture, and identity in Chicano Los Angeles, 1900–1945* (Reprint ed.). New York, NY: Oxford University Press.

Sayles-Hannon, S. J. (2009). In search of multiculturalism: Uncovering "Whiteness" in curriculum design and pedagogical strategies. *International Journal of Learning, 16*(10), 709–719.

Sensoy, O., & DiAngelo, R. (2011). *Is everyone really equal? An introduction to key concepts in social justice education.* New York, NY: Teachers College Press.

Singleton, G. E., & Linton, C. (2005). *Courageous conversations about race: A field guide for achieving equity in schools.* Thousand Oaks, CA: Corwin.

Spandel, V. (2006). Speaking my mind: In defense of rubrics. *The English Journal, 96*(1), 19–22.

Spring, J. (2012). *Deculturalization and the struggle for equality: A brief history of the education of dominated cultures in the United States* (7th ed.). New York, NY: McGraw-Hill.

Stellmack, M. A., Konheim-Kalkstein, Y. L., Manor, J. E., Massey, A. R., & Schmitz, J. A. P. (2009). An assessment of reliability and validity of a rubric for grading APA-style introductions. *Teaching of Psychology, 36*(2), 102–107.

Takao Ozawa v. U.S., 260 U.S. 178 (1922).

Tatum, B. D. (2002). *Why are all the Black kids sitting together in the cafeteria? And other conversations about race* (5th Anniv. Rev. ed.). New York, NY: Basic.

Taubman, P. M. (2009). *Teaching by numbers: Deconstructing the discourse of standards and accountability in education.* New York, NY: Routledge.

Turley, E. D., & Gallagher, C. W. (2008). On the "uses" of rubrics: Reframing the great rubric debate. *The English Journal, 97*(4), 87–92.

U.S. Department of Education. (2001). *Introduction: No Child Left Behind.* Retrieved from http://www2.ed.gov/nclb/overview/intro/index.html

United States v. Bhagat Singh Thind, 261 U.S. 204 (1923).

Vaught, S. (2011). *Racism, public schooling, and the entrenchment of White supremacy: A critical race ethnography.* Albany: State University of New York Press.

Wellman, D. T. (1993). *Portraits of White racism* (2nd ed.). Cambridge, MA: Cambridge University Press.

Woodson, C.G. (1992). *Miseducation of the Negro.* Washington D.C.: Associated Publishers, Inc. (Original work published 1933)

Yancy, G. (2004). Introduction: Fragments of a social ontology of Whiteness. In G. Yancy (Ed.) *What White looks like: African-American Philosophers on the Whiteness question,* pp. 1 24. New York: Routledge.

Zinn, H. (2003). *A people's history of the United States: 1492-present (Reprint Ed.). New York: Harper Perennial.*

AN AFTERWORD
IN TWO VOICES

The Tools of Destruction
and Empowerment: Reflections
on Creating a Book About Rubrics

Michelle Tenam-Zemach and Joseph Flynn

MICHELLE

In 2008, I was hired as a new full-time faculty member in a college of education. Having spent the previous 15 years as an adjunct professor at a community college, as well as having been a teacher and curriculum coordinator for a private school, I was new to higher education at this level. Among many other things, I never had to contend with accreditation processes nor the expectations of approved programs of a state's department of education (DOE). Thus, when I was informed that one of my first tasks would be to generate a key assessment rubric to meet both Florida's DOE requirements for English education and NCATE requirements for accreditation, I was confused and overwhelmed. We were explicitly instructed to develop rubrics based on current assessments in extant syllabi—syllabi that I had neither generated nor taught since I had only just begun teaching in the

Rubric Nation, pages 223–228
Copyright © 2015 by Information Age Publishing
223

program. While the details of the process are beyond the scope of this afterward, the effects of that experience are not.

A few years prior to my being hired, I had done rubric training with Heidi Andrade at Harvard University's Project Zero. An authority on rubrics and assessment, Dr. Andrade taught me well about how to develop rubrics, and I had used that knowledge to develop my own rubric professional development training for teachers I was working with at the time. Therefore, coming into my new position as a professor of education, I thought I understood the elements of effective rubric design, but what I was experiencing during the process of developing rubrics to meet accreditation standards did not seem to align with the best practices I had learned.

Over time, and several years later, the sense of confusion and frustration that I had experienced during that time had not diminished. In fact, it increased. The experience of developing assessments and rubrics for DOE approval and NCATE accreditation in particular, left me with two burning questions: (a) Did NCATE accredited institutions actually do a superior job of educating preservice teachers than non-NCATE accredited schools? and (b) How valid and reliable were these rubrics? I had discussed my concerns with several colleagues from various institutions across the country, and while no one seemed to have explicit data to respond to my questions, one point was consistent: They were as frustrated and confused about their experiences as I was, some even more so. In fact, a consistent refrain I heard was astonishment about the overwhelming use of rubrics in teacher education courses and how *everything* seemed to be "rubricized" nowadays. And while I had been a staunch advocate of rubrics (for many of the reasons discussed in several of the chapters in this text), I could not shake the feeling that something was seriously wrong with how frequently rubrics were developed to meet one expectation of assessment or another. From having trained many teachers and administrators on rubric development, I also knew many educators did not fully understand how to develop well-designed rubrics. And as the years passed, I also noticed that more and more educators were expected to develop and utilize rubrics in their syllabi and courses even though they had never been trained on how to do so. Consequently, many syllabi that I read included rubrics that did not align with the research-based guidelines presented in the literature on good rubric design and development.

Overall, my experience with rubrics at the university level led to a constant nagging in my mind about the utilization of rubrics in general. As a curricularist, I ceaselessly argue that all curricula should be considered living documents; they should not be thought of as permanent artifacts to be utilized in perpetuity. As a result, to meet the needs of my students, I regularly alter rubrics for assignments. However, I often teach courses in which the syllabus is not mine; thus, I cannot alter those rubric in any way, shape or form. I consistently grapple with how challenged I feel every time I have to write a rubric that pretends to capture all that I hope and expect from my students' work. These examples illustrate why I have spent many years struggling with the use of rubrics, and these frustrations ultimately informed my conversations with Joseph and inevitably the development of this book.

JOSEPH

I will be completely honest. I have never been a fan of rubrics. When I was a preservice teacher in the early 1990s, my professors rarely gave rubrics for assignments. When I was a high school teacher I also rarely gave them, and I always told students what my professors told me, "If you have a question about the assignment or my expectations, ask me and we can talk about it!" Finally, when I was a graduate student (during both my master's and doctoral programs) they were rarely ever used, and when an assignment was given that included a rubric most of my colleagues and I looked at the rubric once and turned back to the assignment description as the primary guide. I always felt that rubrics were too confining for me—the teacher—and too proscriptive for students. They minimized risk and hampered developing strong relationships with teachers, especially in higher education.

When I began teaching preservice teachers in 2007 I noticed a stark difference from my own experiences as a student. Many of my students wanted a rubric. They wanted to know *exactly* what needed to be done to get an A, and they seemed to have a difficult time sending an email or asking for clarification in class. Then, typically a few weeks before a major project was due, students would offer a deluge of clarifying questions, mentioning that they had been confused or unclear about expectations for weeks. I never had a problem talking through either the requirements or my expectations for an assignment, but I found myself growing increasingly impatient with the lack of will to take risks and the level of certainty students expected. To me, in my ruminations, the presence of rubrics seemed to be having an effect on students' needs and dispositions; it was all about the rubric. This was made clear to me when one day after a session of clarifications, a student opined, "This would have been much easier if you had given us a rubric." I do not necessarily blame this need for a rubric solely on students. As I found out, most of their other courses used rubrics for practically every assignment in their preparation programs: rubrics for classroom observations; rubrics for essays; rubrics for critical reflections; rubrics for lesson and unit plan assignments; rubrics, rubrics, rubrics. In effect, many—if not most—of the students became hard wired to following the rubric, and it can be argued that the suspension of risk and the willingness to engage faculty is an unintended outcome of standardization and accreditation forces. (Or, is it even an unintended outcome)? The phenomenon forced a challenging and troubling question: What impact does the proliferation and ubiquity of rubrics have on students?

To my dismay it seemed as though a new ethos emerged in teacher education: If ideas and expectations are not codified into a rubric, there is something inherently wrong, unfair, suspicious, disquieting, and ineffective. Moreover, for students, the primary focus was getting the credential with the cleanest (i.e., the most A grades) transcript possible rather than a consideration of full scope of their learning and what one learns from challenge and risk. When did this shift happen, and, more importantly, what does this sea change mean for teaching, learning, and the whole enterprise of education writ large? As I began to share these issues with Michelle, she too was asking similar questions. From our conversations about our struggles with rubrics, we determined that we needed to investigate the phenomenon of rubrics more deeply.

OUR FINAL WORD

Dealing with the institutional phenomenon of rubrics and the critical questions that arose for both of us prompted a discussion between two colleagues. We both lamented about the situations and trends that led us to conduct independent research and what we found was that there was scant literature that critically examined the *impact* of rubrics, let alone historical analyses of the rise of rubrics use in education generally, and teacher education specifically. We then decided to create this book, an edited volume, that could add to the research and scholarship about rubrics that was beyond the one dimensional questions of whether or not they are good or bad and how does one make a better rubric? Over the course of two year's work on this project, we have come to realize that rubrics are in fact mere tools and are only as effective as the hands that wield them. What are far more substantial issues though are the notions of the ways in which various stakeholders frame the use of rubrics, and that rubrics *always* have unintended consequences.

The essays in this volume have centered on a few challenging questions: How do rubrics work? Why are they so prominent in the United States' education system today? What roles do rubrics play in education and teacher education, and whose interests do they serve? And, since a rubric is nothing more than a fixed set of limited and ultimately subjective criteria, what challenges and opportunities might lie in evaluating educators' value and quality based on the atomized procedures of their basic jobs, rather than the holistic entirety of their complex professional practices? Individually, each chapter of this book has taken a different approach to considering and mining these questions. Collectively, the essays make an important overarching point. Rubrics should never be judged as simply good or simply bad. Rather, rubrics should always be considered within the context of their use and the motives behind the actors using them or requiring their use. As previous research and research detailed in this volume show, the ways in which rubrics are structured and the purposes of their use are significant factors in whether or not their use is helpful or destructive. Using rubrics as a way of framing a discussion about practice with a teacher is a far cry from using rubrics as the primary tool for assessing the quality of a teacher.

The chapters of this edited volume have also presented a range of essential issues education professionals and stakeholders ought to be aware—not necessarily to *do away with* rubrics, but to be mindful of the intended and unintended consequences of rubrics in order to better inform our practices and policies, and to establish research agendas that not only seek to discover best practices for creating rubrics but also to critically examine the social, economic, psychological, political, and cultural implications of rubrics. Finally, this volume, being more focused on the use and impact of rubrics in the K–12 and teacher education arenas, generates a number of recommendations for future research and theorizing. For example, how are rubrics being utilized across institutions of higher education? What are the expectations of rubrics in relation to academic quality, course evaluation, tenure, etc.? Due to the widespread reforms taking place in higher education, teacher education, and K–12 education, do rubrics promote a hidden curriculum that further neoliberal and corporatist agendas, and if so how? What is the range of unintended consequences for the use of rubrics in higher education? And, if rubrics are in fact spreading across institutions of higher education, what kinds of professional development programs do universities offer faculty and administrators that encourage best practices and critical considerations about the role of rubrics in their institutions? Ultimately, the chapters offered in this volume are an introduction to a complex phenomenon and encourage the development and investigation of more questions. Only through appropriate research and critical inquiry will we discover answers to these questions and be able to understand the larger impact of rubrics on higher education and the field of education as a whole.

A hammer can be used to drive nails or break glass. A hammer can be used to break down a wall or barrier. It can also be used to build walls and barriers. A hammer can be used to make music. Or, a hammer can be used to kill. Again, it is dependent upon the intention of the hand using the tool. Such is the reality of rubrics. A rubric can be effectively used to frame a discussion between teacher and student or administrator and teacher. It can also be used to marginalize students or deskill a teacher or teacher educator. And by extension, it can be used to close a school entirely. As we have learned through the process of creating this book, our community of teacher educators and researchers must not blindly use rubrics but, like every other phenomenon in education, continue to critically interrogate them; lest we realize we are wielding weapons of destruction rather than tools of empowerment.

ABOUT THE EDITORS

Michelle Tenam-Zemach is Program Professor of Curriculum and Instruction at Nova Southeastern University. She teaches courses on curriculum theory, research and practice, assessment, instructional theory and practice, and English Education. Her scholarship offers a critical examination of science standards in relation to an ecological paradigm, constructive assessment practices, and the influence of language on curriculum.

Joseph E. Flynn, Jr. is an Associate Professor of Curriculum and Instruction at Northern Illinois University. He teaches courses related to social justice and multicultural education, curriculum studies, and educational change and reform. His scholarship offers critical examinations of curriculum, Whiteness Studies, and media and popular culture. Previously, he has guest edited a special edition of The Black History Bulletin on the role of African Americans in popular culture, and currently he is co-editor of the Woodson Review.

Rubric Nation, page 229
Copyright © 2015 by Information Age Publishing
229

ABOUT THE CONTRIBUTORS

Robert Boostrom is Professor of Education at the University of Southern Indiana where he teaches courses in the social foundations of education. Author of several books on thinking and moral life, he recently co-edited (with Hugh Sockett), *A Moral Critique of Contemporary Education, A National Society for the Study of Education Yearbook.* He has been an associate editor of the *Journal of Curriculum Studies* since 1997.

Leslie David Burns, PhD is an Educationist and Associate Professor of Literacy at the University of Kentucky. He is a co-author of the *National Council of Teachers of English/National Council for Accreditation of Teacher Education's Standards for English Language Arts Teachers, Grades 7–12,* and he is the recipient of multiple awards for his work at the local, state, and national levels related to policy, standards, curriculum, literacy research, and English language arts teaching. Dr. Burns' research interests include curriculum studies, literacy studies, English studies, discourse, policy analysis, education reform, teacher professionalism and identity, and techniques for responsive teaching and learning in diverse classrooms.

Susan Dreyer Leon, EdD is the Director of the Experienced Educators M.Ed Program for working teachers at Antioch University New England. In addition to teaching school leadership and administration, Dr. Dreyer-Leon oversees programs in Problem-Based Learning, Mindfulness for Educators and Educating for Sustainability. She is also a National Facilitator for School Reform Initiative and on the board of the QED Foundation and the Making Community Connections Charter School.

Rubric Nation, pages 231–234
Copyright © 2015 by Information Age Publishing

David J. Flinders is Professor in the School of Education at Indiana University, Bloomington. He is a former AERA Vice President for Division B and has served as President of the American Association for Teaching and Curriculum. Flinders is also co-editor of *The Curriculum Studies Reader 4th and Teaching and Curriculum Dialogue.* His interests include curriculum theory, secondary education, qualitative research, and peace education.

Conra D. Gist, PhD is Assistant Professor of Curriculum and Instruction at the University of Arkansas. She has served in various leadership capacities such as a NYC Teaching Fellow Selector and Advisor for the New Teacher Project, and professional development designer for the Office of Teacher Effectiveness in Brooklyn, NY. Currently she is working on a research project exploring how teachers of color are prepared to teach in theory and practice. She teaches courses on race, multicultural perspectives on literacy, teacher education, and curriculum design. She has written articles on teacher development, racial literacy, and culturally responsive teacher educators.

David Gorlewski is the assistant professor of Educational Administration at the State University of New York at New Paltz. He has served as a teacher, teacher educator, and senior-level administrator in the Western New York region. David is coeditor of *English Journal,* a publication of the National Council of Teachers of English. He has published numerous articles and chapters related to school reform and school leadership.

Julie Gorlewski is assistant professor of Secondary Education at the State University of New York at New Paltz. Her books include *Power, Resistance, and Literacy: Writing for Social Justice* (2011, Information Age), *Making it Real: Case Stories for Secondary Teachers* (2012, Sense) and *Left Behind in the Race to the Top: Realities of School Reform*(Information Age, 2013). She is currently coeditor of *English Journal.*

Dana L. Haraway is an Associate Professor at James Madison University, Harrisonburg, VA. She currently serves on the executive committee for the Association for Teaching and Curriculum and on the board Virginia Middle School Association. Her interests include teacher evaluation and quality, assessment, safe school climate, and resiliency.

Catherine Lalonde is an Assistant Professor of Education and NCATE Co-ordinator at D'Youville College. She teaches "Critical Issues and Future Trends in Education," "Multiculturalism and Cultural Diversity," and "Research in Education," and her research interests include multicultural theory, social foundations of education, food distribution and consumption issues, and critical media literacy and pedagogy.

Tom Liam Lynch is the Assistant Professor of Education Technology at Pace University. A former English teacher and schools official in New York City, Dr. Lynch led online learning programs for both students and teachers. His research sits at the intersection of critical discourse analysis, literacy education, learning technologies, and software studies. Learn more at www.tomliamlynch.org.

Kim Marshall was a teacher, central office administrator, and principal in the Boston Pubic Schools for 32 years. He now advises and coaches new principals (mostly with New Leaders for New Schools), teaches courses and conducts workshops on instructional leadership and time management, and publishes a weekly newsletter, the *Marshall Memo*, which summarizes ideas and research from 44 publications (www.marshallmemo.com). Kim has written several books and numerous articles on teaching and school leadership. His most recent book is *Rethinking Teacher Supervision and Evaluation* (Jossey-Bass, 2009). He is married and has two children, both teachers.

Amy Masko is an associate professor at Grand Valley State University in Allendale, Michigan. She earned her PhD from the University of Denver in Curriculum and Instruction with an emphasis in Urban Education, and her M.Ed. from Lesley University in Curriculum and Instruction with an emphasis in Literacy Education. Her research interests include the intersection of race, poverty, and schooling, Critical Race Theory, and comparative international education. She has written articles about urban and rural education in both the United States and Ghana, West Africa. She has worked for public schools and community based educational non-profits. She currently teaches courses in English education at Grand Valley.

Paul Parkison is a chair of the School of Education at the University of Evansville in Evansville, Indiana. He works in the field of teacher preparation with a focus on curriculum design and assessment. He has been involved in accreditation and program assessment for the past ten years. His primary research interest involves the influences that empower educators to engage in authentic identity formation and curriculum design. Finding space within the high stakes accountability climate of education makes this type of empowerment challenging.

Nancy Patterson earned her PhD in English at Michigan State University and teaches in the Literacy Studies Program in the College of Education at Grand Valley State University in Grand Rapids. MI. She taught secondary English for almost 30 years before taking a position at GVSU where she chaired the Literacy Studies Program for eight years. She has been a contributing editor for NCTE's journal *Voices from the Middle* and recently served as co-editor of the Language Arts Journal of Michigan. She is an avid gardener and a trained singer.

Lisa M. Perhamus is an Assistant Professor of the Foundations of Education and the Padnos/Sarosik Endowed Professor of Civil Discourse at Grand Valley State University. Her interdisciplinary work draws upon critical pedagogy; the sociology of education; political sociology; postmodern theories of power; and feminist theories of the body. Her teaching interests include anti-oppression education; the sociology of urban education; kinesthetic experiences of schooling; and issues of race, class, gender and sexuality in education. Her qualitative research asks questions about the human experiences of oppression across multiple contexts. She is particularly interested in how young children, their families and community members create emotional and material conditions of resiliency.

Laura Thomas, MEd is Director of Antioch University's Center for School Renewal and Faculty in the Department of Education. She has been a school change coach and adult learning facilitator since 1995, following a career as a high school English, speech and theatre educator. She is affiliated with the Coalition of Essential Schools and the School Reform Initiative and is proud to be an organizer for Edcamp Keene. She is the author *Facilitating Authentic Learning* (Corwin Press, 2011) as well as multiple articles and currently writes for *The Critical Skills Classroom* (http://antiochcriticalskills. wordpress.com/).

Printed in the United States
By Bookmasters